AF473823

The Book Art of Richard Minsky

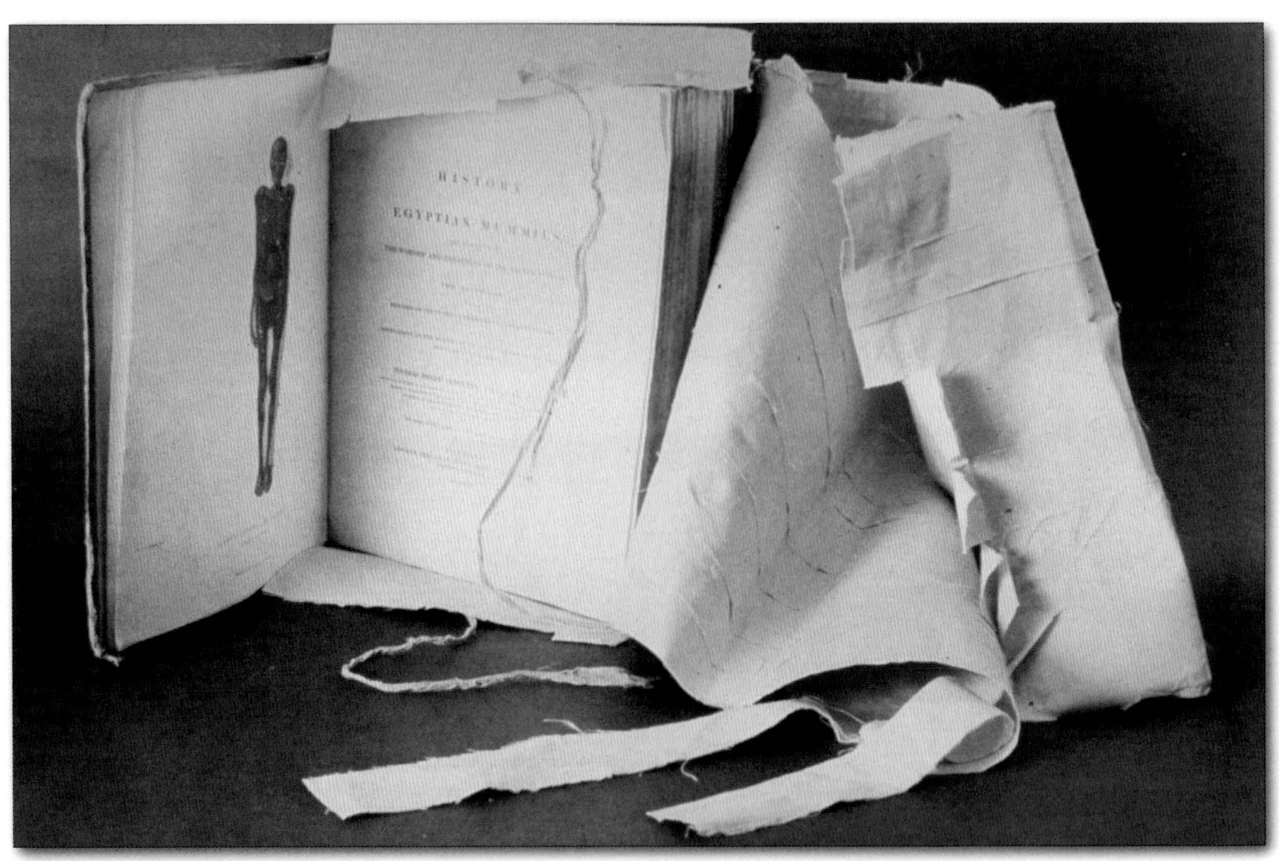

A History of Egyptian Mummies
by Thomas J. Pettigrew. Longman, London, 1834
Bound by Minsky 1973. Linen, turquoise. 12 x 9
Collection of Barbara and Donald Bady, New York

RICHARD MINSKY
MY LIFE IN BOOK ART

New York
George Braziller, Inc.
2011

Published in the United States of America by George Braziller, Inc., New York.

For information, please address the publisher:

George Braziller, Inc.
277 Broadway
New York, New York 10007

Library of Congress Cataloging-in-Publication Data

Minsky, Richard.
The book art of Richard Minsky.
p. cm.
Includes bibliographical references.
ISBN 978-0-8076-1606-2
1. Minsky, Richard--Themes, motives. 2. Artists' books--United States. I. Title.

N7433.4.M56A35 2011
700.92--dc22

2011018074

Printed and bound through Asia Pacific Offset (China)

First Edition

ACKNOWLEDGEMENTS

GEORGE BRAZILLER has long been an inspiration to me, both as a fearless independent publisher and a paragon of fitness. He suggested doing this book after seeing the exhibition *Material Meets Metaphor: A Half Century of Book Art by Richard Minsky* at Yale University's Robert B. Haas Family Arts Library. The exhibition was curated by Jae Jennifer Rossman, Assistant Director for Special Collections, with the assistance of Mia D'Avanza, 2009 Kress Fellow in Art Librarianship, and Molly Dotson, 2010 Kress Fellow in Art Librarianship. Thanks are due to them for organizing the chaos of material that now occupies 36 linear feet (57 boxes) of the library's Special Collections shelf space as The Richard Minsky Archive.

Thanks also go to the Director of the Haas Arts Library, Allen Townsend, for his support of the exhibition, which the library presented from August 2–December 21, 2010, and to Dr. Robert Carlucci, Manager of Visual Resources at Yale, who provided high resolution scans of many slides.

Without the guidance of Ina Saltz, the typography of this book would have been less refined. Barbara Slate has been listening to my stories for over 20 years and encouraged writing them. She reviewed many versions of the manuscript and brought her critical acuity to the layout. More than that, she and Samantha put up with me disappearing into the studio for the second year in a row to do a Braziller book. Their love and encouragement keep me motivated.

Richard Minsky

All dimensions are in inches.

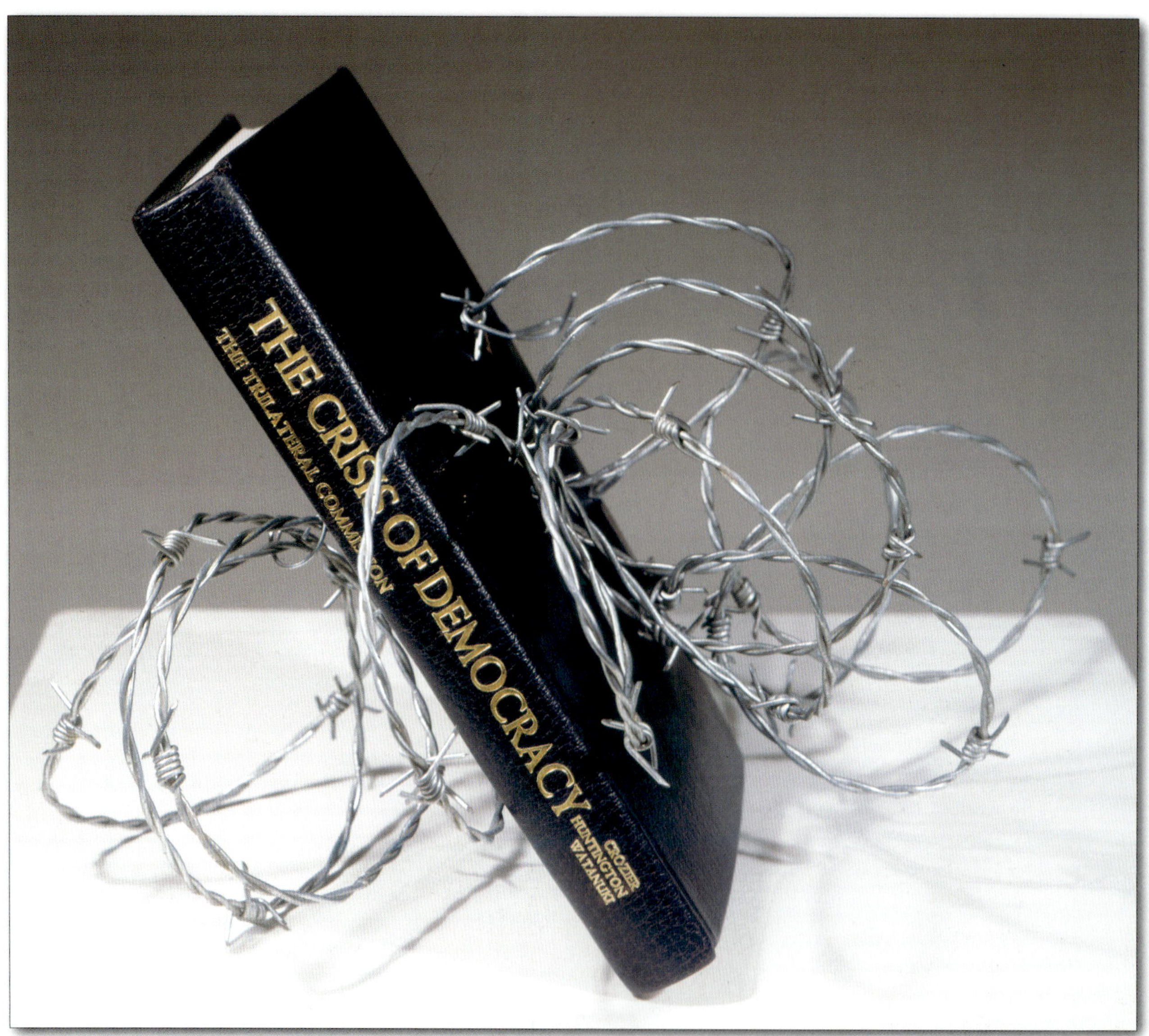

The Crisis of Democracy
by Crozier, Huntington and Watanuki for the Trilateral Commission.
New York University Press, 1975.
Binding by Minsky, 1980. 8¾ x 6 x 11
Sheep, gold, barbed wire.
Photo: installation at the Allan Stone Gallery, New York, May, 1981.
Collection of the Haas Family Arts Library, Yale University

FOREWORD

IN 1980 RICHARD MINSKY created a binding for the book *The Crisis of Democracy*. After binding it in dark blue sheepskin with the title gold-stamped on its spine, Minsky encircled the book with barbed wire. Thus entangled, *The Crisis of Democracy* provokes stares and generates questions, such as, What is the crisis? Where is the threat? Those questions transform a passive viewer into an active interrogator. Eventually, the questioner learns that the book itself poses the threat; the book's authors argue that it is necessary to curtail personal freedoms in order to preserve the governability of a democracy. Under Minsky's hands the book has leapt from the bookshelf and into the gallery, its artistic transformation exposing the contradictions and potential consequences of its premise.

Richard Minsky turned his passion for letterpress printing and binding into his life's mission as he worked to help establish the field of book art, coining the name itself along with an organization to nurture the concept. His efforts were part of a wave of activity in the United States and abroad in the 1960s and 1970s as artists, writers, publishers, and artisans pieced together a crazy-quilt community.

The Center for Book Arts (CBA), founded by Minsky in 1974, served as the standard-bearer of independent nonprofit book arts organizations. The expansive spirit generated by Minsky and others at CBA was emulated by later book art centers in the United States. It is a spirit rooted in sharing information and encouraging collaboration, which in turn builds community among its varied participants. That openness is a characteristic often noted by art world outliers who visit and stay to thrive at book art's invigorating intersection of books, language, media, and structural invention.

This writer's focus on book art should not suggest that it represents Minsky's singular interest, however. The reader will soon learn from him about his myriad pursuits, including musical composition, collaborations, scholarly book collecting, and publishing. Those of us with a lengthy tenure in the book art field are grateful as well for Minsky's tireless proselytizing on behalf of early book artists—such as Barton Beneš and Stella Waitzkin—whose innovations and influence might otherwise have gone unrecognized.

In his own work, Minsky advocated for craft practice sited in an art context long before the concept of interdisciplinarity grew fashionable. He realized that a craft-art convergence could produce memorable disjunctions—or perhaps a more complicated conjunction. For example, for *The Crisis of Democracy*, Minsky chose to execute a leather binding in order to highlight the abraded effect of the barbed wire on the book. He described the effect as exposing "the inner flesh that contrasts with the grain of the leather" as the barbs "slowly erode the decorative surface of the skin." [1]

Map the Territory

To name is to exercise ownership, an empowering act. Minsky's naming of book art in 1974 is a lesson in purposeful simplicity. He wished to distinguish such work from "art books," a term that calls to mind illustrated books *about* art. Instead, the identity of book art revolves around books that are *themselves* works of art, in which imagery, text, materials, and some kind of paginated structure cohere. It also designates work in sculpture, installation, and performance that responds to cultural metaphors of the book, even as those metaphors are in flux due to the dominance of digital and video media in culture today.

Minsky further specified that the Center for Book Arts carry the plural of "art." In so doing, he chose to expand the center's mission to teaching and to providing studio facilities for related craft disciplines such as bookbinding, printing, and papermaking. However, in naming the center's exhibition space,

1 *Material Meets Metaphor: A Half-Century of Book Art by Richard Minsky*. Jae Jennifer Rossman, curator. An exhibition at the Robert B. Hass Family Art Library, William H. Wright Special Collections Exhibit Area, Yale University, 2010: 36.

Minsky held to the singular of "art," calling it the Book Art Gallery. Minsky has curated numerous exhibitions for the gallery over the last thirty-six years that explore historical as well as contemporary material.

Some of the practitioners who taught and exhibited at CBA also innovated in methods and materials for work in book and paper conservation, and then applied those new structures, materials, and techniques to their own artistic output.[2] The boundary between the practical and artistic aspects of book art has always been a permeable one. Today, CBA offers classes and hosts visiting artists in its studios, organizes exhibitions in its gallery, and sponsors too many programs to enumerate. The content of book art can be anything, literally, and it can take form as a familiar bound book that is printed (or handwritten or lettered), and then bound along one edge or assembled with or without sewing or adhesive; or it can open out into a table-top sculptural screen, or even expand into a room-sized installation.

The Art of Book Art

The properties and strategies of art movements from over a century resonate within Richard Minsky's fusions of book and art. Artists have mined the expressive material and structural potential of the book form since the avant-garde period of the late nineteenth and early twentieth centuries. Inventive appropriations of materials and formats resulted in, for example, a 1932 Futurist book whose tin pages clatter when turned, and a long poem about an interminable journey that opens out from a foldable map format, from 1913.[3] Note, however, that knowledge of these progenitors and others was little known in the 1970s and only began to circulate among book artists through exhibitions beginning in the 1980s.[4]

If Minsky's work can be said to align with one predecessor, it is found in its interplay between intellectual content and a theatrical presentation. One discerns a similar dualism, if more subtle in delivery, in the elusive but omnipresent influence of Marcel Duchamp, whose playful erudition influenced both the avant-garde and postmodernism. In particular, Minsky's altered books inhabit a related if distinct domain where Duchamp's readymades reside. Readymades were found objects that Duchamp appropriated and re-presented in an art context, such as a snow shovel that he rechristened *In Advance of the Broken Arm*, from 1915. In 1919 Duchamp even created an environmental bookwork when he asked his sister Suzanne to hang a textbook outside her Paris window. He titled the work *Unhappy Readymade*, and it developed—disintegrated—over time.

Duchamp's book and box incursions dealt with ideas about art, value, and originality, such as a breast-bedecked exhibition catalogue,[5] and his *Boîte-en-valise* (Box in a suitcase, 1936-1941), which housed small reproductions of his artworks, like a portable exhibition. His works undermined art world norms and often were delivered with an underlying wit. Without diminishing Duchamp's extraordinary and continuing influence over contemporary art and culture, many of Minsky's appropriations also proffer humor or the unexpected along with critical content. From this shared trait, however, Minsky's bookworks diverge in two ways.

First, Minsky's works result from his conscious and strategic choice of a book for its content, unlike the studied indifference claimed by Duchamp in his selection of readymades. For example, take an early transformation by Minsky, his infamous shocker, J. H. Studer's 1888 *The Birds of North America*, which Minsky altered in 1975 by affixing a pheasant skin to his leather binding of the book. The work, submitted to an exhibition of finely tooled leather bindings, produced a satisfying uproar in a true Duchampian

---

2 For example, over the last thirty years CBA has offered classes and exhibited book art by book conservators Hedi Kyle and Gary Frost, both of whom have shared innovative structures with the field. See also "Innovation from Tradition in the Book Arts," by Richard Minsky. *American Craft*, October/November, 1993.

3 The two books referenced here are, first, F. T. Marinetti's *Parole in libertà futuriste tattili-termiche olfattive* (1932) and, then, Sonia Delaunay-Terk and Blaise Cendrars's *La prose du transsibérien et de la petite Jehanne de France* (1913).

4 A key early exhibition (and catalogue) that revealed book art antecedents was, Jaroslav Andel, *The Avant-Garde Book: 1900-1945* (New York: Franklin Furnace, 1989).

5 Duchamp adorned each catalogue cover with a latex rubber falsie. The catalogue accompanied the 1947 *Exposition Internationale du Surréalisme* in Paris, organized by Duchamp and André Breton.

manner. We will leave it to Minsky to tell the full story later in this volume, except to note that the action succeeded on several fronts: it tweaked expectations of fine binding (after all, the leather binding *was* well executed); it demonstrated the vibrant consequences of the conflation of craft with artistic expression, and it drew attention to a practice of early naturalists, which was to shoot the animals they would later painstakingly study and draw.

That underlying social critique constitutes a second key attribute in many of Minsky's works—unlike Duchamp's, whose targets tended to be the art world's power structure. Minsky's strongest voice is heard in works that expose injustice or cry out for change. Sculptural bookworks provide Minsky with a vehicle that draws equally on his expertise as a master binder and his iconoclastic aesthetic. The resulting collisions between craft and art, often infused with humor, irony, or an incisive skepticism, produce works that engage a viewer's intellect after delivering an unforgettable visual punch.

Beginning in 1993, Minsky channeled his longstanding commitment to human rights into a series based on the Bill of Rights. In response to the individual first ten amendments he produced ten works, nine of which involve an existing book. He has since developed these works into an edition that sells as a set. Each work embodies Minsky's response to a particular amendment through the lens of today's social and political landscape. For example, in response to the First Amendment, which protects freedom of expression, Minsky burned a copy of Salman Rushdie's *The Satanic Verses.* The book's publication in 1988 led to Rushdie's denunciation in several Muslim countries and the undermining of freedoms of the press, religion, and speech.

After burning *The Satanic Verses* and so enacting the threat to the author and his book, Minsky constructed a reliquary (as he called it) to house the resulting charred remains. The structure is adorned with dense and vivid imagery suggestive of fretwork, and stained glass panels provide a glimpse of the destroyed book sealed within. The work arrests one's attention and then compels reflection on how human rights can be curtailed or overthrown when caught up in the vortex of societal forces.

Minsky's response to the Fourth Amendment, which protects against unreasonable search and seizure, confronts threats to freedom that have arisen along with new technologies. Minsky altered a copy of William Gibson's *Neuromancer,* the 1984 science fiction novel that presents cyberspace as a realm vulnerable to intrusion by corporate, governmental, and criminal interests. Gibson's storyline exposes the consequences of that unfettered government interference. Minsky's binding incorporates a metallic shuriken (a star-shaped throwing weapon) on the cover, an image that recurs in the novel. A pink slipcase includes the text of the Fourth Amendment hot-stamped in hologram foil on one side. The hologram shifts into illegibility when viewed at a distance, as the text scrambles into a pattern suggestive of digital code. That confusion in legibility evokes the biological/digital commingling in the novel's protagonist, who jacks into the cyberspace network through a neural interface. As if in invitation, on the opposite side of the slipcase glitters an embedded network interface card. Time to plug in.

Minsky's transformation of *Neuromancer* marks a lifelong fascination with technology. He continues to be an avid explorer of the Internet and cutting-edge computer software, and participates in the virtual world of Second Life, where he founded a Book Art Museum (naturally).

As demonstrated by the considerable critical success of the Bill of Rights series, Minsky continues to connect micro actions in the economic, political, artistic, and social spheres to macro effects on society. He is the quintessential artistic entrepreneur, a maestro of material and metaphor in book and art hybrids that demand our attention and inspire reflection. Read his story, study his work, and follow his life's compass that has pointed him to true north for over fifty years: let nothing prevent you from giving voice to your truth.

Betty Bright
Author, *No Longer Innocent: Book Art in America 1960-1980*

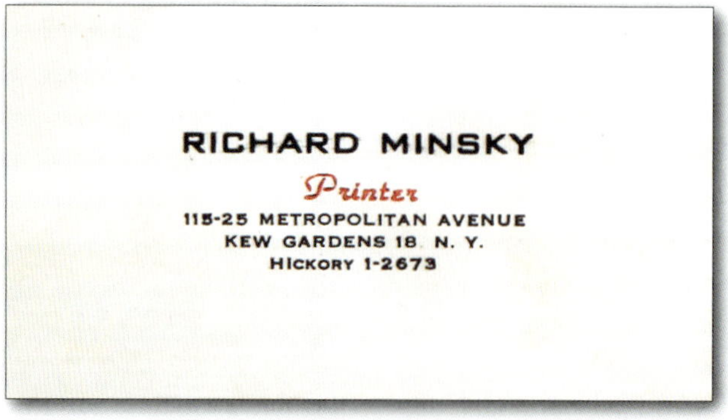

Business Card, 1960
Letterpress from hand set type. 2 x 3½
Collection of the Haas Family Arts Library, Yale University

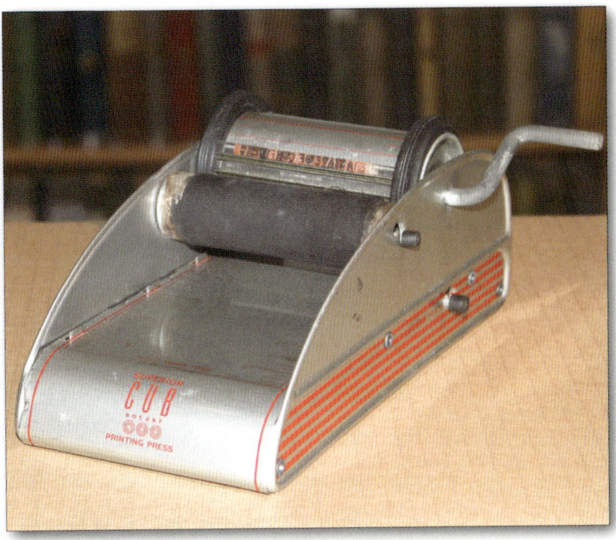

Superior "Cub" rotary printing press, 1957

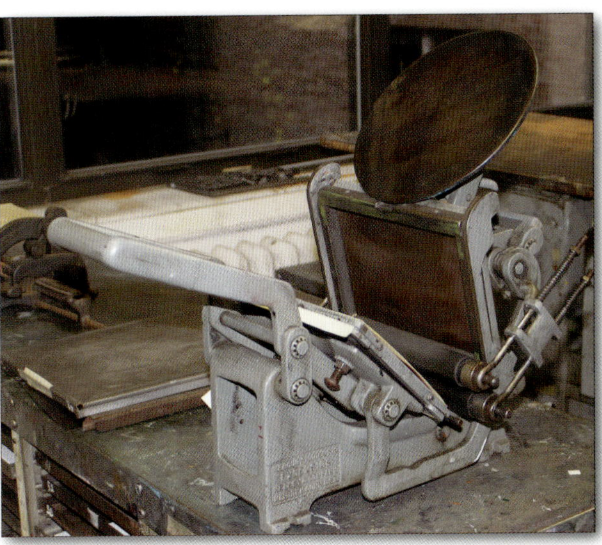

Kelsey 5x8 platen press, 1960

Early Years

ON CHRISTMAS MORNING, 1957 my favorite gift was a Superior Cub Printing Press. It prints postcard size, using rubber type that is similar to foundry type in appearance. You set it in lines into metal type holders that assemble onto the press cylinder. The booklet that came with it has lessons on everything from typography to drumming up business. I was in heaven!

A week later my mother woke me up later than usual. She said, "This morning daddy passed away. He had a heart attack." I was confused and in shock. I wanted to see him, but they had already taken his body away. The funeral was quickly arranged, but I was not allowed to go. My mother said that at ten I was too young. For years I didn't believe he was really dead.

In 1934 my father, Louis Minsky, was the Founder of Religious News Service, which he thought would help reduce prejudice. He had 500 correspondents around the world with teletype machines. Saturday mornings I would ride into Manhattan with him from our apartment in Queens, listening to classical music on the car radio. When we got to his office on 57th Street in the Building for Brotherhood I would write on the Royal typewriter. I loved that machine, and the magic of the letters appearing on the paper as the keys struck the ribbon. The Cub printing press substituted for the Saturdays I spent at his office writing on the Royal typewriter.

When my father died, my mother, Roberta, went to work for the Anti-Defamation League, continuing the mission of reducing prejudice. She was politically aware, and held meetings of The League of Women Voters in our apartment.

In 1958 I took Graphic Arts shop at Russell Sage Junior High in Forest Hills, Queens. The teacher, Mr. Caputo, was inspirational. We learned hand type composition and letterpress printing, dry point etching, linoleum cutting, basic bookbinding and paper marbling. The shop had Pilot hand presses and a motorized 10x15 Chandler & Price platen press.

In August of 1960 my mother died. The doctor thought she had hepatitis but it was cancer. Now 13, I was able to go to the funeral. I saw her body in the coffin and for the first time understood the meaning of life.

Within a month I had to come to terms with many things. My 72-year-old grandmother, Edna, was my guardian jointly with the Guardianship Clerk of the Surrogate's Court. I needed to earn money.

In September I cashed in all the savings bonds I had received in January for my Bar Mitzvah, which yielded $350. That was enough to buy a 5x8 Kelsey platen press, 6 cases of used foundry type and some ink.

I printed my first business cards, and passed them out in my homeroom, inviting all my 9th grade classmates to become 15% commission sales representatives. The orders started coming the next day. I continued printing on that press through high school and college.

JUNIOR ASTRONOMY CLUB
35th Annual Public Lecture Series
Dr. Donat G. Wentzel
Visiting Professor of Astronomy
Princeton University
will speak on
The Origin of Spiral Arms
Waverly Building, New York University
24 Waverly Place Room 170
February 21, 1964 8 P.M.

GUEST LECTURE TICKET

Guest Lecture Ticket
Junior Astronomy Club, 1964.
Letterpress from hand set type. 2¼ x 3¾
Collection of the Haas Family Arts Library, Yale University

The last year at Russell Sage I developed an interest in astronomy. A distinguished astrophysicist was presenting a lecture at New York University one Friday evening. I took the hour-long bus and subway trip to Washington Square, and was surprised that only about two dozen teenagers were in the audience. The event was sponsored by the Junior Astronomy Club, which had been in existence since 1929.

I joined that day, and suggested that they could fill the 300-seat auditorium if they sent free tickets to the Science Department chairmen at all NYC high schools and asked them to award them to their best students. That week I printed tickets for the next lecture. It worked—the hall was filled with smart kids. I continued printing the tickets until graduating from high school in 1964.

The JAC published a bimonthly *Junior Astronomy News*, and needed a member to be responsible for printing it. I readily volunteered. In the spring of 1961 we moved the Gestetner mimeograph into my apartment. Others wrote the articles, edited them, and gave me the typed stencils. I printed 350 copies. These were mailed to the members and to subscribing libraries. I designed the covers, which were usually reproduced from Gestefax stencils made at a service that scanned the artwork and burned a stencil with an electric spark. The following year I became the Editor, and also continued producing it. I printed the May, 1963 cover on my Kelsey press in red and black [facing page].

I bought a 4x5 Crown Graphic camera, and at Richmond Hill High School became the photographer for *Domino*, the school newspaper. They gave me keys to the darkroom, but took them away after I was accused of taking girls in there. I only took one girl in there, Barbara Krooss, and all we did was talk. She became my first girlfriend a year later.

Occasionally I did covers for other school publications—*Dome*, the literary magazine, and *Nucleus*, the science magazine. *Dome* was a properly printed publication, since it circulated to the entire school, and *Nucleus* was done on a Ditto spirit duplicator, since only a small number of copies were needed. I loved the Ditto machine because you could draw in several different colors on one stencil.

As a loner and a dork I was an easy target for some of the tough kids. One day a particularly obnoxious one was taunting me, trying to pick a fight, and hit me a few times to get me to hit back. I knew that if I did that he would cream me. But I'd had enough. Since I was about six I had played with electronics, and had built all sorts of things from kits. That afternoon I rigged a zapper with a 300 volt portable TV battery that fit in a jacket pocket, some capacitors, and lengths of wire that extended to my fingertips. The next day was assembly, when jacket and tie were mandatory.

I saw him in the stairwell between periods and zapped him on the back of his neck. "What the fuck was that?" he yelled. "Stay away from me or it'll get worse," I replied, and walked away. Five minutes later my name was called over the loudspeaker to report to the Boy's Dean. That was Mr. Beller, who looked exactly like Clark Kent in the TV show Superman. "Hand it over," he demanded. I took the device off and gave it to him. He gave me a lecture about using my brain for the betterment of humanity.

At the end of the day I retrieved my zapper and wired myself. But there was nobody laying in wait for me. To the contrary, all harassment ceased, and the leader of that gang asked me to join them at their lunch table and help them with their homework.

What does this have to do with book art? In 2003, the 100th birthday of Eric Arthur Blair (whose pseudonym was George Orwell), I used those electronic wiring skills in a binding for the first edition of *Nineteen Eighty-Four* [page 14], and in 2009 the zapper became an electric chair for *Freedom of Choice* [page 126].

VOLUME XXXIV MAY, 1963

JUNIOR ASTRONOMY NEWS

THE ANDROMEDA GALAXY

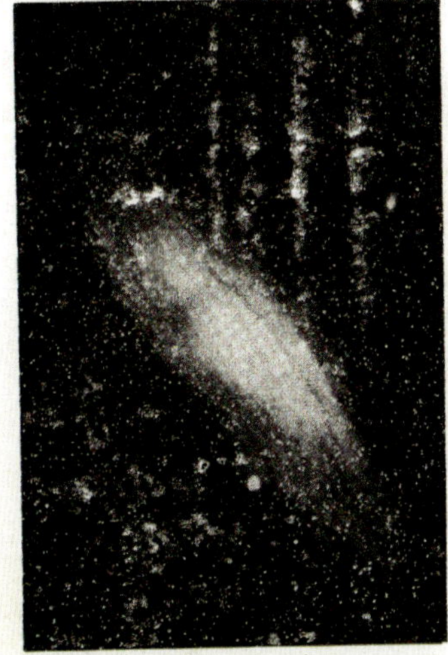

NGC 205

NGC 224
M 31

NGC 221
M 32

Mt. Wilson and Palomar Observatories
48 inch Schmidt Telescope

THIS MONTH:

Ballots for election of officers for 1963 - 1964, with candidates' qualifications.

Thermonuclear Fusion by Len Swec

The Andromeda Galaxy by Richard Minsky

Junior Astronomy News
Junior Astronomy Club, New York, Vol. XXXIV, May, 1963.
Letterpress from hand set type and Ludlow. 11 x 8½
Collection of the Haas Family Arts Library, Yale University

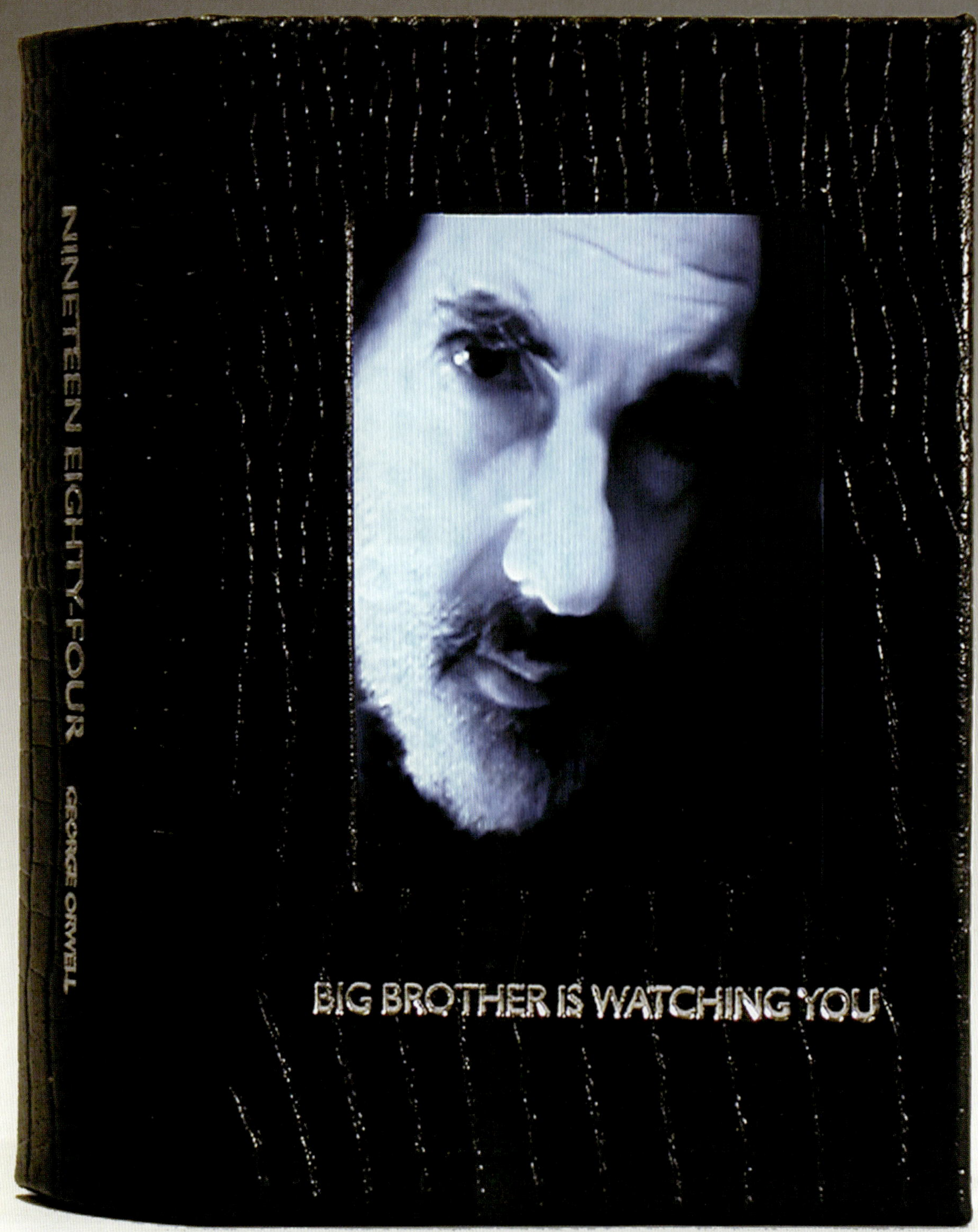

Nineteen Eighty-four
by George Orwell. Secker & Warburg, London, 1949. First Edition.
Binding by Minsky, 2003-2006. 7½ x 5 x 2½
Lizard-grained cowhide, white metal foil stamped title and slogan. LCD monitor embedded in cover with miniature video camera hidden behind leather with ⅛" hole for lens. When you hold the book you see yourself on the screen.

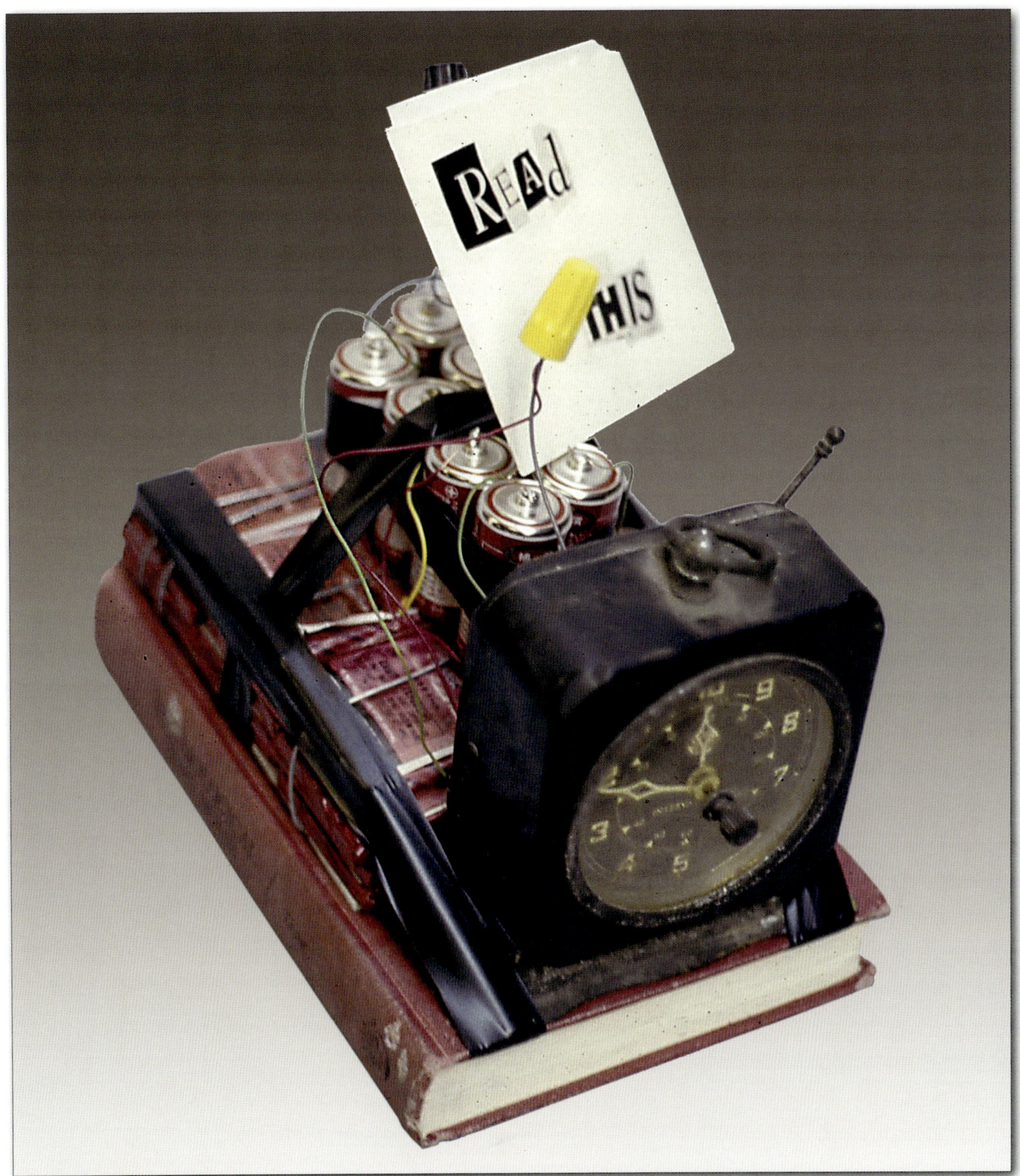

The Biological Time Bomb
by Gordon Rattray Taylor. The New American Library, 1968.
Binding by Minsky, 1988. 8 x 5 x 6
Live explosives, batteries, timer, electrical tape,
photocopy, envelope, collage.

The perils of genetic engineering.

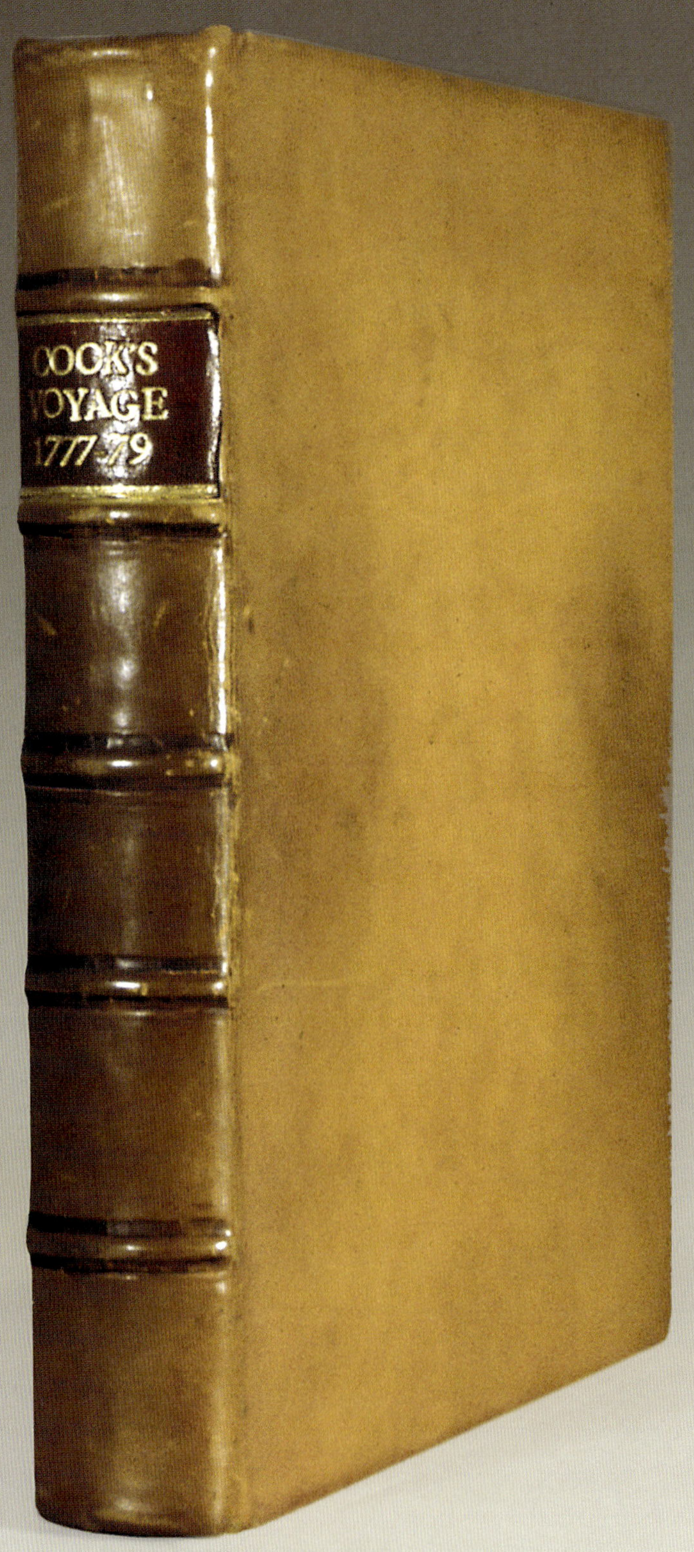

Cook's Voyage 1777-79
Binding by Minsky, 1968
Full calf binding in period style, sewn on five raised cords, goatskin label tooled in gold with brass handle letters.

After Richmond Hill I enrolled at Brooklyn College as a physics major, planning to become an astrophysicist. I had thought about going to medical school and becoming a psychiatrist, but at my nephew's bris I nearly fainted when I saw the mohel cut off his foreskin.

Brooklyn College was a two-hour trip each way by bus and subway. Driving would take 25 minutes, but I couldn't afford a car. To make money I became a door-to-door salesman for *Collier's Encyclopedia.* There was a week of intensive training memorizing the pitch, learning to handle all sorts of situations, and how to close the deal. In five weeks I made enough to buy a 1960 SAAB, which had a three-cylinder, two-cycle engine. That education in sales became important to my book art, as you will see.

The car helped me get to Brooklyn my sophomore year. I was an A student as a freshman, but when I had a head-on collision with a truck, my grades plummeted to D+. I couldn't concentrate. When taking a test I would spend the entire time writing one sentence. My English teacher sent me to the college psychologist for evaluation.

The psychologist referred me to a psychiatrist who prescribed anti-depressants. After a year of writing down my dreams and taking increasing doses of medication I didn't get any better. My pharmacist finally refused to refill the prescription because the dosage was so high. Completely off the medication, I started to improve.

I became a varsity sabre fencer. That helped to get me into shape both physically and psychologically. My interests expanded and I switched majors to economics, spending two years researching an honors paper debunking the notion that rationality was a necessary assumption in economic theory.

At class registration my process was to look for teachers who used their own book as a text, no matter what the subject. That led me to a class in Readers' Theater with Prof. Melvin R. White. At the end of the semester he asked me to join the Readers' Theater group that toured the east coast giving performances. That training in vocal presentation and entertainment has been useful in everything since, particularly when working as an itinerant lecturer.

Fencing and theater were not enough to keep me busy, so I joined the Brooklyn College Chorus, which was under the direction of Robert Hickock. In addition to performing the great choral works—Bach's *B Minor Mass* and Mozart's *Requiem,* we performed in costume with action for the BC Opera Theater in a full production of von Weber's *Der Freischütz.* I had been playing violin in school orchestras since 4th grade and singing in the chorus since 8th grade, so it was a natural continuation of interest. This was the background for my composition of the music for *Adventures in Ku-Ta-Ba Wa-Do* [page 28].

Everything changed on October 19, 1967. Anti-war sentiment had been growing. While the Brooklyn College President was away, an administrator called in NYC Police to break up a student protest of Navy recruiters on campus. Nearly a thousand students came to the support of the demonstrators, and 200 cops came to quell the riot. Forty students were arrested, and more were left bludgeoned and bloodied.

A student boycott followed, and a few days later thousands showed up for a rally led by Columbia University student organizer Mark Rudd. Two large flags were carried across campus, one red and one black, symbolizing revolution and anarchy.

I had two mentors at Brooklyn College—Professor Nordstrom and Professor Birkenhead. Both were economists who had earned their PhDs at The New School. Professor Nordstrom had long white hair and sparkling blue eyes. He credited his rise through the army in WWII from an enlisted Private to a Colonel in charge of a division of tanks to writing clear orders. He said most officers wrote orders that any fool could understand. He wrote orders that no fool could mistake.

Professor Birkenhead was an activist. After the October riot he invited the CIA to recruit on campus. He followed up by advising students to protest CIA recruitment on campus. He advised me to apply to the CIA for a job to avoid being drafted to Vietnam. I followed his advice. It required a 17 page application, an interview, and a background check that included FBI agents interviewing my neighbors.

Despite my disastrous sophomore year, I was able to finish Brooklyn cum laude with honors in Economics. Brown offered me a University Fellowship with full support and a stipend for five years to enter a PhD program in Economics. Taking my chances on going to Vietnam, I withdrew my CIA application and in September 1968, packed my bags and moved to the new Brown Graduate Center in Providence, RI.

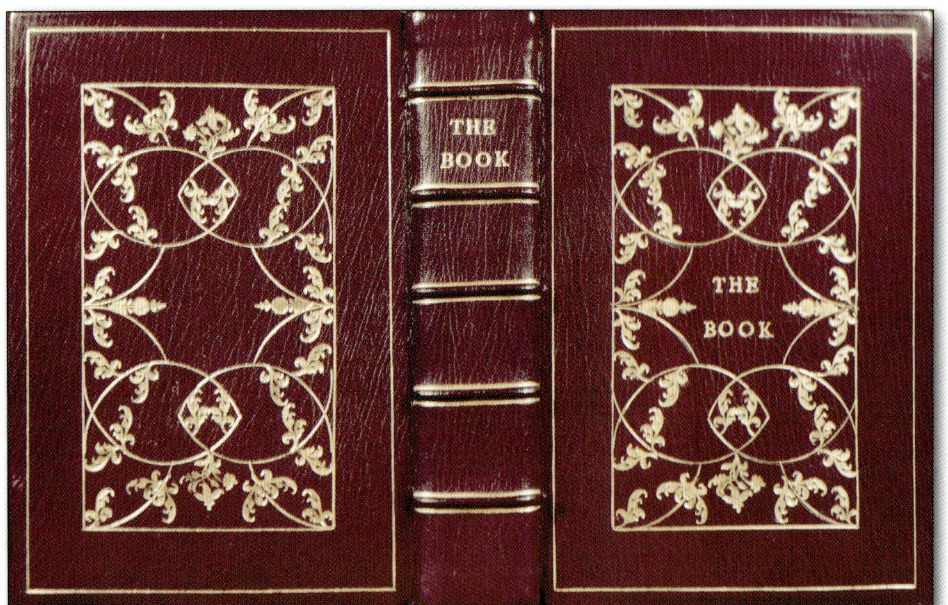

The Book
by Douglas C. McMurtrie.
Covici-Friede, New York, 1937.
Binding by Minsky, 1968. 10 x 8
Goatskin, gold tooling, silk endbands, marbled endsheets.

When I arrived at Brown University to begin graduate school in Economics I had no idea that my direction would quickly be changed. The week before classes began I explored the campus and discovered the Annmary Brown Memorial, a windowless mausoleum that had its walls lined with one of the largest collections of incunabula (15th century printed books) owned by an American university. After a short conversation, the Curator sent me to basement B of the Rockefeller Library to meet Daniel Gibson Knowlton, the University Bookbinder, who had spent the previous few years conserving and restoring that collection.

The bindery immediately appealed to me. Books in various stages of repair were on the counters and the smell of leather permeated the room. I enrolled in his bookbinding class and bought some equipment from him. There was an old wooden lying press and plough, a sewing frame, a cast iron nipping press, and hand tools. I installed a bindery in my tiny dormitory room.

By the end of 1968 I completed two full leather bindings. *Cook's Voyage* used 18th century style tools, materials and techniques to achieve the look and feel of that period. *The Book*, Douglas McMurtrie's 1937 history of books, had been on the bookshelf in my home since before I was born. It seemed the right choice for my first gold-tooled binding design. The pattern uses brass tools based on those created in the 16th century for the great bibliophile Jean Grolier [above].

That winter I started binding the 1931 Cheshire House edition of *The Georgics of Virgil* [facing page]. The copy I bought had no covers but immaculate pages. My design called for cream Hewit's calf with a thin border in brown Oasis goatskin onlay, with a single gold line outside the border and gold filigree inside. Onlay is done by paring leather exceptionally thin using a curved knife, pasting it on the cover, and pressing it flat. In keeping with the theme of the Georgics, the corners were to be red goat onlay flowers with gold stems and green onlay leaves, with tan drawer-handle onlays, outlined in gold, fencing in the flowers. The title was to be blind-tooled (without gold) in the center of the cover.

Everything went smoothly until I got to the title. Blind tooling is done by pressing a warm wooden-handled brass tool into damp leather so the impression darkens. My tool was too hot and the leather too wet, and in a moment it burned the delicate skin. I showed it to Dan. "Oh, dear," he said. I asked, "What can I do?" "Fill the burned lettering with auto body filler and sand it flat," he replied, "and design an onlay to go over it."

It took three months to pare a piece of black goatskin the size I needed without making any holes in it. I designed the onlay with drawer-handle corners at the same angle as those already on the cover, and tooled the title in gold. The result was better than the design I initially envisioned. It was an important lesson in craftsmanship—take a mistake and make it an improvement.

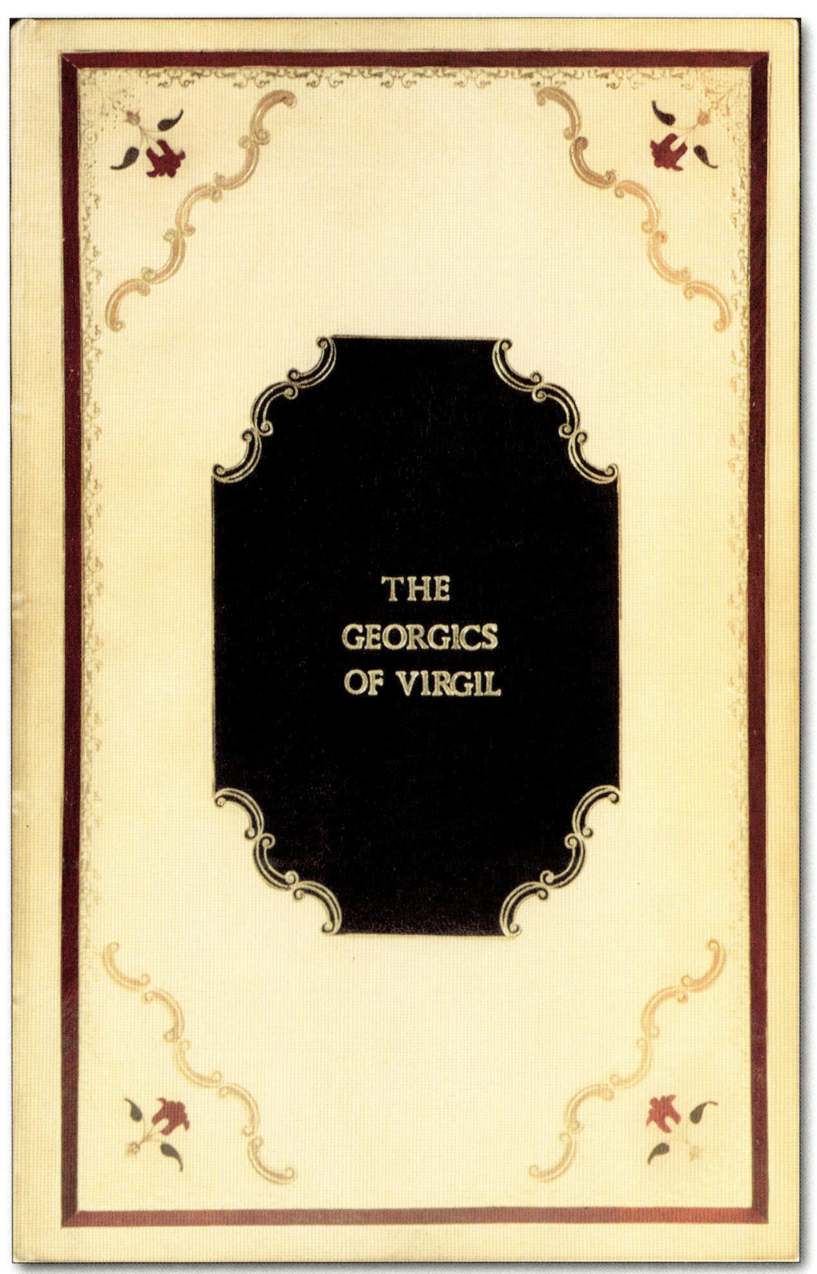

The Georgics of Virgil
Translated by John Dryden. Cheshire House, New York, 1931.
Binding by Minsky, 1969. 14 x 9
Hewit's fair calf with onlays of Oasis Nigerian goat, gold and blind tooling. Sewn on 5 raised cords. Swedish marbled endsheets. Calf hinges. "MINSKY" tooled in gold, inside front cover, "1969" in gold, inside back cover.
Collection of Clare Stone, New York

Much of my time was spent binding, and I began skipping economics classes. That seemed fine with the faculty, because I was disruptive, disagreeing with much of what they were teaching.

Each weekend I drove my baby blue Plymouth Belvedere back to Queens, where I would spend some time with my grandmother, who was then 80, and whose favorite thing to do was cook for me. A group of musical friends would come for a jam session, where we played mostly blues and rock, with some free-form jazz.

At Brown I spent my study time reading in the library. As an undergraduate I had become immersed in the history of economic thought, which was not taught in the Brown graduate program. I had read Adam Smith's *Wealth of Nations* in several editions. Brown had a copy of the original from 1776, signed by its first owner, a French Director-General of Finances. That copy changed the way I understood Smith's text and changed my relationship with books as objects.

It transported me into 18th century France. New questions came to me—what had he thought before reading this? The library had copies of François Quesnay's *Tableau Économique* in French, and no English translations. It took several months at my carrel with Cassell's French-English dictionary to understand how that had influenced Smith and what changes in thought had taken place.

The intellectual questions that this copy of *The Wealth of Nations* suggested were not as unusual as the metaphysical experience. I felt the presence of the French finance minister when holding the book. It was a spiritual or psychic phenomenon. That got me started collecting early printed books based on their vibes, without regard to their language or subject. This attention to the book's feeling and transmission of emotion and consciousness through the material became a central element in my work.

It was clear by the end of the first semester that the faculty and I had very different notions about economics. For the spring semester, the Chairman, Ben Chinitz, approved my registering for a four course program of independent study and research. I spent much of my time in Dan Knowlton's bindery, and also joined the Brown University Chorus, singing in a concert performance with the Rhode Island Philharmonic.

The Vietnam War continued, and graduate school deferments were eliminated. I was sent a draft notice at the Queens address. I filed a change of address, which switched my Draft Board to Providence. In New York City, everyone was trying to avoid the draft, so the board was taking many misfits to fill their quota.

The order to appear for a pre-induction physical quickly came to my Brown mailbox. The line of naked men proceeded through all the stages of examination. At the end a Captain asked, "Is there anything else we should know?"

I said, "I don't know—is this something you should know about?" and handed him the three yellowed Thermofax copies of my psychiatrist's report on the aftermath of the 1965 car collision. It had been prepared for the lawsuit against the truck driver and detailed the permanent damage to my brain, with the results of psychological tests, including that my drawings of males and females showed confusion between them.

They scheduled an appointment with the army psychiatrist a week later. I wore a Harris Tweed jacket and an ascot, and didn't shave. He asked, "How are you?" I replied, "Much better, thank you."

After a few more questions, he said, "Do you think you would like being in the army?" This was obviously a trick question. I looked at the corners of the ceiling. "Would you like being in the army?" he reiterated.

"I don't know," I replied, "I never thought about it." He gently said, "Think about it." I pictured myself in a foxhole in Vietnam with explosions going off all around me, being shot at with machine guns by people who considered me an invader, and bodies and blood everywhere. "I think there would be too much excitement," I finally answered.

"You don't like excitement?" he asked.

"No, I would rather be in the library with my books." That was the end of the interview. He gave no indication of what he was thinking.

A week later I received a draft card with the status 4F—Unfit for Military Service. That car crash may have saved my life. After that, I began to believe in the wisdom of the divine creator.

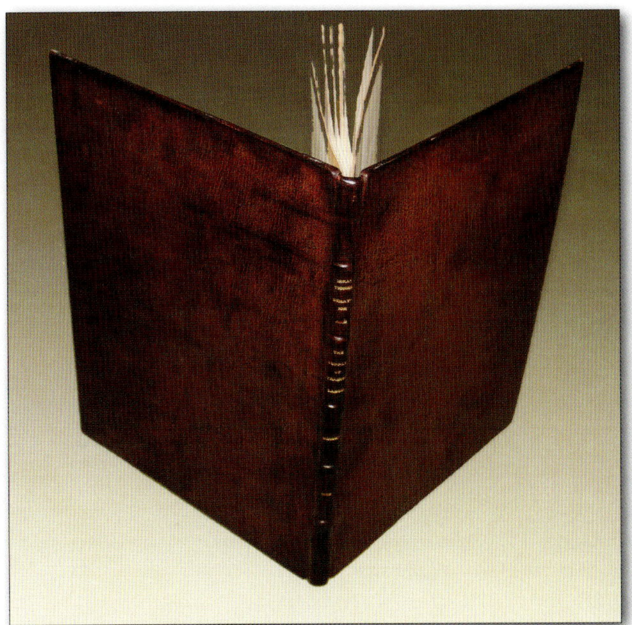

Irrational Behavior and the Supply of Trained Labor
by Richard Minsky. 1969. 11¼ x 8⅝
Thesis for MA in Economics at Brown University, Photocopy bound in brown goatskin, gold title.
Collection of Clare Stone, New York

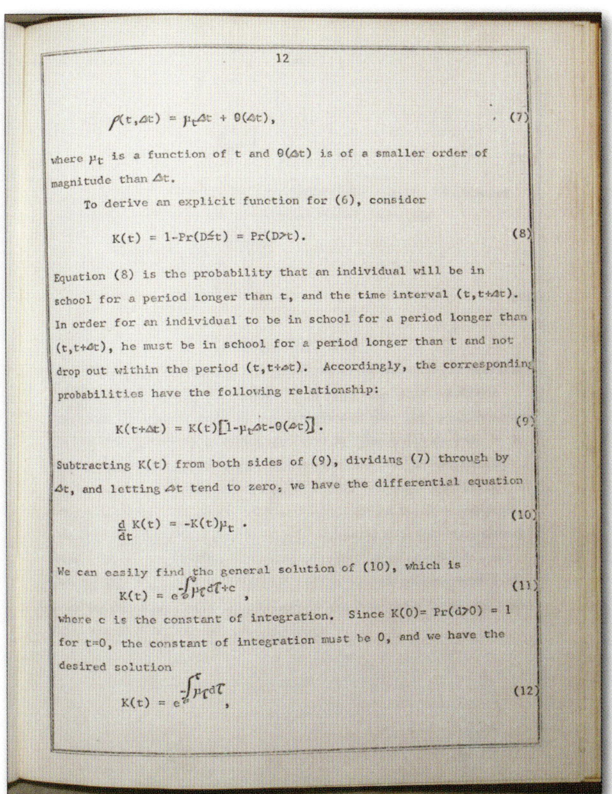

12

$$\rho(t,\Delta t) = \mu_t \Delta t + \theta(\Delta t), \quad (7)$$

where μ_t is a function of t and $\theta(\Delta t)$ is of a smaller order of magnitude than Δt.

To derive an explicit function for (6), consider

$$K(t) = 1 - Pr(D \leq t) = Pr(D > t). \quad (8)$$

Equation (8) is the probability that an individual will be in school for a period longer than t, and the time interval $(t, t+\Delta t)$. In order for an individual to be in school for a period longer than $(t, t+\Delta t)$, he must be in school for a period longer than t and not drop out within the period $(t, t+\Delta t)$. Accordingly, the corresponding probabilities have the following relationship:

$$K(t+\Delta t) = K(t)[1 - \mu_t \Delta t - \theta(\Delta t)]. \quad (9)$$

Subtracting K(t) from both sides of (9), dividing (7) through by Δt, and letting Δt tend to zero, we have the differential equation

$$\frac{d}{dt} K(t) = -K(t)\mu_t . \quad (10)$$

We can easily find the general solution of (10), which is

$$K(t) = e^{-\int_0^t \mu_\tau d\tau + c}, \quad (11)$$

where c is the constant of integration. Since $K(0) = Pr(d>0) = 1$ for t=0, the constant of integration must be 0, and we have the desired solution

$$K(t) = e^{-\int_0^t \mu_\tau d\tau}, \quad (12)$$

I reworked my undergraduate honors paper into a master's thesis titled "Irrational Behavior and the Supply of Trained Labor." The thought behind it was that economic theory had been based on the notion of rationality for centuries. The thesis demonstrated, through a mathematical model, that rationality was an unnecessary assumption.

I bound a copy in polished goatskin. The gold title had to be in 6 point type because the spine was so thin. The mathematical model was just 16 pages, including the bibliography. It may have been the shortest thesis ever submitted. Two years later I sold it as a work of book art to gallery owner Allan Stone.

I gave an unbound copy to my thesis advisor. Soon he called me into his office. "I've read your thesis, but am not sure that I understand it," he volunteered. "It doesn't matter whether you understand it. Will you sign it?" I'm not certain why he did. Perhaps the thought of having me for another term had something to do with it.

In June of 1969 I left Providence with an MA in Economics, and was offered a full scholarship toward a PhD with the Graduate Faculty of The New School in Manhattan, where my Brooklyn College mentors had studied.

The Chairman of the Economics Department was Robert Heilbroner, historian of economic thought and author of *The Worldly Philosophers* among other works. The two graduate courses on that subject were taught by Adolph Lowe, the great socio-economist who had been an economic architect of the Weimar Republic. Together they created the first graduate course on Ecological Economics. I continued there though the spring of 1971, and credit my studies with that department for the institutional economics that enabled me to create the Center for Book Arts in 1974.

One day I saw a most peculiar figure striding down the hallway—a man wearing a cape, high button shoes and a bowler. I stopped in the nearest office and asked a woman, "Who is that?" "Professor Horace Kallen," she replied. "I want to take his course. What does he teach?" She answered, "Philosophy of Art, and you have to take it next semester, because he's 88 and is retiring." I immediately registered for it, and that experience changed the way I think about art and the methodology in my approach to making things.

The first day of class he started the lesson by saying, "What is creation? When you take a shit it's a creation." Professor Kallen changed me from a bookbinder to a book artist.

On May 4, 1970, four unarmed students were killed by Ohio National Guard troops at Kent State University during a protest of the US invasion of Cambodia. This precipitated a national student strike. I joined a guerrilla theater group and became active in what used to be called agitprop—agitation propaganda—and later was called street theater.

We took on many charged subjects, not just military/political themes. Racism was an issue. In one skit another player and I would fall down on a crowded sidewalk or in a bank and a group would gather around us. "Someone's been shot," yelled one of the standing circle. "Call the police," yelled another. "One of them's a nigger and the other's a spic," yelled a third. And the fourth voice yelled, "Never mind, business as usual." We then quickly dispersed. The whole scene took about 20 seconds.

My sister, Susan, changed her name to Astra Wolf and was living in a loft on Henry Street in Manhattan. Astra was the Executive Secretary to Abram Lerner, Director of the Joseph H. Hirshhorn Museum. The collection was being stored in a Chelsea warehouse while the building was under construction in Washington.

I was living with my grandmother in our apartment in Queens. I still had my printing press, but now also could bind and repair books. Dan Knowlton had suggested that I join the The Guild Of Book Workers, an organization that had started in 1906. I became active in it, and was the youngest person at committee meetings.

Astra suggested I show Mr. Lerner my bindings, and I was awarded a contract from the Smithsonian to bind and repair books for the museum. Once a week I would drive to their office to pick up books and deliver the previous week's work. While binding I would read the books, and that was my art education. They also commissioned some special bindings, including a full leather presentation volume for Mr. Hirshhorn.

Within a year I had completed all the books that needed work, and it was on to magazines. Reading these I learned about the art world, art politics, and the art market. But after a while it was redundant, and I suggested they get a commercial bindery to finish the job.

The Museum needed a photographer, and I put my experience in that medium to work, taking the Civil Service test and becoming a G7 Museum Assistant. This required setting up a 4x5 view camera in the warehouse, going into the vaults to retrieve the works of art, and photographing about 25 of them a day. Handling some 2,000 paintings and sculptures trained my eye.

Mr. Lerner was often in the warehouse. After a few months of handling the art and familiarizing myself with the collection, I said to him, "There are no books in this collection as art works." He replied, "If you want books to be recognized as art, you'll have to start an organization to promote that and get museum exhibitions." That stuck in my mind. Another thing he said that influenced me was, "Exhibition catalogs are usually too big. They should fit in your pocket."

One day at Jones Beach with Astra I had forgotten to bring anything to read. She said, "Why don't you draw?" "Draw what?" I asked. "Whatever you see," she answered, and gave me a pencil and paper. I did a drawing of all the people on the beach. She said it was good, and that I should do more. I started to spend my time drawing and painting. Some artists I respected told me I should become an artist.

Astra and I began collaborating on books. In 1970–71 we did three copies of *The Traveler*, each with 20 of her poems and 20 paintings that we passed back and forth until they were done. I was experimenting with paper marbling, primarily for endpapers in books, but we also worked on top of the marbled imagery with ink and paint for some of the pictures. We designed the bindings together as well.

The Traveler
20 Poems by Astra Wolf, in her handwriting.
20 pictures and binding by Astra Wolf and Richard Minsky, 1971.
10¼ x 7¾
Goatskin, watercolor, and collage on hand marbled paper.
Collection of Clare Stone, New York

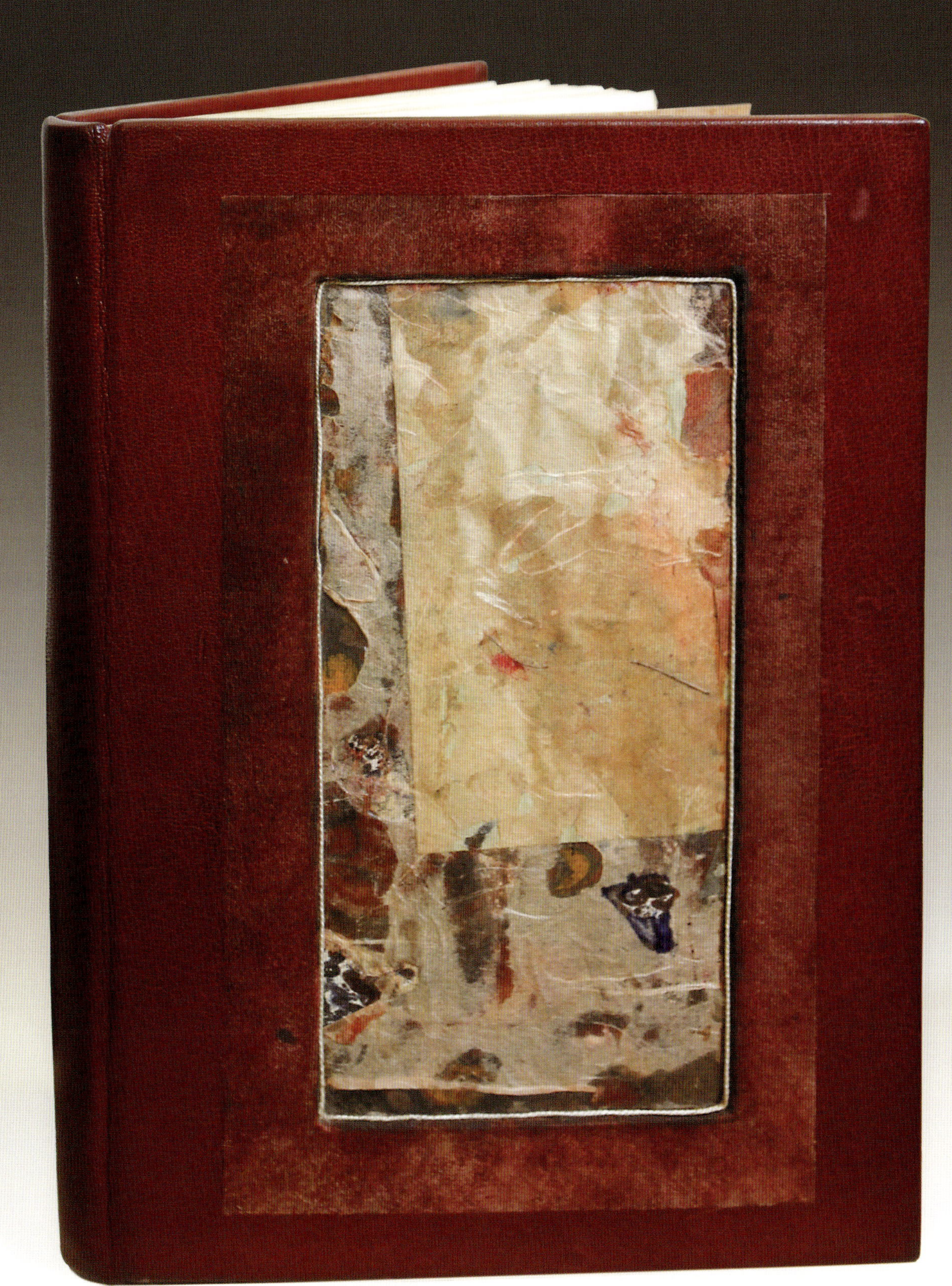

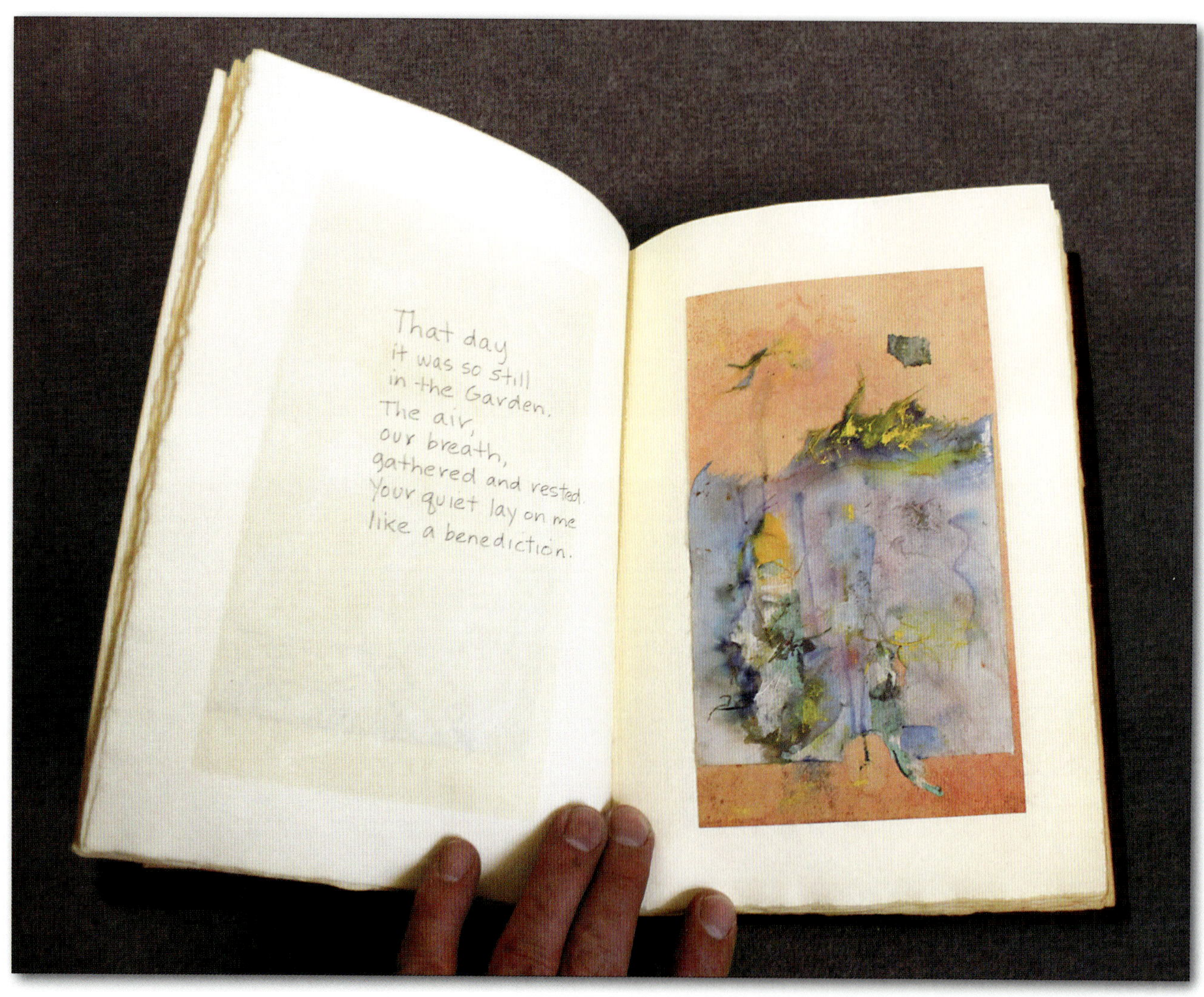

The Traveler
20 Poems by Astra Wolf, in her handwriting.
20 pictures and binding by Astra Wolf and Richard Minsky, 1971. 10¼ x 7¾
Watercolor, ink and collage.
Collection of Clare Stone, New York

I continued at The New School for another year, studying the history of economic thought, operations analysis, advanced mathematical modeling and more. The great disappointment was that the basic textbook at The New School was the same as at Brown, Henderson and Quandt's *Microeconomic Theory.*

It is built on the assumption that profit maximization is the goal of the entrepreneur. The "Marxists" disagreed with the "Capitalists" on how the profits should be distributed. This narrow focus on profit maximization ignored ethics and trained people to do what subsequently collapsed the economy. My father was a not-for-profit entrepreneur, as am I. The theories they espoused did not include my family.

At the end of the spring 1971 semester I would have been one credit short of the course requirements for the PhD, but had no need of that degree to pursue my work in book art.

By April of 1971 I had had enough of Richard Nixon. After two years of his Presidency I didn't want to live in the USA. I gave notice at the museum, bought a backpack and a tent, and took my violin to Europe. The semester was not quite over at The New School, but I didn't care. Starting in England, I visited the master bookbinders Sydney Cockerell and Bernard Middleton, and went to the tannery of Russell Bookcrafts, where the Oasis Goat skins were tanned and dyed.

Hitchhiking from the tannery, I was picked up by a lorry [British truck]. The driver was in a rock band and stopped because he saw my fiddle case. I lived and played with the band for two weeks before heading to Paris. I set up my tent in the Bois de Boulogne, and started visiting bookbinderies. Each binder does things slightly differently, and I learned a lot by observing them.

I also started hanging out at the American Center on Boulevard Raspail, where many musicians gathered. Within a week I was playing in three bands, and moved into a house in Vincennes shared by musicians, artists, actors and mimes. The folk-rock band, Come with Us, played gigs of all sorts, including a performance before a huge audience at the Faculté de Droit. That one was memorable not just for the thousands who came, but for the armored police who lined the street to the concert, with body shields, full visored helmets and submachine guns, indicative of the lasting impact of the student riots of 1968. In June, two of the bands played in the Festival de Montparnasse.

Astra came to Paris. We bought a used Skoda, a small Czech car, and drove to Italy on a meandering excursion, stopping at binderies in Nice, Marseilles, and other spots along the way. Nice has a wonderful beach with a wide variety of colored stones. I took a few with the notion that I would make a Nice Stone Book.

In Florence we visited the Biblioteca Nazionale Centrale, where a team of book conservators was restoring the damage from the Arno flood of 1966. We drove back to Paris by way of Venice, with a stop at the Centro del Bel Libro in Ascona, Switzerland, sold the car, and flew to New York.

I made a blank book with the stones from Nice, adding some blind, gold, and colored tooling to the composition. The marbled endpapers evoked the stones and water of the Nice beach. The day it was done I sold it to Allan Stone.

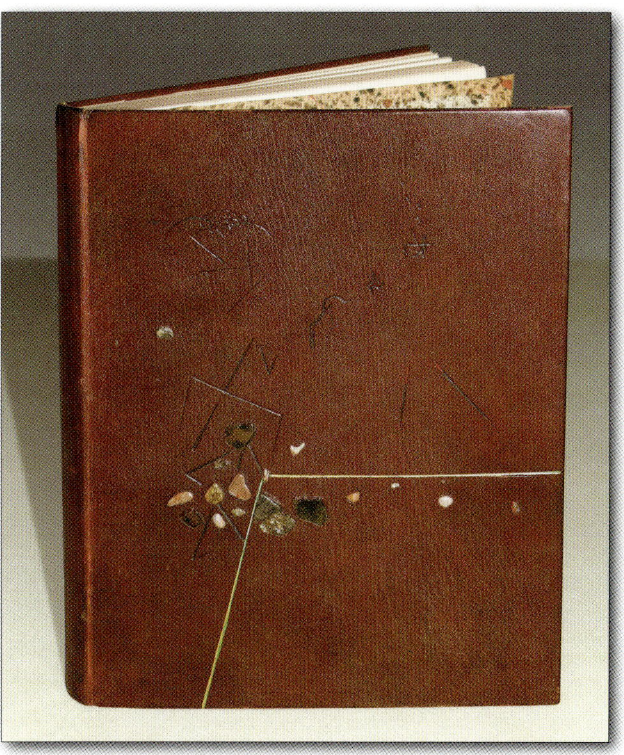

Nice Stone Book
Bound by Minsky 1971. 11½ x 9
Oasis goatskin, stones from the beach in Nice (France), gold, blind and colored tooling, hand marbled endpapers by Minsky.
Collection of Clare Stone, New York

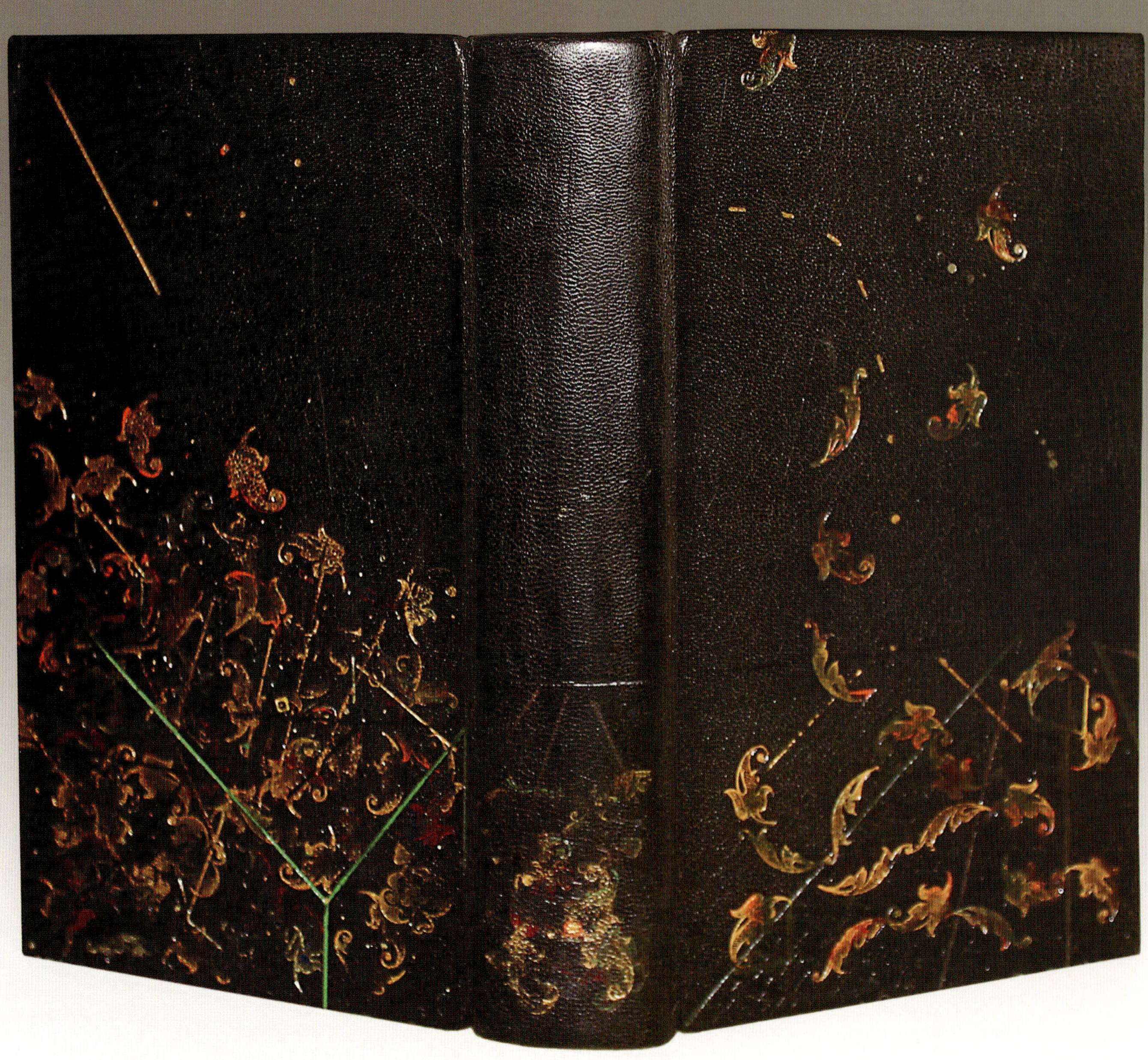

Blank Book
Binding by Minsky, 1972. 9¼ x 6¾
Gold, blind and colored tooling, watercolor endpaper.
Collection of Clare Stone, New York

Working from my apartment was not bringing in enough business. It was time to open a shop. There was an attractive storefront for rent about a half mile away in Forest Hills. With no money to pay the rent or drum up business, I approached The Small Business Administration for a loan. I filled out the forms and they sent someone to look at the equipment in my apartment and at the storefront.

The loan was quickly approved and I painted a new face on translucent white plastic for the 20-foot illuminated sign in three panels: The center, in large letters, RICHARD MINSKY / BOOKBINDING AND REPAIRING; this was flanked by two smaller panels: ART GALLERY and PRINTING.

An auction at a typography shop enabled the purchase of a cabinet with 20 cases of foundry type, and a local printer offered a good deal on an 8x12 motorized Chandler and Price platen press he wasn't using. By the spring of 1972 it was all set up, and people started coming in.

I asked Allan Stone who did his catalog printing. "Lou Meisel at Moak Printing," he advised. I designed a pocket-size catalog with black and white photos of my work. It included books done with other artists, including Domenick Turturro and Roy Newell. A week later the catalogs arrived.

Advertisements in all the art magazines' summer issues used up the remaining funds from the SBA loan. Only one customer came from the ads, but it was exactly the right person. I got a call from someone who wanted three copies produced of a catalog for a private art collection.

Customers were bringing a variety of work into the shop. A dietician had a cookbook she had used for fifty years, and although it cost ten times as much to repair the stained and tattered volume than it would to buy another copy, each of those stains was a memory to be preserved. Every copy of a book is different, and the information it contains about its history is often more valuable than the original text. In the age of screen reading and e-books, that sort of memory is lost.

In May I sent out press releases. *The New York Post* published an article about my shop titled "Art Scene Comes to Queens." That was picked up the same day by CBS-TV. Reporter Rolland Smith came with a crew and put me on the 6 o'clock news in a segment that he ended by saying, "Richard Minsky—modern work with an ancient art."

One local resident who saw the sign and walked in was Paul Shanley, publisher of *Art in America*. He told his friend Philip Dougherty, the New York Times columnist, who devoted an entire column titled "Another Chapter In Ancient Art of Binding."

Evenings and weekends I taught printing and bookbinding classes, which quickly filled. These not only provided income, but also assistants and girlfriends.

I continued creating new non-commissioned bindings. Mostly these were blank books, which I liked because there were no constraints of subject matter and could be pure abstraction. Allan Stone bought almost all the non-commissioned bindings I produced during that period.

One evening a man walked in who said he had noticed the sign while driving by. We talked for a while, and made arrangements for him to bring in some books for bindings and for boxes. These were not ordinary books, but were magnificent works—Vollard editions with prints by Rouault, and André Gide's translation of Goethe's *Promethée* with prints by Henry Moore.

One day he brought Pettigrew's *History of Egyptian Mummies* into the bindery for repair, because the cover was loose. I told him he could pick it up the next week.

The next day this book was lying on top of a bolt of airplane linen that I was cutting into strips for hinges, when it struck me that wrapping this text in the strips would make it look like a mummified book. Without asking permission, I created this binding [frontispiece], using reversible adhesives. Donald loved it. In 1977, critic and curator Rose Slivka included it in the landmark exhibition *The Object as Poet* at the Smithsonian Institution's Renwick Gallery.

An artist named Ed Plunkett came to the shop. He had coined the term "The New York Correspondence School" for a group of artists whose medium was mail art. This group had connections with Dick Higgins and the Fluxus movement. Ed introduced me to Ray Johnson, the leading artist in the genre, and other members of this circle.

I started putting my training as a door-to-door book salesman to use, going to art galleries every Wednesday, their least busy day. An old steel suitcase became my companion for two years and we visited 400 galleries. After painting it with black enamel and gold corners, I added a large green leather panel and hand tooled "RICHARD MINSKY / BOOKBINDING AND REPAIRING" in large 23K gold letters. It looked like a magician or ventriloquist's box, and the inside was lined with maroon velvet.

Filled with books, the trunk weighed about 60 pounds. Carrying it up and down subway steps was challenging, but kept me in shape.

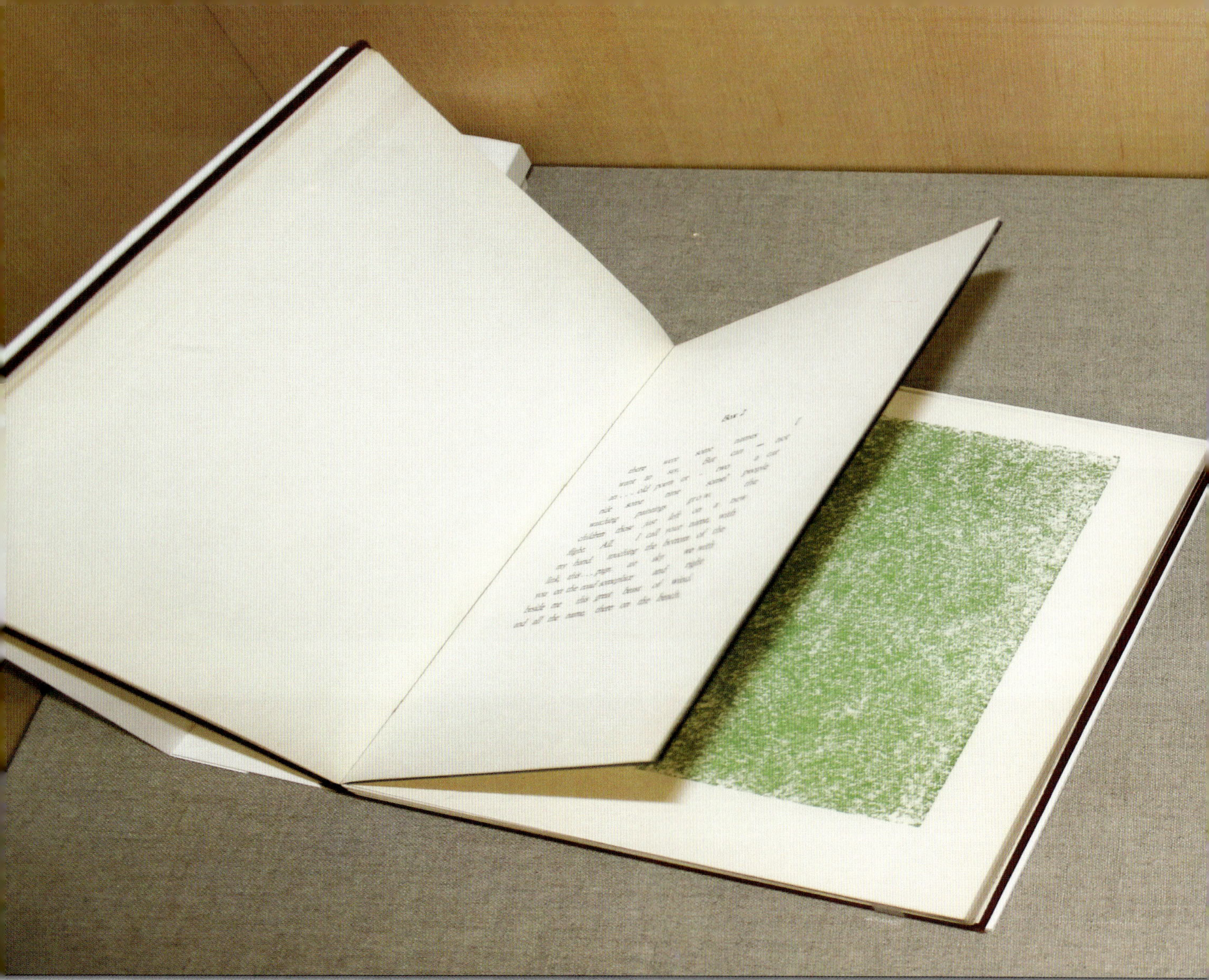

Adventures In Ku-ta-ba Wa-do

GERALD JACKSON, AN ARTIST whom I had always admired, showed me a book he had created with pages of pastel color fields interspersed with pages of his poetry. I thought it would be a great project to undertake as a small edition, and developed a method for creating color field images by printing a flat linoleum block on the motorized 8x12 Chandler & Price platen press, using crumpled paper and bits of paper collage as makeready. [1]

To translate the handwritten poetry into typography and retain the intentionally varied word spacing of the original, I hand set the text from foundry type in Goudy Oldstyle. To coordinate the impression quality of the type with the color prints, I made offset plates from a proof of the typography and printed the poems on a Multilith at the nearby printing shop of Fred D'Alauro, from whom I had gotten the C&P.

Peggy Kelly, one of my printing students, did much of the presswork on the color prints, hand-feeding the paper after I did the makeready and Gerald had approved it.

The original manuscript had no title, and Gerald suggested *Adventures in Ku-Ta-Ba Wa-Do*, based on one of the poems. As I read the book I heard music in my head, and moving through the colors was like listening to an oratorio or opera.

I wrote a score, assembled a group of musicians, and booked time at Mercury Studios on 57th Street, with recording engineer Chuck Irwin. The score follows the color sequence of the prints and uses the poems as a

1 Makeready: Thin paper placed under the tympan sheet of a letterpress, normally used to eliminate unevenness in the impression.

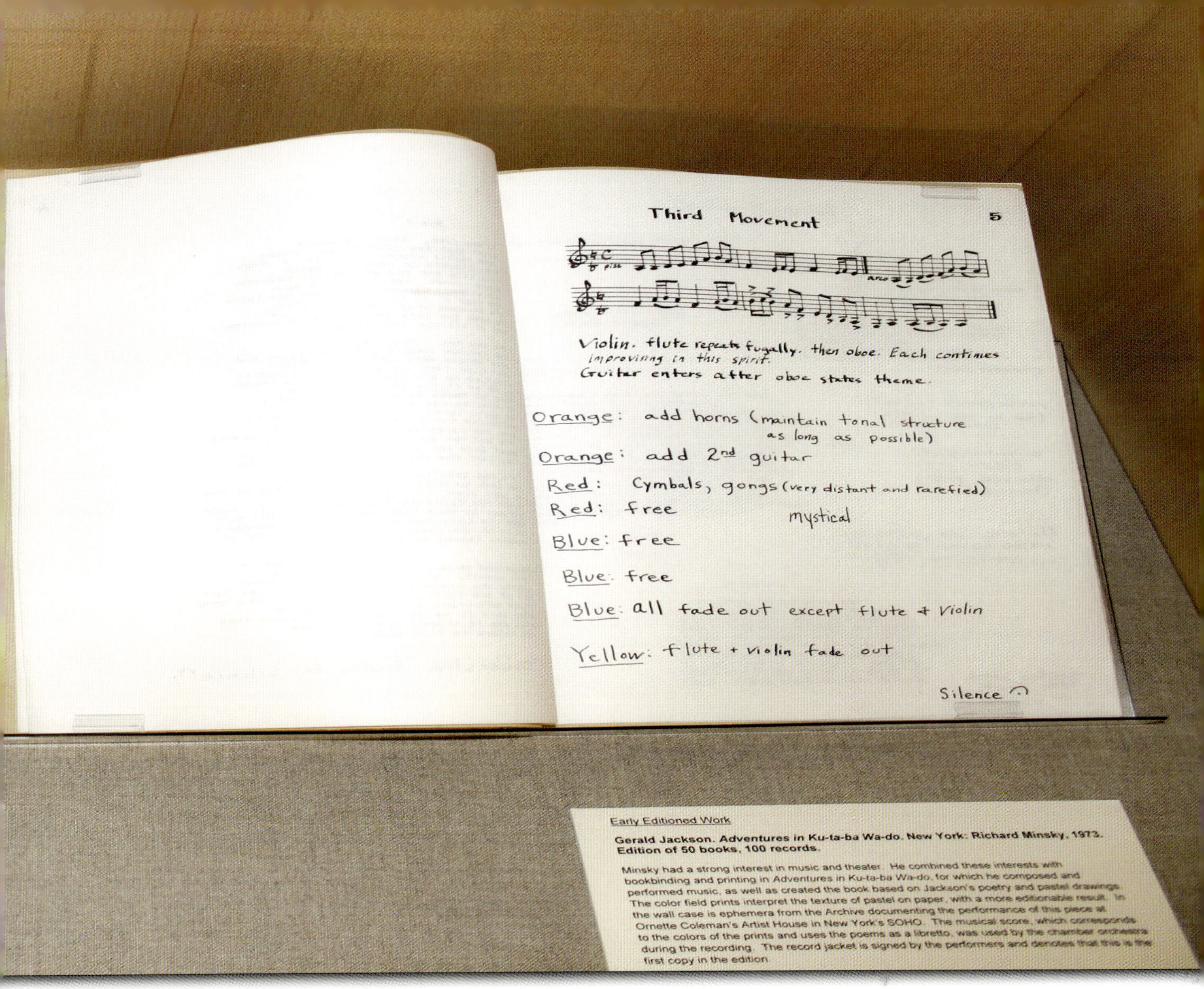

libretto. The musicians had the color prints on their music stands, as the score called on them to interpret the colors.

We recorded four or five takes of each section of the work on 8-track tape, made selections, and mixed down to a stereo master just under 40 minutes long. I had 100 copies made as LP records—50 to go with the edition of the book and 50 to sell separately and to send to radio stations. I hand set type for the record jackets, printed them letterpress in silver ink, and the musicians signed each one.

In 1973 the book, record and score were issued. I sent copies of the record to three alternative radio stations: WKCR (Columbia University), WNYU (New York University), and the independent WBAI. All three played the recording in its entirety. In January 1975 we staged a performance based on the recording at Ornette Coleman's Artist House, on Prince Street in New York's SOHO.

Adventures in Ku-ta-ba Wa-do
by Gerald Jackson, music by Richard Minsky.
Richard Minsky, New York, 1973.
Edition of 50 books 10 x 8, with score 11 x 8½; 100 LP records, of which 50 were issued with the book and score.
Installation photo at the exhibition *Material Meets Metaphor*, Haas Family Arts Library, Yale University, 2010.

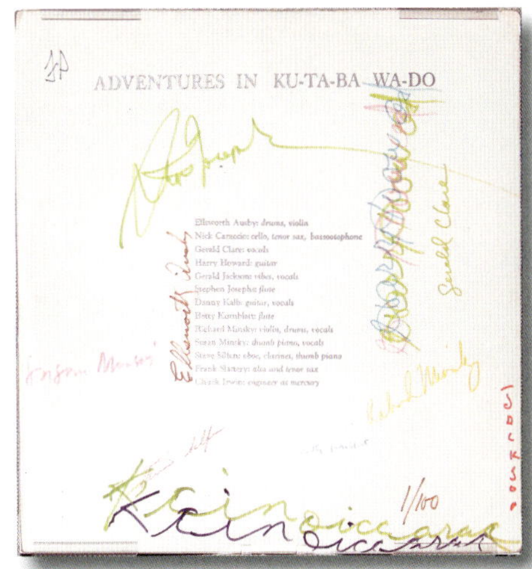

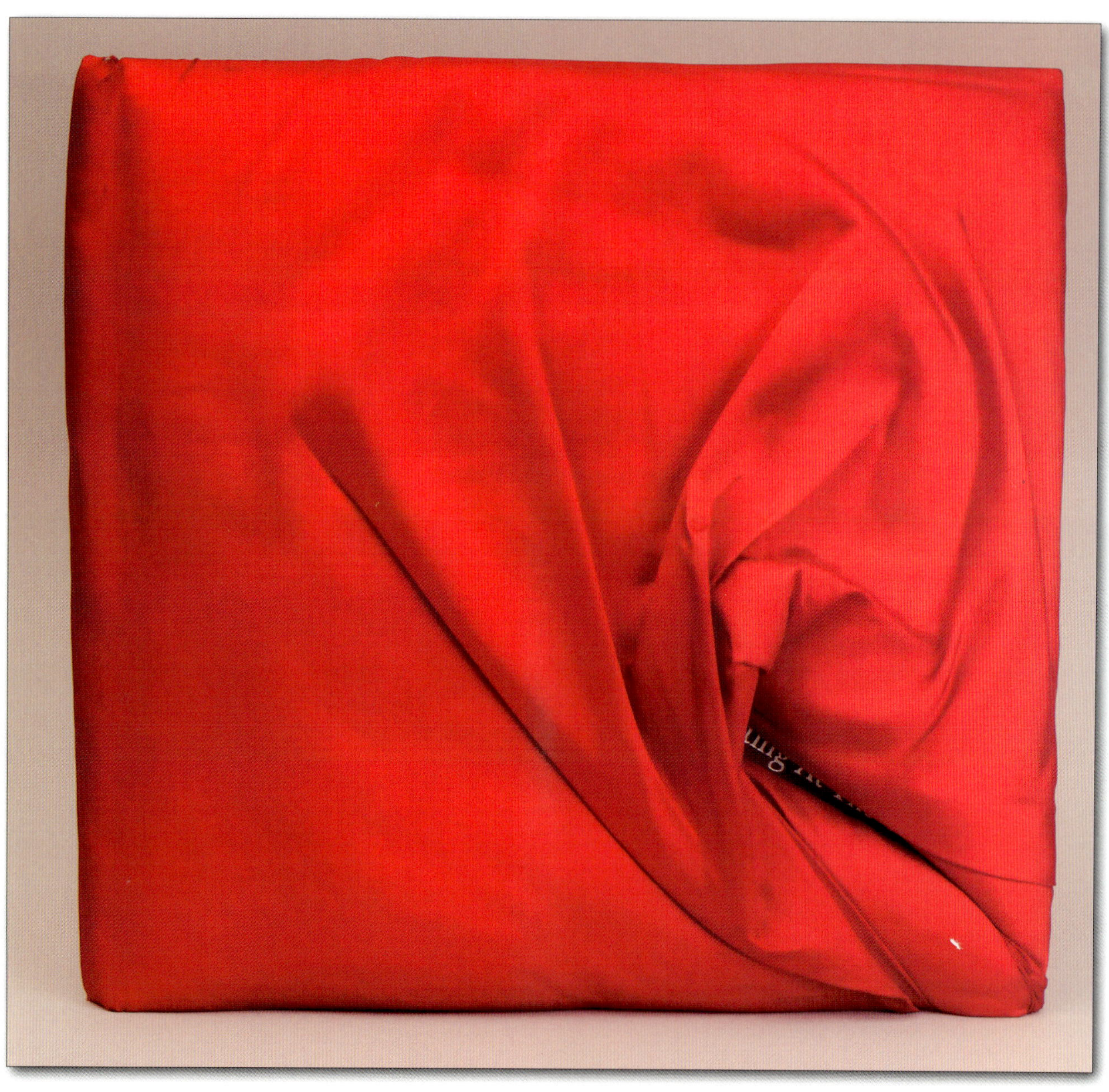

Eating At The Y: Pornographics by C. Bible
Etchings by Charles Bible, 1974.
Binding by Minsky, 1974. 14¼ x 14½
Padded satin, foil stamped title on leather label. In order to read the title it is necessary to insert one's fingers in the recess and move the satin folds aside.
Private collection, New York

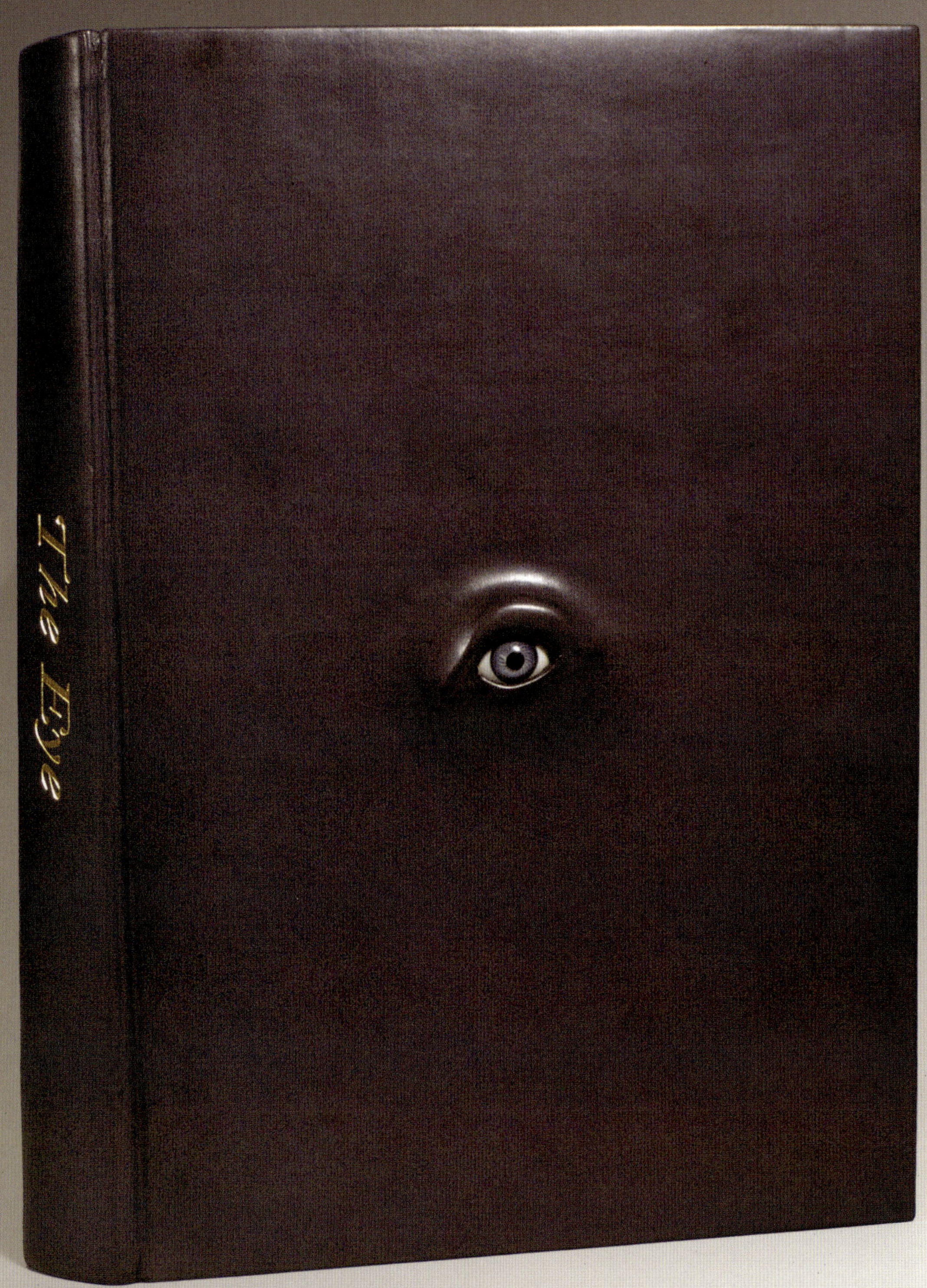

The Eye
by Roanna Martin-Trigona. Tod Volpe, New York, 1994.
Designed, printed and bound by Minsky, 1994.
Calf with inset artificial eye, title stamped in 23K gold.

The story of Salvador Dali's painting "The Eye," which was the basis of the dream sequence in Alfred Hitchcock's movie, "Spellbound." Printed inkjet on Dieu Donné handmade paper, mounted movie stills, other historical photos and ephemera.

Box of Books

DEALERS were constantly being approached by artists with portfolios of slides, and all were booked up months or years in advance. Some had fixed "stables" of artists and did not look at anything that was brought in. I just wanted to sell books. Ronald Feldman bought one of my sculpturally enhanced blank books and gave it to David Smyth, who filled it with drawings, paper sculpture, and poetry.

I developed a time-saving pitch that became performance art. Entering a gallery the first time, I would say to the owner, "Hello, I'm Richard Minsky and have some books I think you'd like to see." While speaking I would open the trunk and look at the dealer's face. If there was a blank stare I would close the trunk, saying, "Thank you for your time," and leave. If, on the other hand, their eyes sparkled or they reached for a book, there would at least be an entertaining conversation.

In November 1973, anticipating the need to produce more work, I sent posters to college art and printmaking departments offering an Apprenticeship in Book Arts. There were a few applicants. But much as I loved the storefront shop, it was not paying its way. The economy was in the worst recession in three decades and interest rates were high, making borrowing expensive. The store lease was up, and I didn't renew. My friends' band, New Cats Pajamas, had been using the basement for rehearsals, and played a concert for the closing party in the empty storefront.

Three of the qualified applicants, Bob Bretz, Gloria Zuss, and Robert Espinosa, wanted to do the apprenticeship even though the shop closed, and we started working in my apartment.

A few customers continued providing work, and I kept making the Wednesday trips to Manhattan with my box of books. In April 1974 I was making the rounds in a gallery building on 57th Street without much success, when I walked into the Zabriskie Gallery. After an hour of looking through everything I had, Virginia Zabriskie said, "I have an opening in June. Would you be able to put together an exhibition of your work by then?" This was something I had not foreseen, but said, "Yes, if it's OK that some of the work will be borrowed from collectors and not for sale." That was fine with her, and I became the first book artist to have a 57th Street gallery exhibition.

Pat Gorman designed a pocket-size catalog for the show, with duotone images of the books. It has my hands oiling the spine of a leather book on the title page, and oiling a girl's spine on the last page.

Polly Lada-Mocarski came to the show. She was a bookbinder who had studied with the great Ignatz Wiemeler in Germany and Douglas Cockerell in England. At the age of 70 she was the most dynamic and inspiring member of the Guild of Book Workers, and one of the very few who understood art. We became dear friends, and Polly, who was well-connected, made many important introductions. One of those was to Rose Slivka, Editor-in-Chief of *Craft Horizons* magazine, for which Polly was the Bookbinding Editor.

I was embedded in the art world, meeting many people who became important in my development. Ray Johnson introduced me to Bobby Buecker, whose West Broadway loft was a meeting place for Correspondence and Fluxus artists. He built harpsichords and mounted art exhibitions. While studying Baroque Music at Brooklyn College I had written a paper on the effect that developments in harpsichord construction had on musical composition. Building one has been an unresolved fantasy for many decades.

On one visit to Buecker & Harpsichords, as the gallery was named, I was playing some improvisations in e-flat minor. A man came up to me and said, "There was only one composer who improvised in E-flat minor." I assumed he meant Beethoven, and played the opening bars of the Moonlight Sonata. He introduced himself, Albert M. Fine. He carried a flute in his backpack, which he played beautifully. We struck a friendship, and he said I must meet Henry Geldzahler.

Henry was the young Curator of 20th Century Art at the Metropolitan Museum. As soon as I sat down in his office, he said, "Who do you know?" Handing him the Zabriskie catalog, I named some artists and collectors of my work. He liked what he saw and encouraged me to come back. This began a friendship that lasted until his death in 1994 at age 59. Henry wielded substantial influence in the art world, and this was a fortuitous meeting. He helped me in many ways, through advice and introductions, as well as purchasing my work for the Museum.

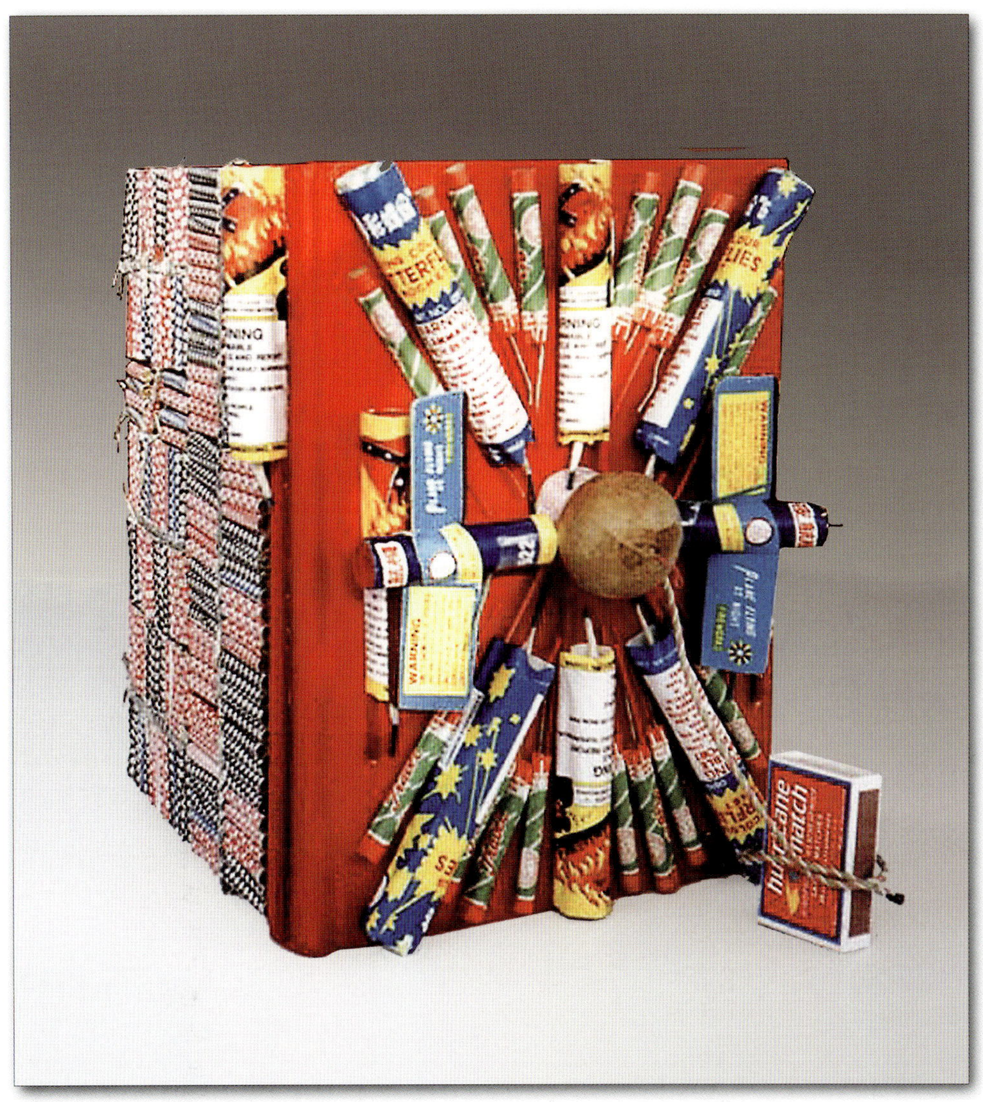

Fireworks: A History and Celebration
by George Plimpton. Doubleday & Co., 1984.
Binding by Minsky, 1992. 10 x 7 x 2
Acrylic paint and live fireworks with hurricane matches.
Private Collection, New York

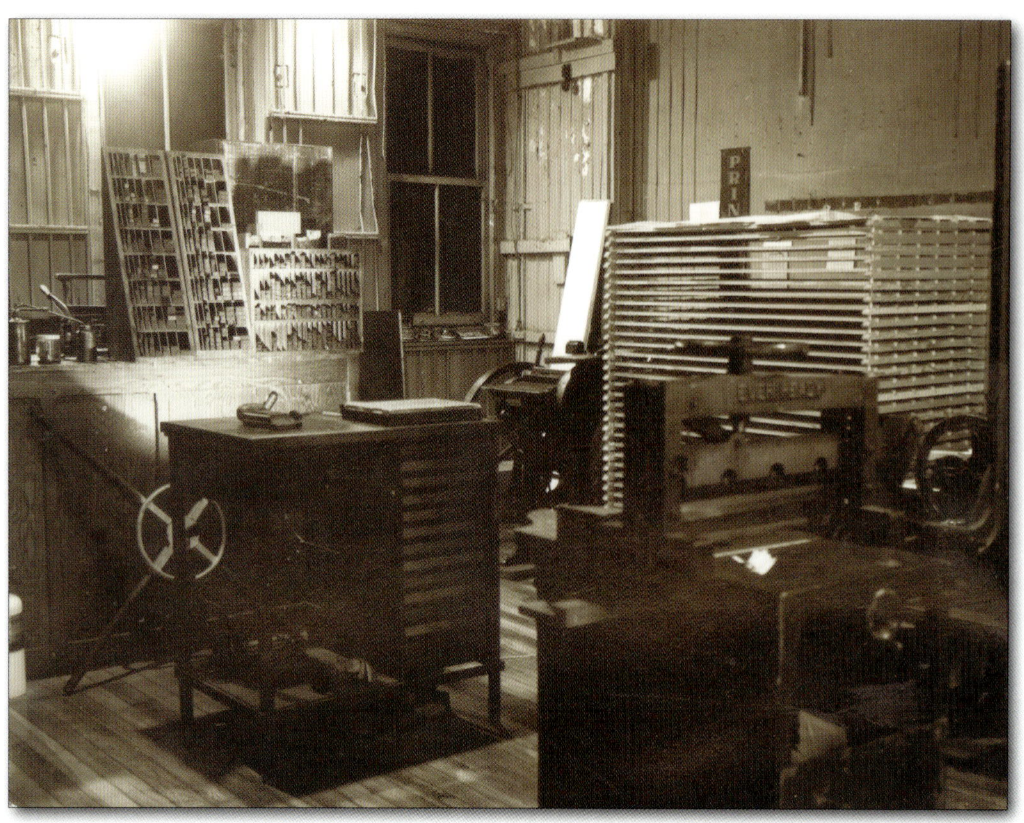

The Center for Book Arts printshop at 15 Bleecker Street, New York City in 1974.

The Center for Book Arts

ONE SUMMER EVENING in 1974, walking down Bleecker Street on my way to CBGB to see the great punk rock singer and poet Patti Smith, I saw a sign "Store for Rent" and thought how nice it would be to have a place nearby and avoid the hour-plus subway trip home to Queens. It struck me that this would be a great location for a Center for Book Arts, between SOHO and the East Village art scenes. I wrote down the phone number, and the next day called the landlord.

I showed up at the inspection wearing cutoff denim hot pants, a red tank top and homemade goatskin sandals, carrying a violin. It's important that a place has good acoustics. Either Charlie (the landlord) liked my fiddling, or he was really hard up for a tenant. He agreed to a two-year lease at $350 a month, with the month of August free to do renovations, and the right of renewal for ten years at a low fixed rate of increase.

The following week my three apprentices came in. We demolished the existing interior walls and sanded the floors. I spent days at the Mid-Manhattan library reading the volume on New York Not-For-Profit Corporate Law, to learn what was required, and called the Volunteer Lawyers for the Arts. They assigned a tall lawyer named Rick Wall to handle the incorporation.

We moved the equipment in and opened to the public in September. It required a minimum of 18 hours a day for the first six months, and I set up an area with a mattress. There was no shower or bathtub, and I would go to Henry Geldzahler's apartment in a townhouse on 11th Street several times a week to shower and freshen up. Henry served on the Center for Book Arts Advisory Board until he became the NYC Commissioner of Cultural Affairs in 1977, where it would have been a conflict of interest.

Fluxus and Correspondence School artists gathered at the CBA in the early days. The Center's first weekend

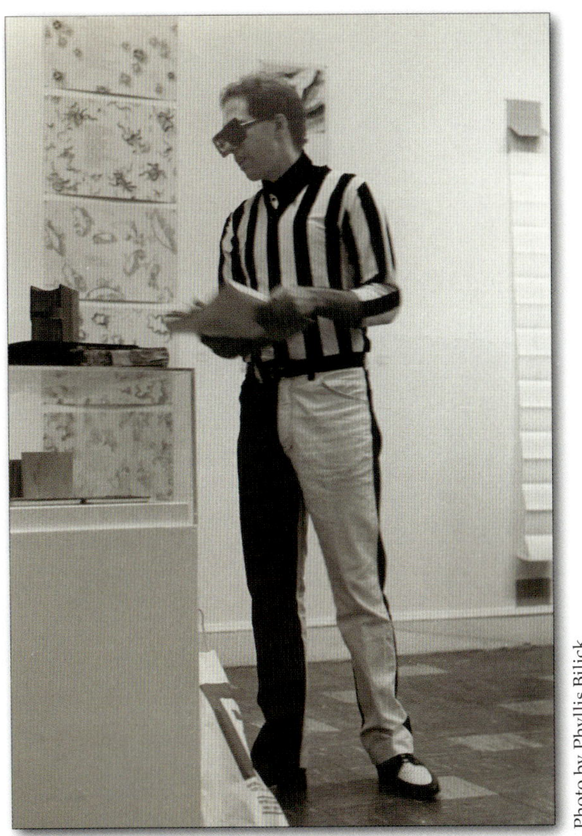

Photo by Phyllis Bilick

Minsky at an Exhibition ca. 1980.

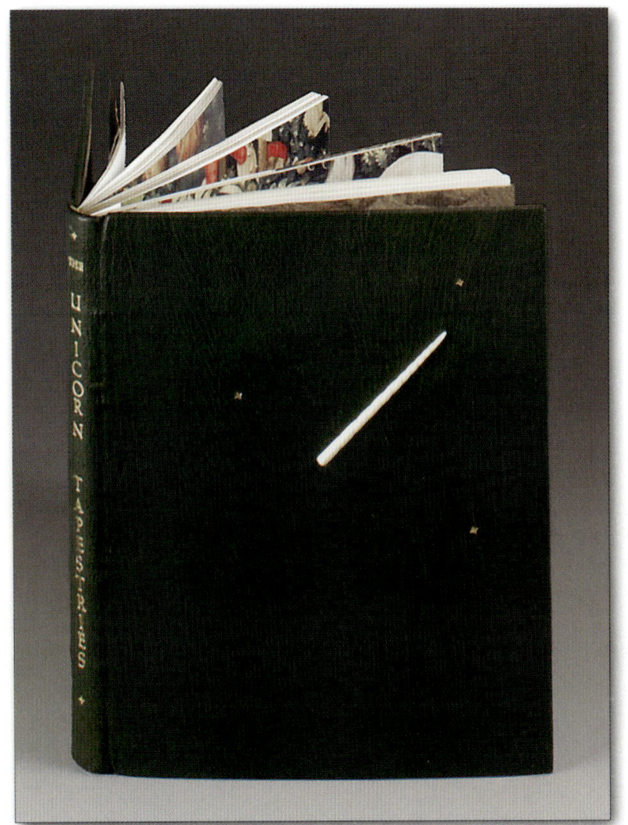

Photos courtesy of Center for Book Arts

The Unicorn Tapestries
by Margaret Freeman. Metropolitan Museum of Art, New York, 1976. CBA/MMA edition binding.
Collection of the Center for Book Arts, New York

event was a meeting of Ray Johnson's Spam Radio Club.

Albert M. Fine took the role of Artist in Residence, which he retained for two years. Every day he would come and do his correspondence, using the CBA as his address, which quickly led to large quantities of mail art coming in. He wrote in an alphabet that he had invented, and illustrated his missives with abstract cartoons. When not writing, he would rant, an activity at which he was a grand master.

Albert's self-assigned title was First Majority Cosmic Elder Consciousness, First Representative, Planet Earth. When he left the CBA and moved to Boston, he bestowed the title on me, with the alteration, Second Representative. I still consider that one of the greatest honors.

Many poets came to the CBA and learned to set type by hand, producing editions of books on our motorized letterpresses. Rick Fields said that it changed the way he wrote poetry when he felt the weight of his words in lead.

In 1976 Henry asked me to create a unique binding on *The Unicorn Tapestries*, a book published by the Metropolitan Museum, for their permanent collection. The result was a green goatskin cover with an ivory unicorn horn within a circle of stars. He showed it to the head of the Metropolitan Museum Shop, and that resulted in an order for 25 copies to be made by the CBA apprentices under my supervision [above]. The ivory was carved by bowmaker Nicholas Caraccio, one of the original three members of the CBA Board of Directors.

The story of the Center for Book Arts would take a book bigger than this one. More apprentices came, and thousands of students. During the past 36 years the CBA has mounted over 200 exhibitions, including some that traveled around the world. It currently offers 100 classes and workshops annually. Several other Centers across the USA and abroad were developed on the CBA model, including the Minnesota Center for Book Arts and the San Francisco Center for the Book. Visit the Center's website at www.centerforbookarts.org.

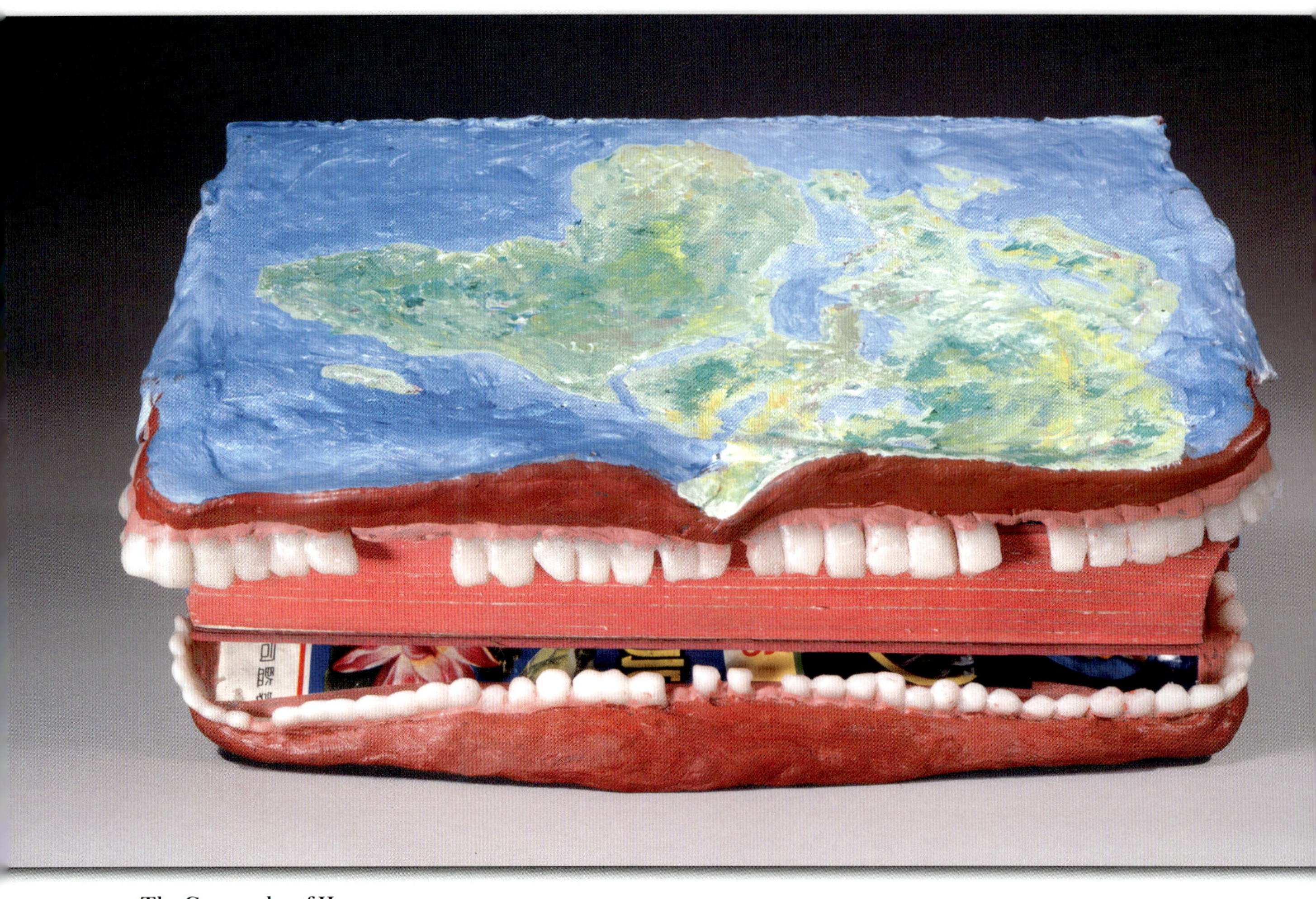

The Geography of Hunger
by Josué de Castro. Little Brown, Boston, 1952.
Binding by Minsky, 1988. 9 x 7 x 3
"Friendly Plastic," acrylic, endpapers of food and dog food labels.

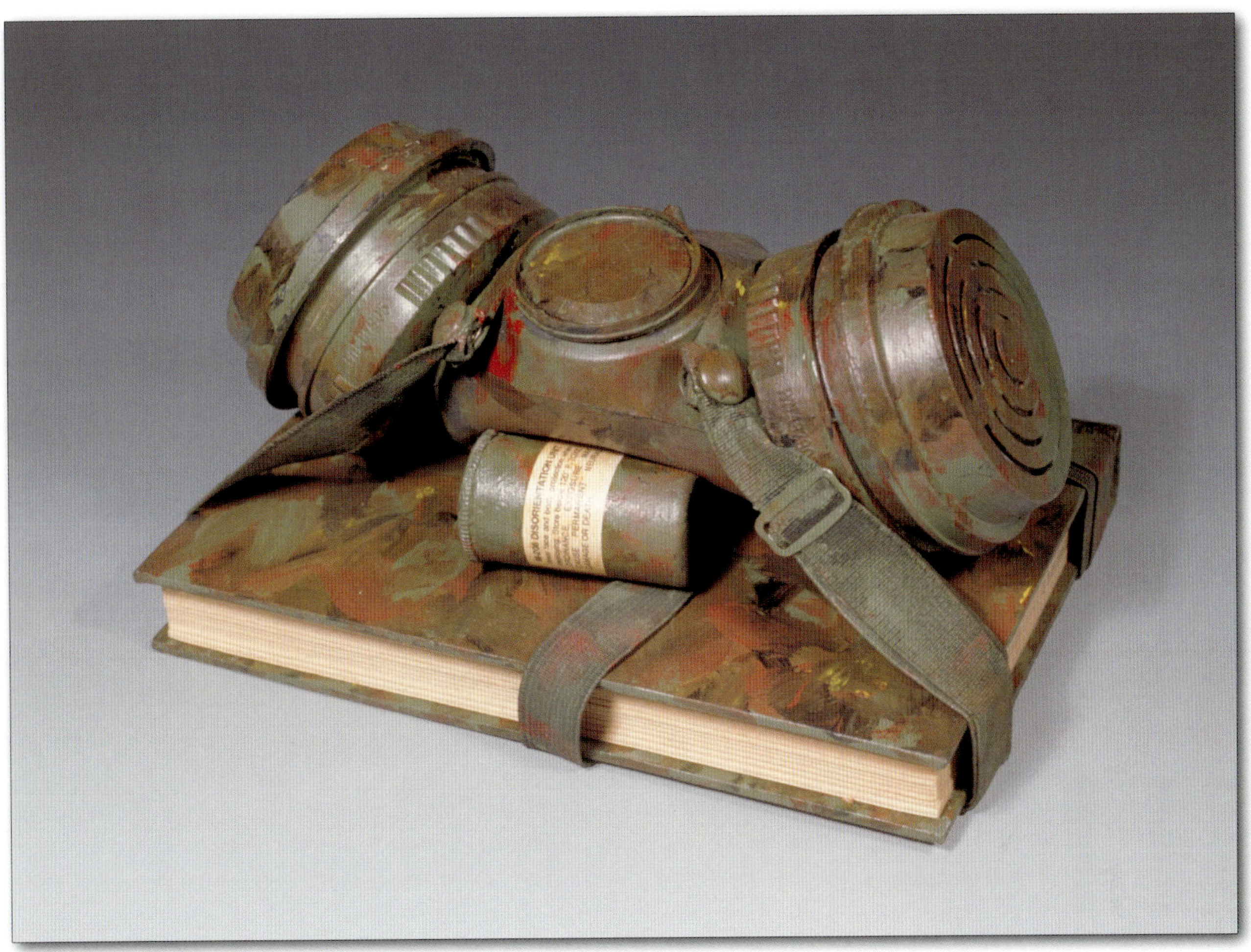

Chemistry in Warfare
by F. A. Hessel. Hastings House, New York, 1940.
Binding by Minsky, 1993. 8 x 5 x 4
Binding painted in acrylic, with matching gas mask and container with toxic ordinance label, printed by ink jet.

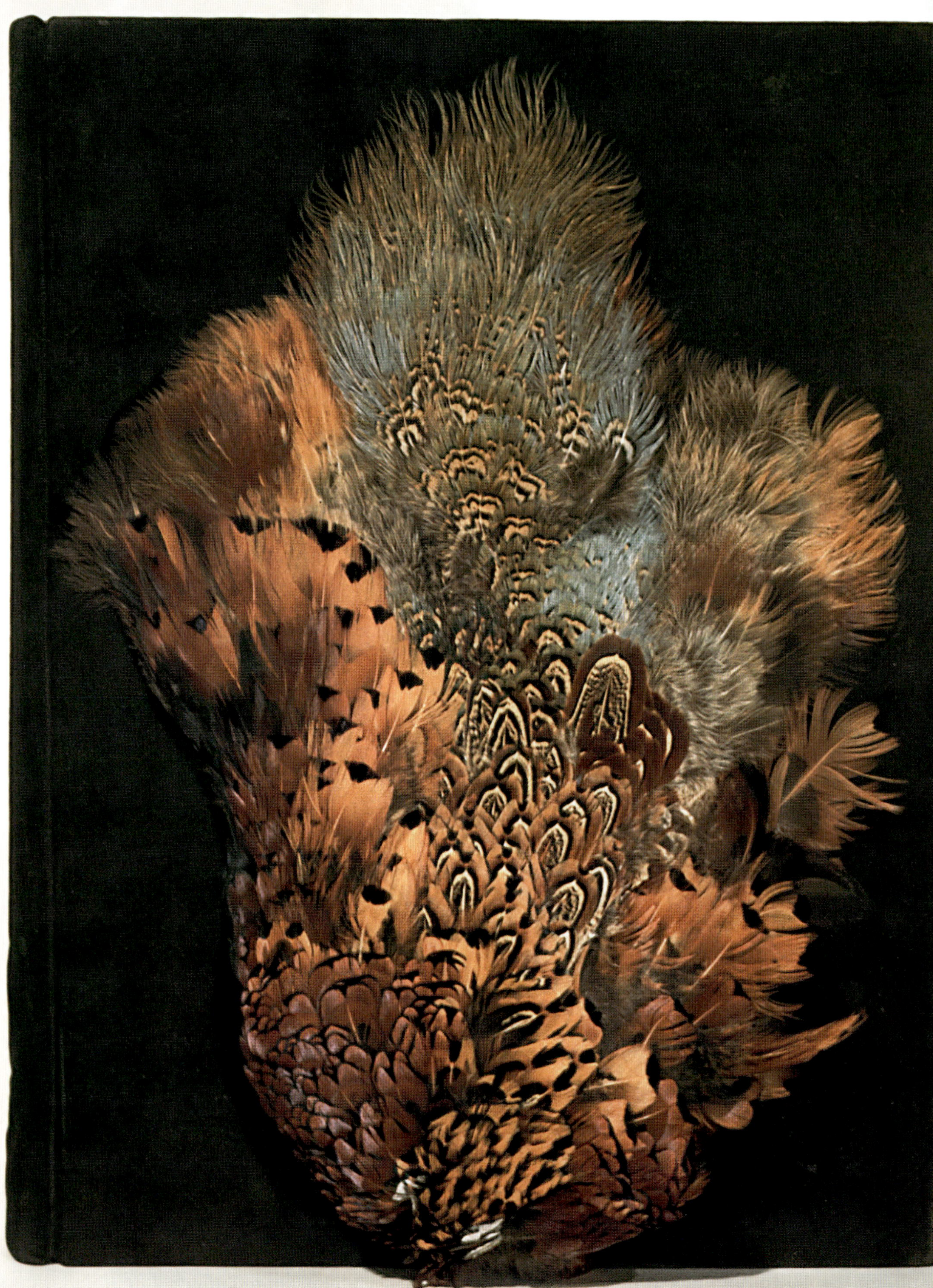

The Birds Of North America

IN 1975 I was asked to submit a binding for a Guild of Book Workers exhibition at Yale. I had just been given a copy of *The Birds of North America* that needed a binding. That day a street vendor on my corner pulled out a pheasant skin, replete with feathers, and said, "you got any use for this?" It was obvious. The Divine Creator was providing material for the cover.

The first report I got was that the conservator screamed when she opened my package and saw what at first glance appeared to be a dead bird. They decided to eliminate my work from the exhibition. But the great bookbinder Polly Lada-Mocarski and Yale Prof. Norman Pearson came to my support. The show opened with *The Birds of North America* in it. The controversy over this book had spread around New Haven, which drew an unusually large crowd for a show of bindings.

I came back to Yale a week later, with one of my apprentices, to photograph the exhibition for a review in *Book Arts* magazine, which we were publishing at the Center for Book Arts. The case that had held my book was empty! I asked the Curator, Dale Roylance, what had happened. "It was falling apart, so we put it in the Beineke Library vault," he answered. "Let's take a look at it," I said. He sent for the book, and it appeared just as I had left it. "See," Dale said, "the feathers are loose."

Some of the feathers had always been sticking out at odd angles. I pulled a few feathers off the bird and scattered them around the exhibit case, and said, "If anybody asks, tell them the bird's molting!"

I didn't get what all the hoopla was about. To me it was a fairly straightforward binding, almost Dada in its simplicity, but more along the lines of "material meets metaphor" that I had started exploring in 1973 with the binding of *Pettigrew's History of Egyptian Mummies* [frontispiece]. So I asked Dale, "What's the problem with this book, anyway?" He said, "How do you store a book like this next to other books on the shelf? And how do you read it?" At that time book-objects were not so prevalent as today, and definitely not in the world of fine bookbinding.

"You don't stick it on a shelf next to other books. It's a work of art, like a sculpture, and you exhibit it like that," I answered.

Fast forward 30 years. In 2004 the Yale Arts of the Book Collection, under the leadership of its new Curator, Jae Rossman, purchased my archive. In 2006 The Guild of Book Workers selected *The Birds of North America* for its 100th Anniversary Retrospective Exhibition at The Grolier Club. I was asked to be one of the three jurors who selected other artists' works for the Contemporary Exhibition. To top it off, after the exhibition the owners of this book sold it to Yale, where it is now safely perched.

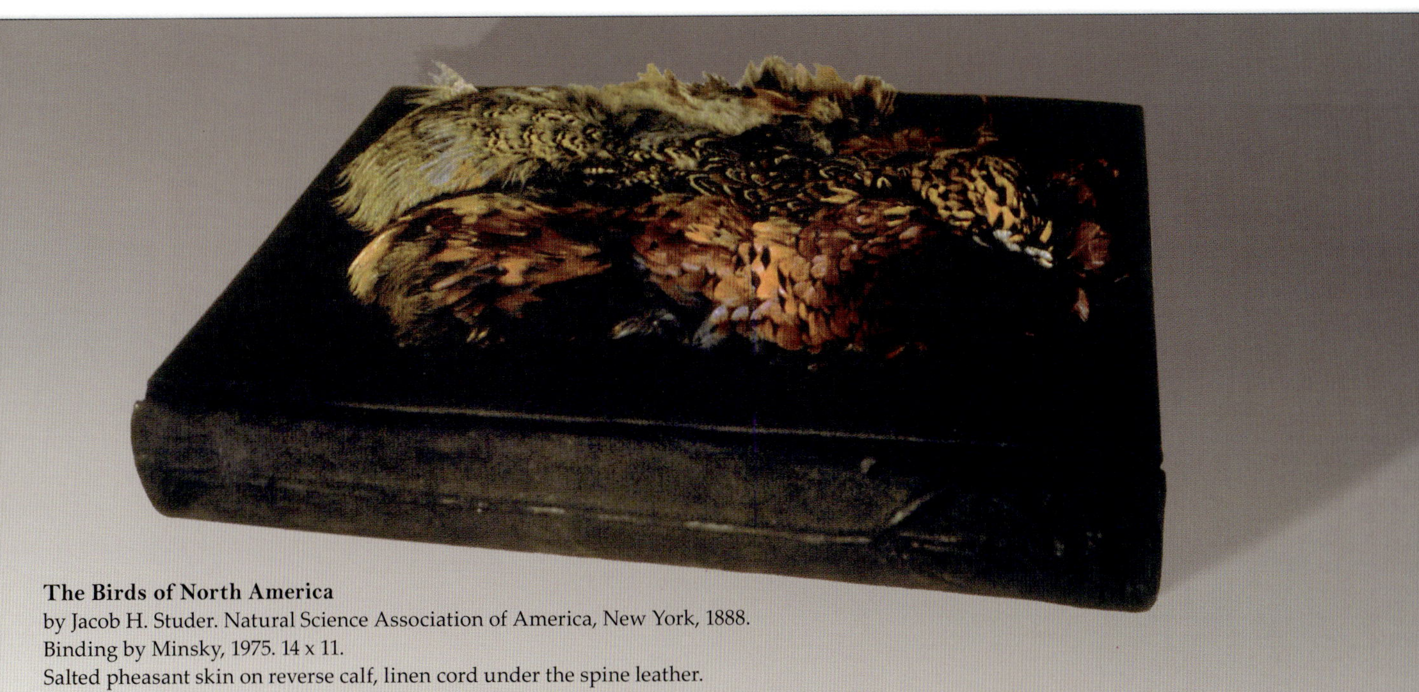

The Birds of North America
by Jacob H. Studer. Natural Science Association of America, New York, 1888.
Binding by Minsky, 1975. 14 x 11.
Salted pheasant skin on reverse calf, linen cord under the spine leather.
Collection of the Haas Family Arts Library, Yale University

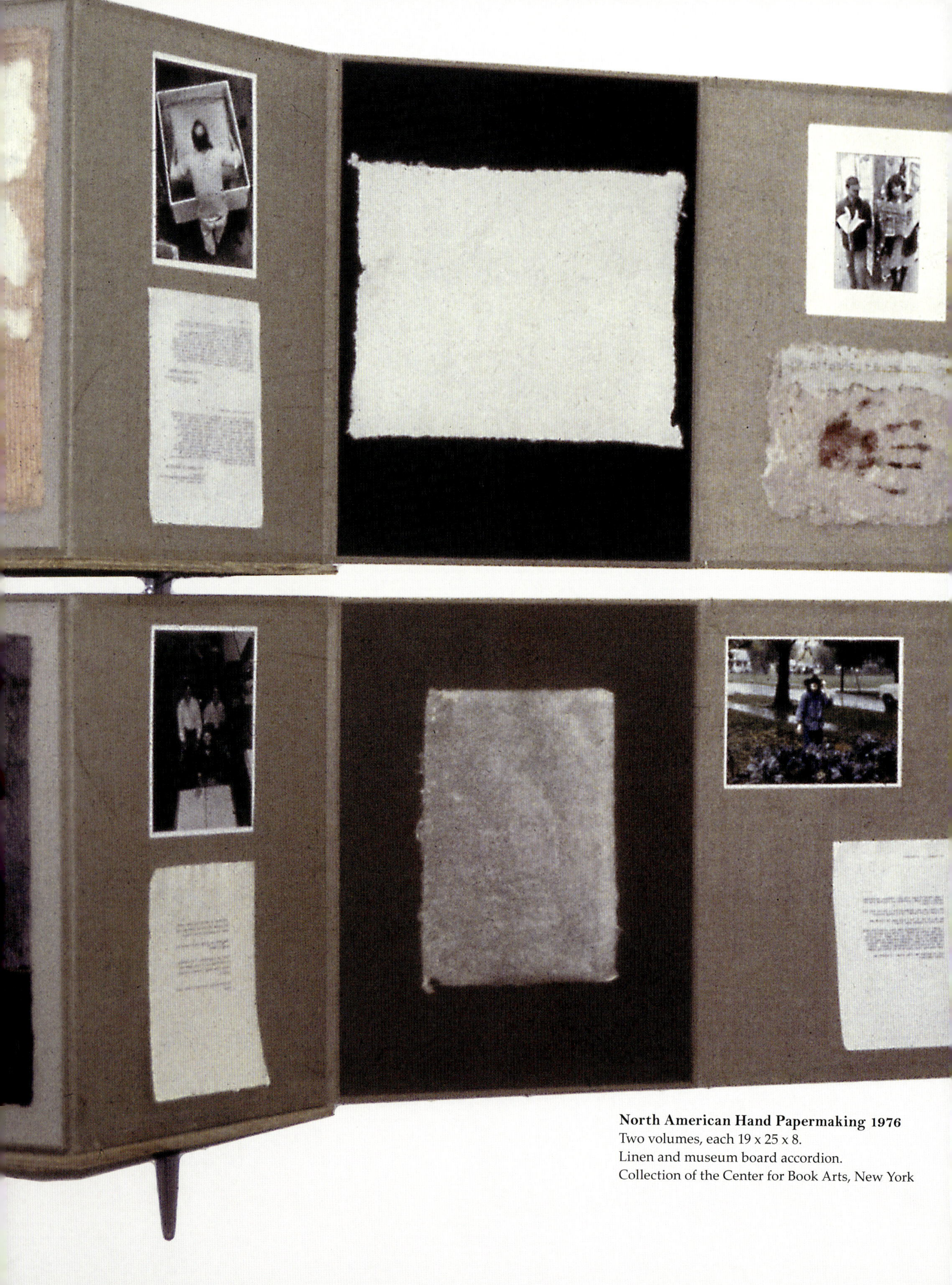

North American Hand Papermaking 1976
Two volumes, each 19 x 25 x 8.
Linen and museum board accordion.
Collection of the Center for Book Arts, New York

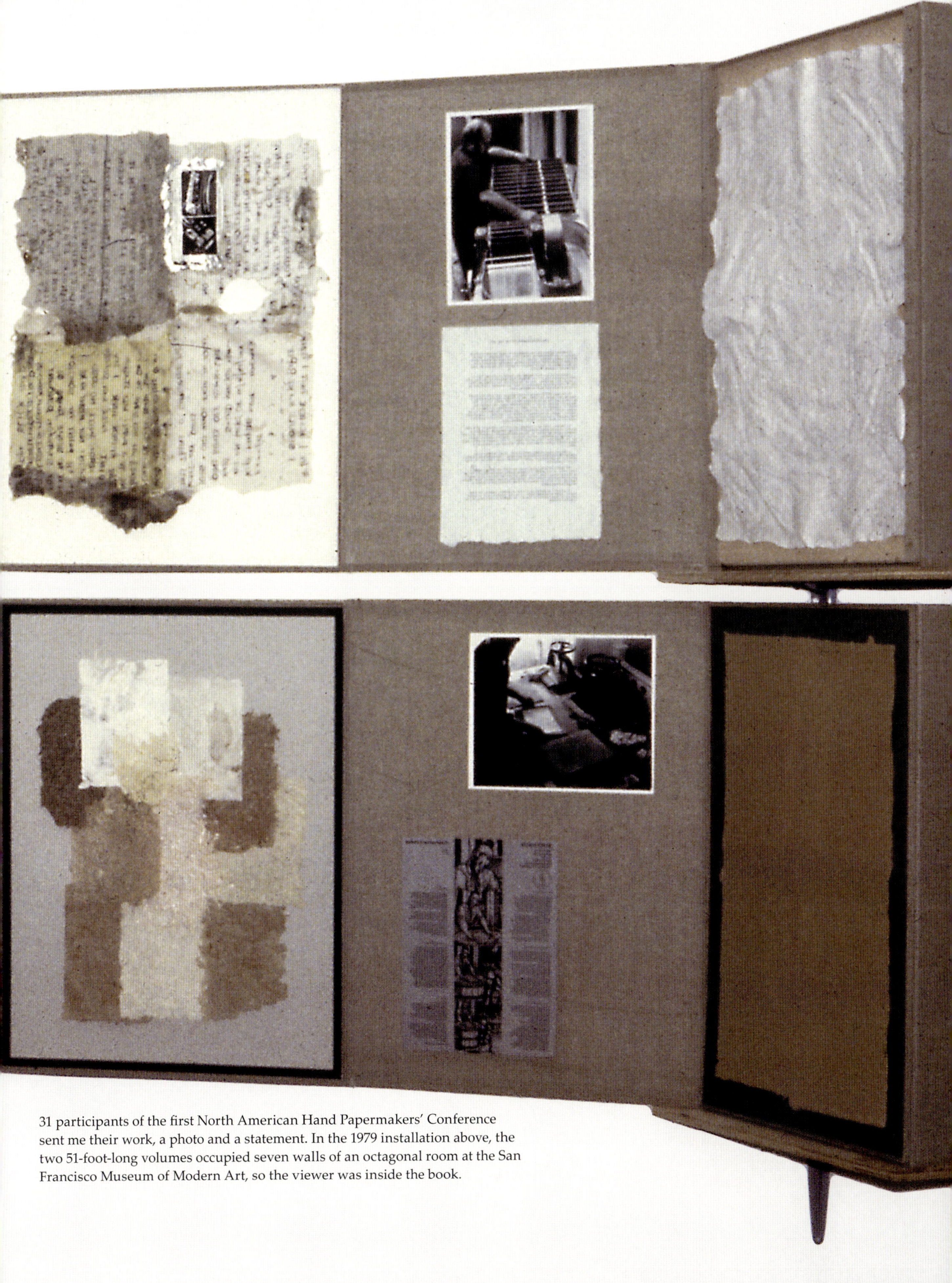

31 participants of the first North American Hand Papermakers' Conference sent me their work, a photo and a statement. In the 1979 installation above, the two 51-foot-long volumes occupied seven walls of an octagonal room at the San Francisco Museum of Modern Art, so the viewer was inside the book.

In 1977 Al Brunelle, an ex-biker who was head of the Printmaking Department at at the School of Visual Arts, asked me to teach an introductory course. It included etching, letterpress, lithography, and screen printing. The students did good work. Al invited me to teach a course in Publishing for Artists.

But in the spring of 1978 I got a phone call from the National Endowment for the Arts. "You have been selected as a semi-finalist for the US/UK Bicentennial Fellowship in Visual Arts. Would you like to submit an application?" I did, and they awarded me a grant to live in the UK for ten months.

Al graciously said I could teach the course the following year. In October I moved to London, set up a studio, and started lecturing at art schools and colleges. The activities of that time are the subject of *Minsky in London* (p. 46). When I returned, I taught the SVA course. It was an exciting challenge, covering everything from developing content and production methods to marketing and copyright law. The Copyright Act of 1979 had just gone into effect, so there was a lot to learn. In addition to the basic material that had to be covered, I added what I then called the Theory of Museum Finish, and now call Material Meets Metaphor. This is a system of tools for the creation and evaluation of artworks that seem to vibrate or shimmer the space around them.

Material Meets Metaphor

THE ILLUSION is created by balancing the material, image, and metaphor, so the viewer's mind keeps moving from observation of the physical object (paint, stone, wood or whatever material it is) to the representation of something, whether abstract or figurative, to the internal experience that the work evokes. Like the shutter of a movie projector, a slight flicker or shimmer occurs as the viewer's attention shifts back and forth many times each second from the internal to the external.

For fifteen weeks the students were encouraged, through a series of exercises, to create works that cause this effect. In the process they learned color theory—not the Itten, Albers, Goethe sort (which were taught in other classes), but color meditations based on the chakras, color healing, and color stimulation of the endocrine system. This helps in the manipulation of the biological, emotional, and perceptual states of the viewer.

They also produced examples of good work without "museum finish." That includes work with strong object and image properties but not metaphor, which is decorative art, and work with strong image and metaphor but not object properties, which is illustration. This also helps students to understand why a reproduction or copy of an artwork does not create the same sensation as the original. A picture of a painting in a book is an illustration, and lacks not only the factors communicated by the original materials, but any psychic energies the object may have accumulated either in its creation or over time.

In book art, this method is used to create sculptural bookworks that address social, political, and economic issues, books that are merely beautiful, craft work that is functional, and works that embody spirits as fetish objects.

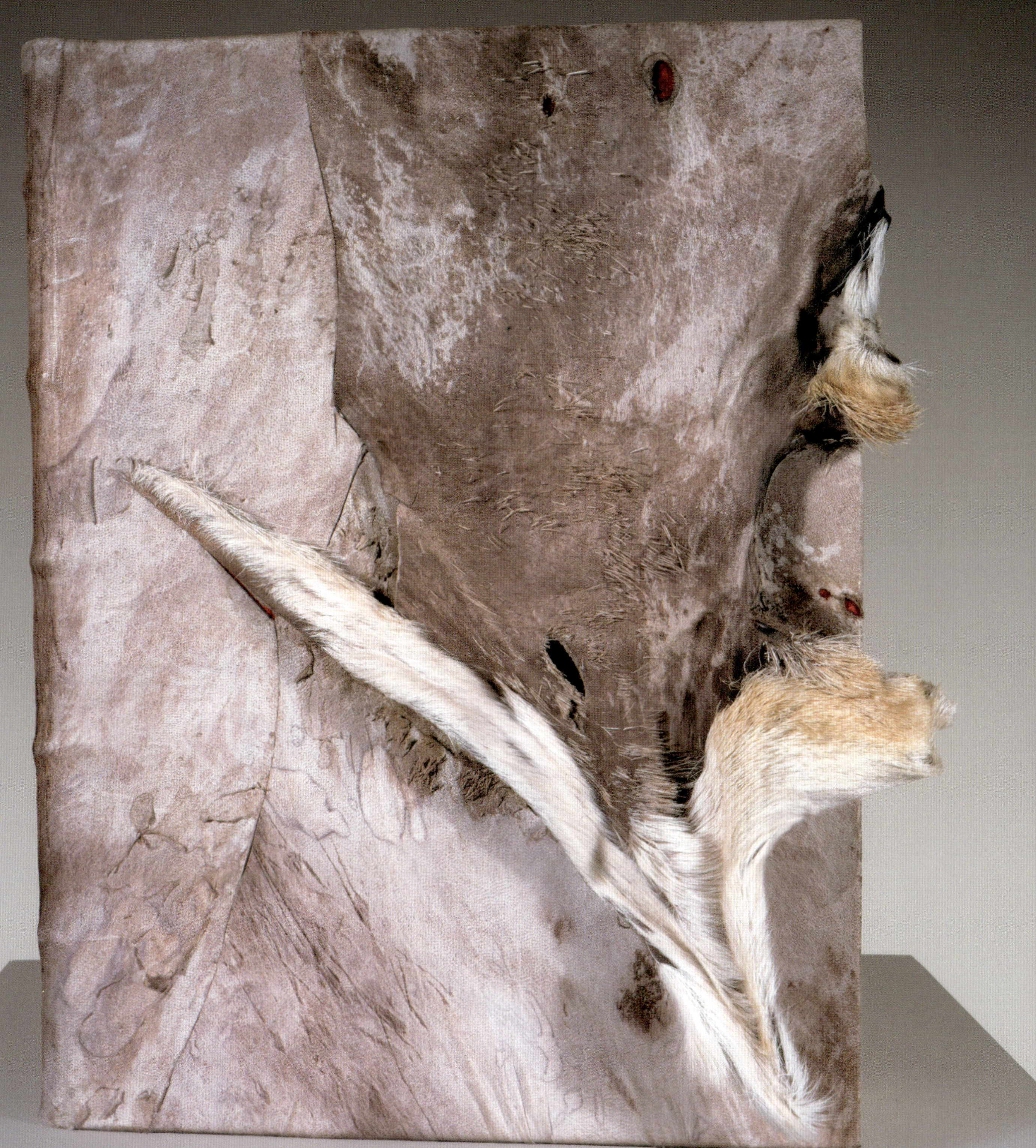

The Dog Bite
by Barton Lidicé Beneš.
Plain Wrapper Press, New York, 1970.
Binding by Minsky, 1977. 13 x 11 x 2
Skin of unknown origin, endsheets of Amatyl bark paper.
Collection of Barton Lidicé Beneš

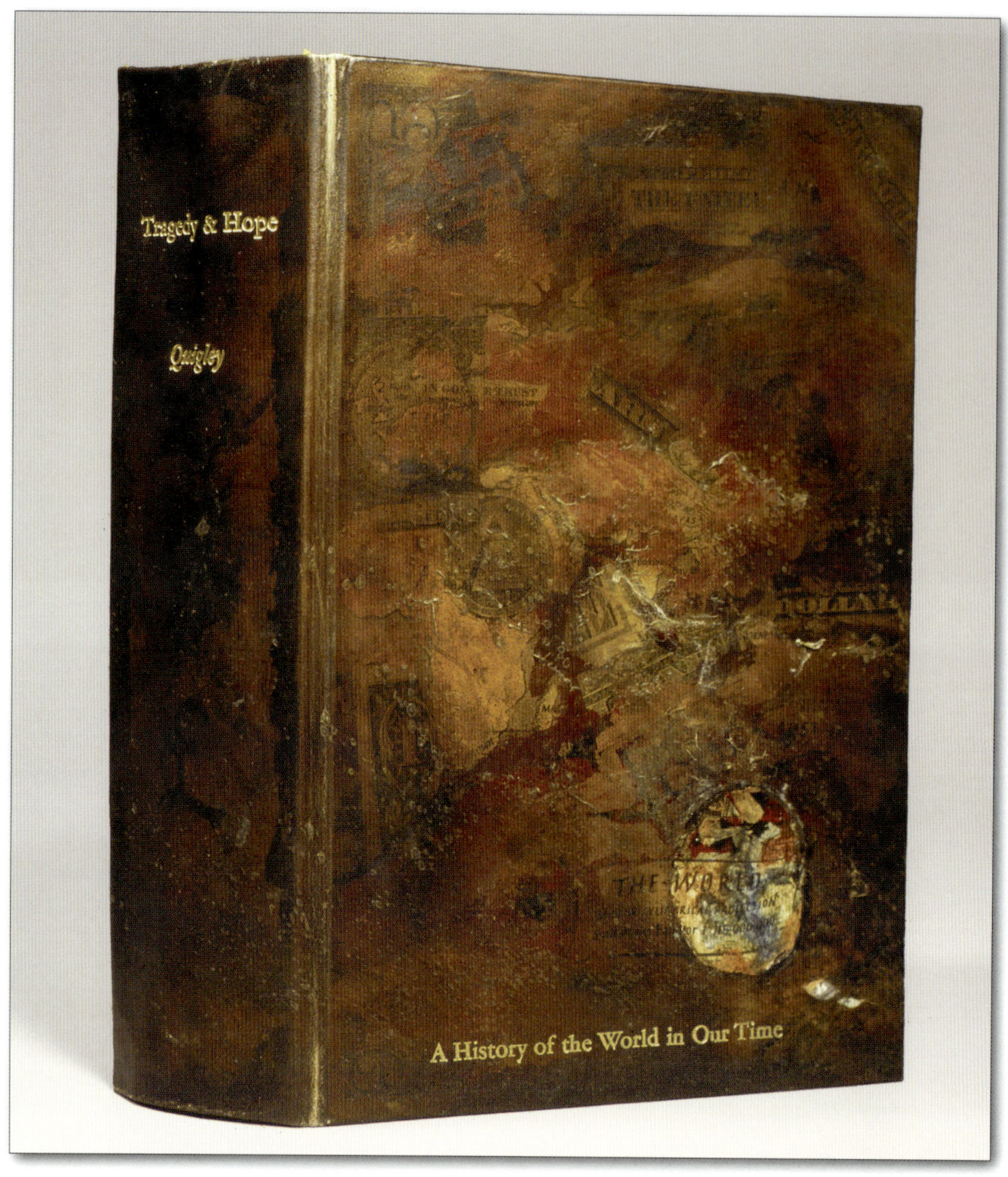

Tragedy and Hope: A History of the World in Our Time
by Carroll Quigley. Macmillan, New York, 1966.
Binding by Minsky, 1988. 9 x 6¾
Kid vellum (tanned by the artist) over collage and acrylic, gold title.
Pine box with oil-base stain, acrylic, lacquer and gold leaf, felt lining.
Private Collection, New York

This history book names some of the generally ignored villains in world events. In the 1988 Zabriskie Gallery exhibition [see p. 112], the book was displayed open to the page naming the German industrial cartel members who became naturalized American citizens in the 1930's. They sat on the Boards of major American corporations and supplied Hitler with materials needed for armaments. The collage under the kid skin, which is translucent lampshade vellum, consists of American currency cut into swastikas, placed on a world map that was the endpaper of this edition.

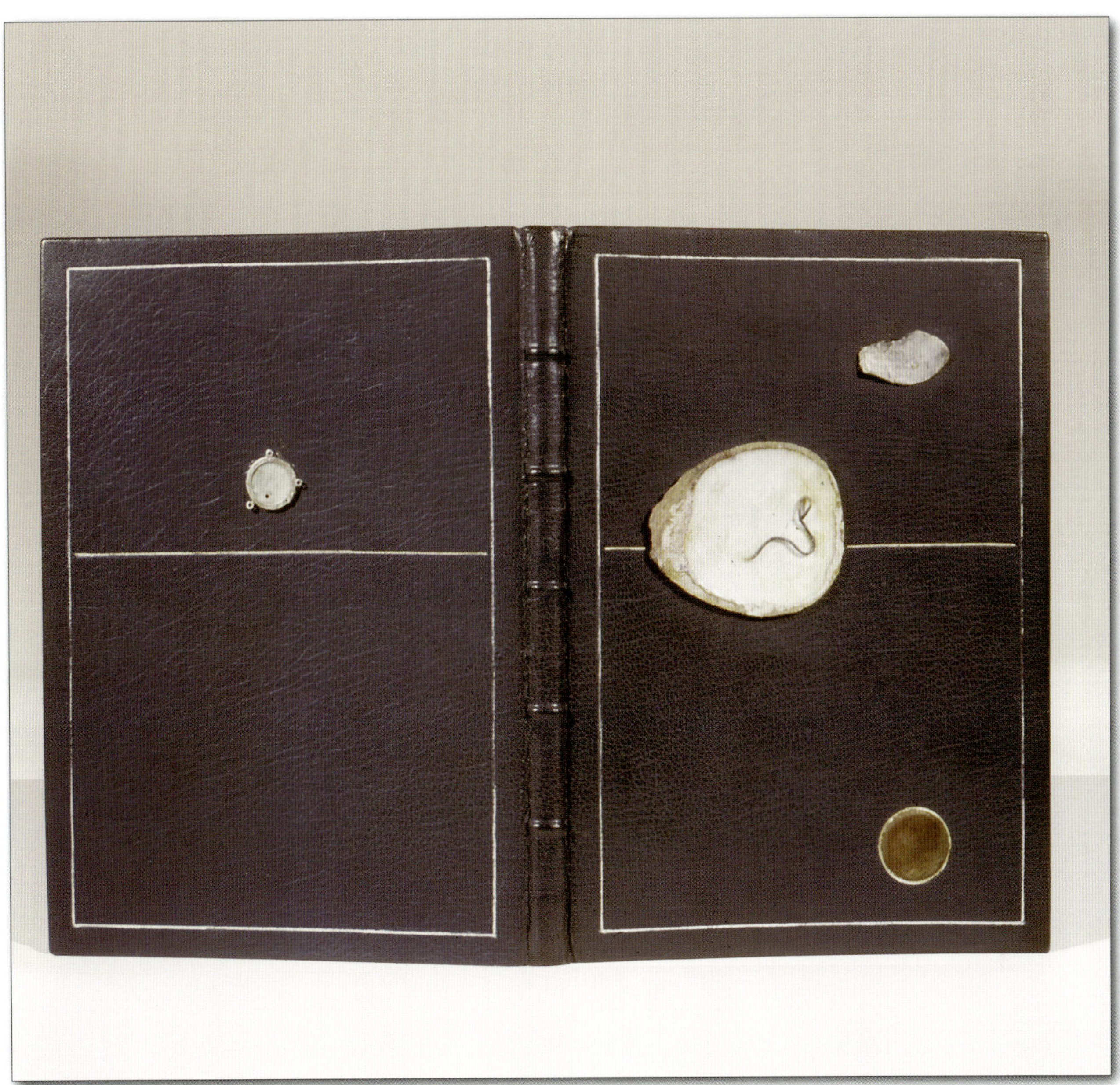

The Traveler
20 Poems by Astra Wolf, in her handwriting, 20 pictures and binding by Astra Wolf and Richard Minsky, 1970. 9 x 7
Goatskin and object collage, hand tooling; watercolor, ink and collage on paper and marbled paper [see also pp. 22-24].

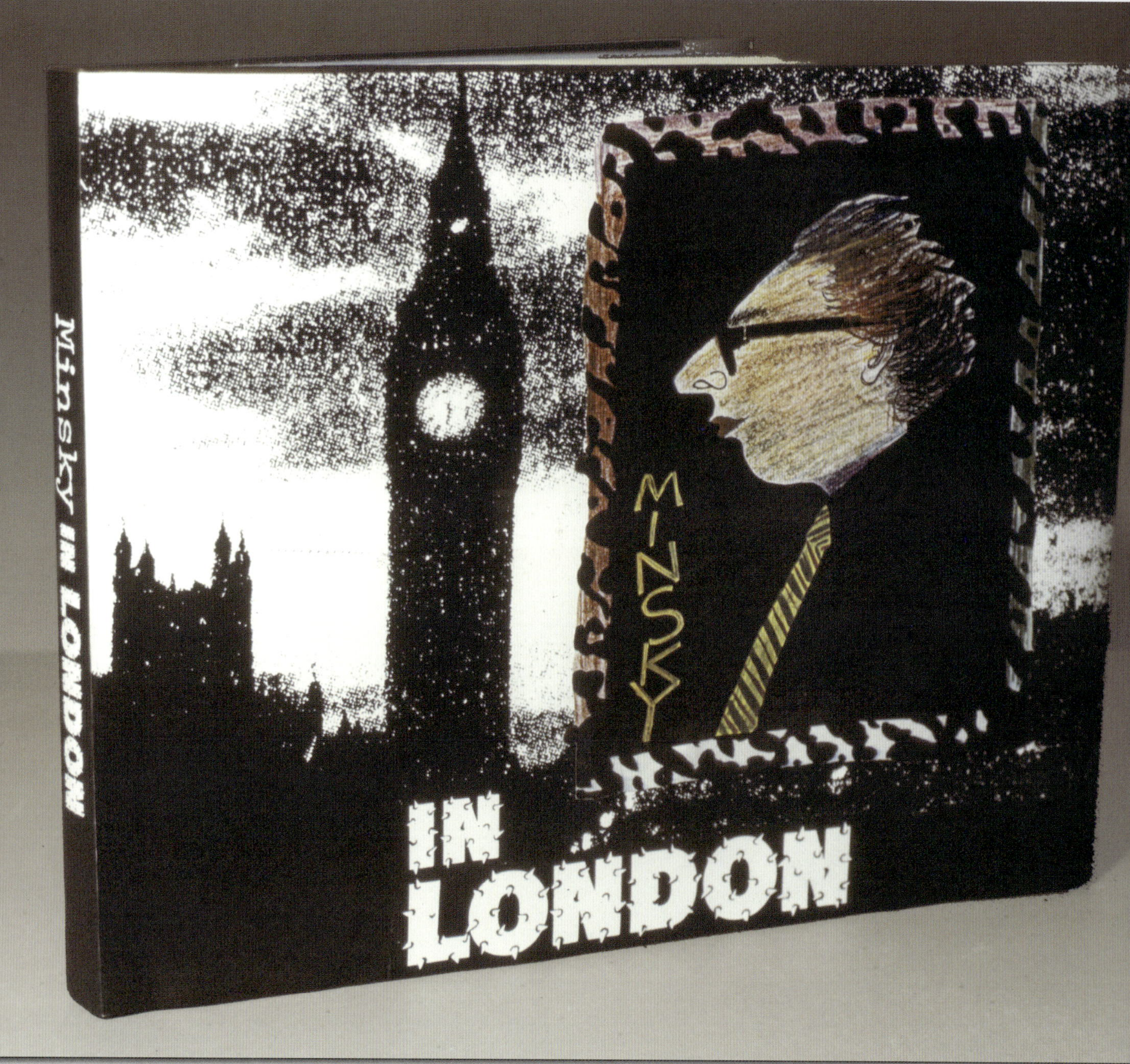

Minsky in London
Edited by Pamela Moore. 90 photographs by Richard Minsky.
Richard Minsky, New York, 1980. 14 x 11
Cover and record label design: Pat Gorman
Cover caricature of Minsky: Gerald Mynott
Rear endpaper photo: Pat Gorman
Rear endpaper lyrics by Kathy Fire
Libido by Kathy Fire, performed by Kathy Fire and Reverse
Ode to a Dead Sheep by Tommy Weitzel
Vandercook presswork assisted by Dikko Faust

Letterpress from Monotype and handset type on Mohawk Superfine paper, with dry mounted photographic prints and 45 rpm record. Foil stamped leather spine, screen-printed bookcloth boards with color Xerox transfer.

Minsky in London

OCTOBER 1978 I moved to London, set up a studio and started lecturing at art schools and colleges. The London College of Printing (LCP) and the Camberwell School of Art gave me adjunct faculty positions, which allowed me full use of their facilities. The activities of that time are the subject of *Minsky in London*. It includes tanning ratskins [p. 48] for my punk binding of Patti Smith's *Babel* [p. 50] and goatskins for the manuscript book [p. 51] that Tom Phillips used for his translation of *Dantes Inferno* [p. 119].

In addition to my narratives, there are those by the editor, Pamela Moore, who was there for most of the events, and observations by 15 people I encountered. It is a no-holds-barred account, including the story of Tom Phillips' *Dante's Inferno* giant fire disaster at Editions Alecto, and meetings with many people in different parts of British society—from the Heralds at the Garter Service to artists, punk rockers, and bookbinders.

My New York roomate Tom Weitzel came for a few weeks and we drove throughout England, Wales and Scotland visiting artists and writers, particularly those with bookish interest. Among the stops we made were John Latham, who was famous for chewing up Clement Greenberg's *Art and Culture* and returning the spit-out version to the library [which cost his job]. He was then doing altered books and conceiving of a book three stories high. Poet Jonathan Williams' Corn Close cottage had an antique set of brass rectal dilators on a shelf in the bathroom. Ian Hamilton Finlay's garden was a book with words carved in stone and other materials as situated sculptures.

There are 90 photos, including some large color prints that I made in the LCP darkroom, and black and white prints I made in New York. There also are commercial 4x6 prints made at various "one-hour photo" shops.

I was living in a building with thin walls, and couldn't play the Les Paul guitar without getting complaints from neighbors. At the conclusion of a lecture at LCP I asked, "Does anyone know of an available situation that has sex, drugs and rock'n'roll?" A woman came up to the stage and said, "I have just the place for you." I moved into the top floor of Jay Landesman's house in Islington. His sons had a band in the basement. Jay and his mistress (who had attended my talk) lived on one floor, and Fran, Jay's wife [lyricist of "Spring Can Really Hang You Up the Most"], was on another floor. Jay started the magazine *Neurotica* in 1948, and founded The Crystal Palace nightclub, hosting talent from Lenny Bruce to Woody Allen, in St. Louis in 1952. Jay traded a month's rent for a binding of *Neurotica* in grey flannel and black leather.

I started a series of "Seminars Dansants," a salon that attracted artists and those who liked to talk about art. There was enough sex and drugs to keep me happy.

The endpaper of *Minsky in London* features the lyrics my other NY roommate, Kathy Fire, wrote about my lifestyle, titled "Libido," with a recording mounted in the back cover of the book. On the flip side is a recording of Tommy playing the guitar next to a dead sheep in Scotland.

The Victoria and Albert Museum included three of my works in *The Open and Closed Book* exhibition in 1979, and ordered copy No. 1 of *Minsky in London*. I presented the National Endowment for the Arts with a copy in lieu of a final report on the fellowship.

The front and back of each page are printed on separate pieces of heavy paper that are laminated together with bookcloth hinges, which creates a stiff substrate for the mounted photos. In order for the book to lie flat when opened, each folio is sewn to an N-guard with linen thread, and the N-guards are then sewn with the same thread onto linen tapes. It is possible to open this book into a complete circle for exhibition.

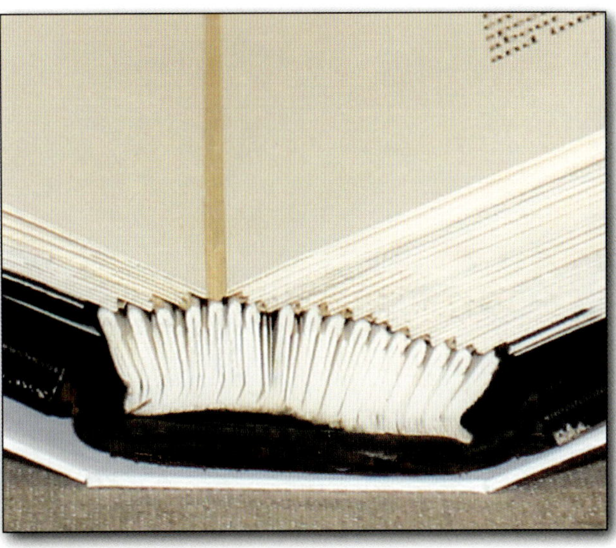

tanning ratskins

Richard Minsky, Tanner Extraordinary

Of the many fascinating facets of the character of Richard Minsky, his interest in bookbinding led him to The National Leathersellers Centre in
Northampton. He walked into my office early in 1979, and his innocent guile
gave no hint of the cross examination I was to face in the coming weeks. I
should perhaps begin by explaining that we normally take two years to train
leather technologists in the science and practice of leather manufacture.
Richard could only spare me two weeks and so the string of questions and an-
swers began, and went on and on and on. He has an enormous capacity for
rapid learning and rapidly became familiar with the work, and the question
of bookbinding leathers in particular.

He had been working only two days in our experimental tannery (clad in
protective clothing and gum boots he looked like a space man), when he came
and said to me 'David, what do you know about tanning rat skins?' I have been
in the leather industry some forty years and made leather from almost every
type of skin, including human skin, during that time, but I never had tanned
a rat skin in my career!! He continued, 'I have need of some alum tawed ratskin leather for a punk book I am making. Can you help me please?' With
some misgivings I agreed, after all I thought all hides and skins are basically
the same, both chemically and somewhat physically constructed.

Shortly, two ratskins arrived and we commenced tannery operations, using
conventional procedures to remove the hair and convert the skins into leather. The skins were quite small, so at no stage could we put them through the
normal mechanical operations. Richard very labouriously scraped off the ad-
ipose fatty connective tissues from the flesh side and carefully nurtured his
precious skins through every stage of the process like a hen with a brood of
tiny chicks. Due to lack of time, Richard took his wet dressed skins back to
London, to dry them on his own premises. A few days later, some of my
worst secret fears were confirmed; our mutual lack of ratskin processing experience had produced a disaster, the skin had dried out hard, horny, trans-
parent and greasy, looking just like wrinkled oil silk, quite useless for bookbinding purposes.

So back they came to me by post, turning the envelope yellow with fat on
the journey, but the G.P.O. did not complain. I degreased the skins, redressed
them and finally Richard collected them, pronouncing them OK this time.

His experiences at the leather centre in no way dampened his interest in
leather manufacture; on the contrary he is determined to open his own small
tannery in the USA, to produce bookbinding leather by a special process designed to yield leathers of high durability.

So, in addition to all his many interests and activities, Richard Minsky, tanner extraordinary may one day be with us all. The best of luck be with you.

D H Tuck

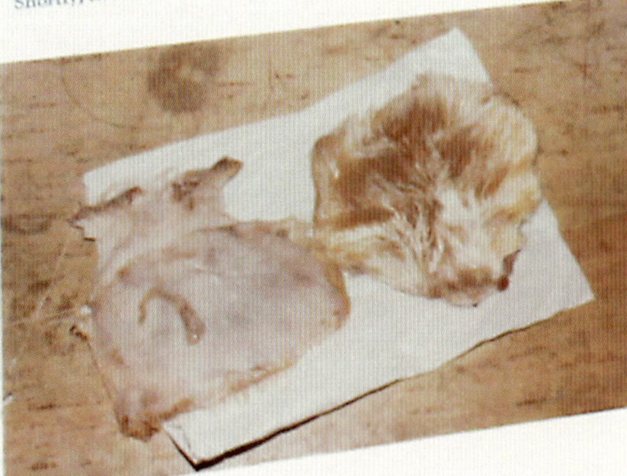

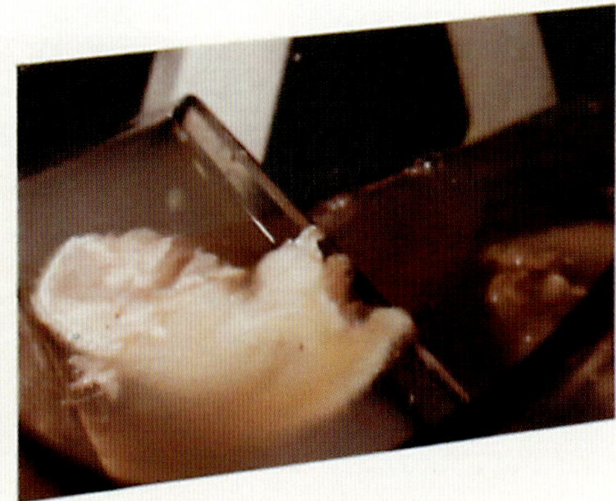

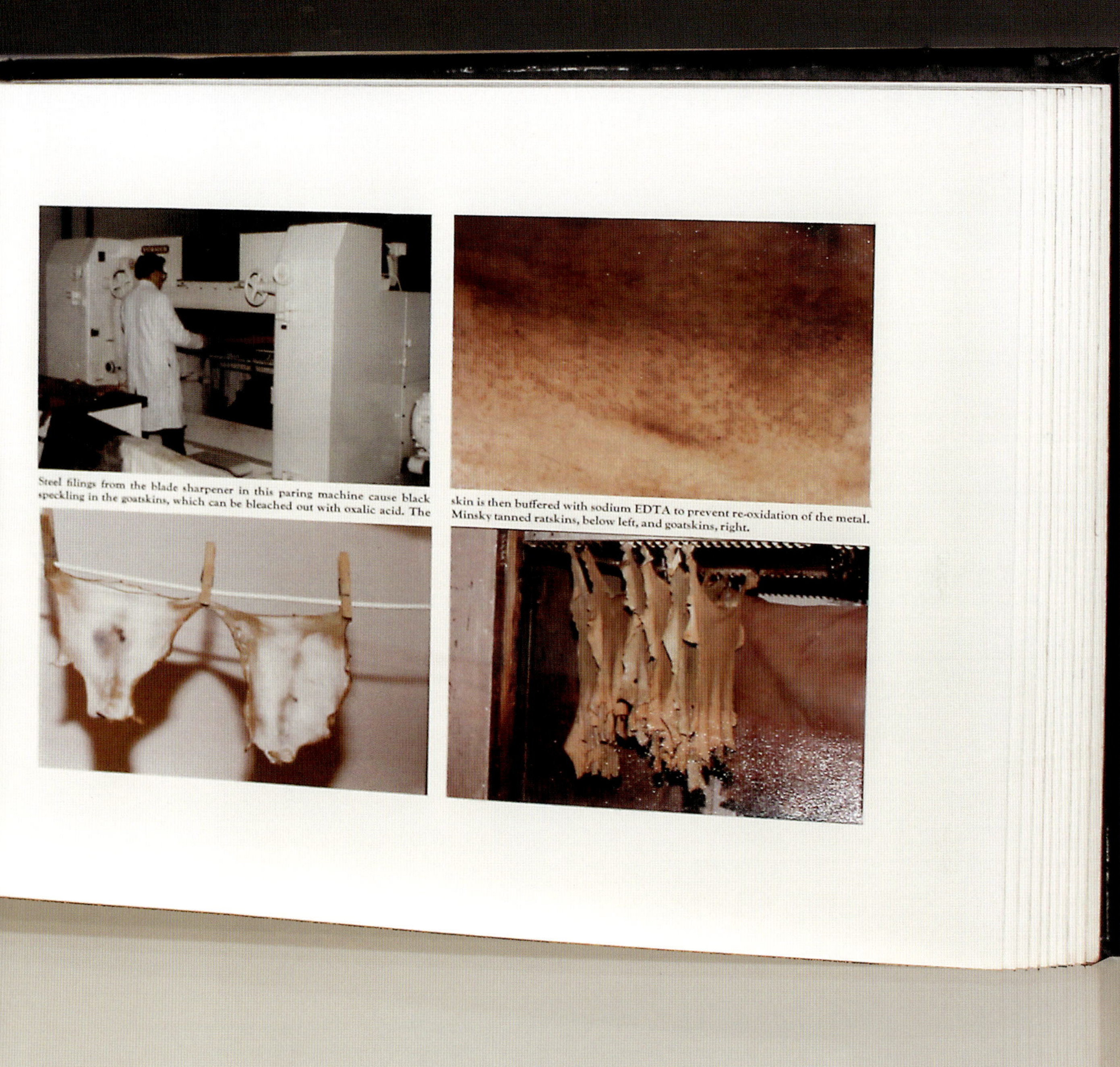

Minsky in London

Photos by Minsky, 1979. The letters written by others are printed in blue. This one is by David Tuck of the National Leathersellers' Centre in Northampton, England, and tells the story of my time there tanning the ratskins (left) for the *Babel* binding [p. 50], and the goatskins (right) for the *Dante's Inferno* manuscript book [p. 51].

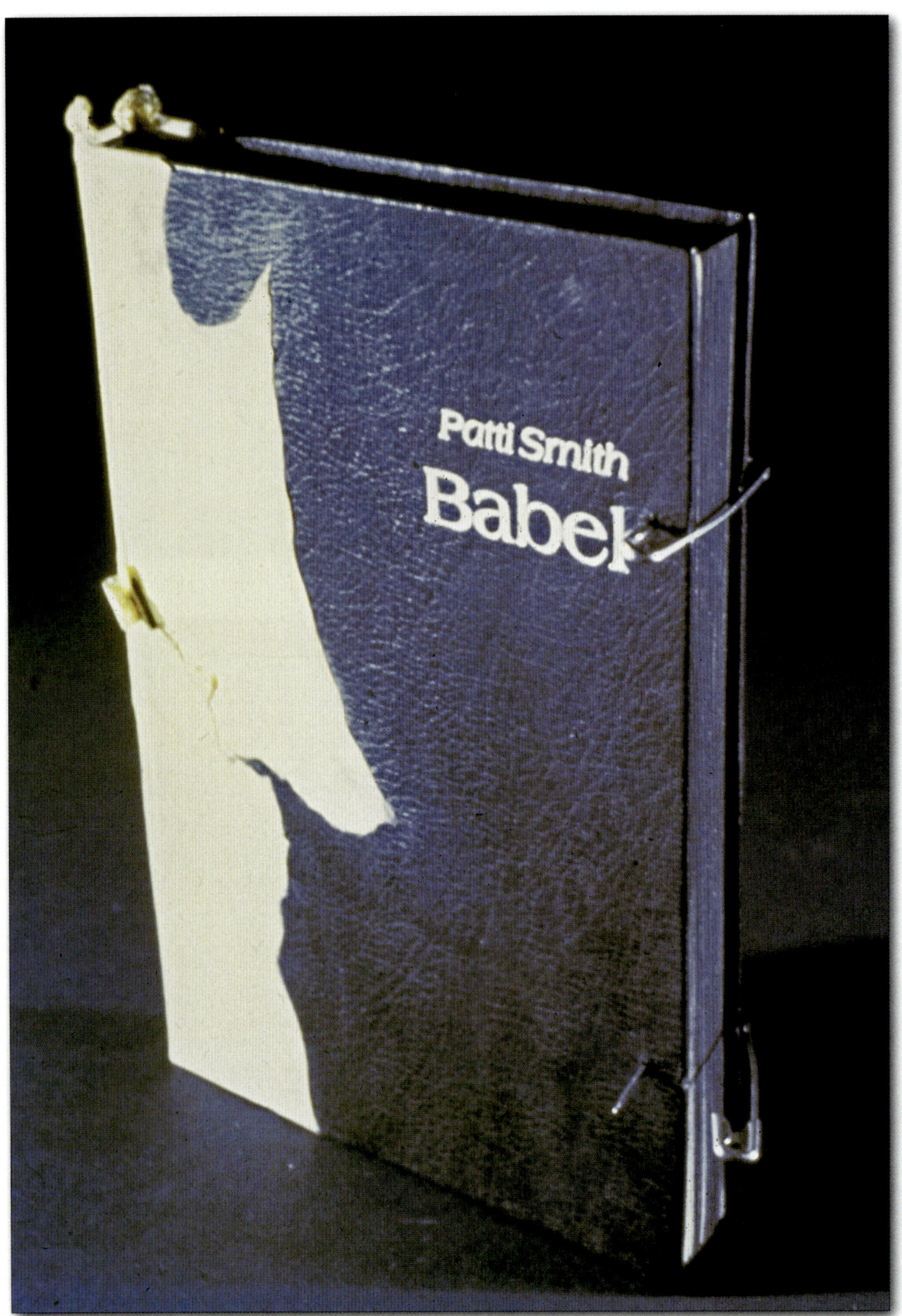

Babel
by Patti Smith. G. P. Putnam's Sons, New York, 1978.
Binding by Minsky, 1979. 9 x 6
Alum tawed ratskin, sumac tanned goatskin [see p. 48], safety pins, foil stamped title. Endsheets: rubber stamped safety pin motif by Barton Lidicé Beneš. Black suede box with padded satin lining.

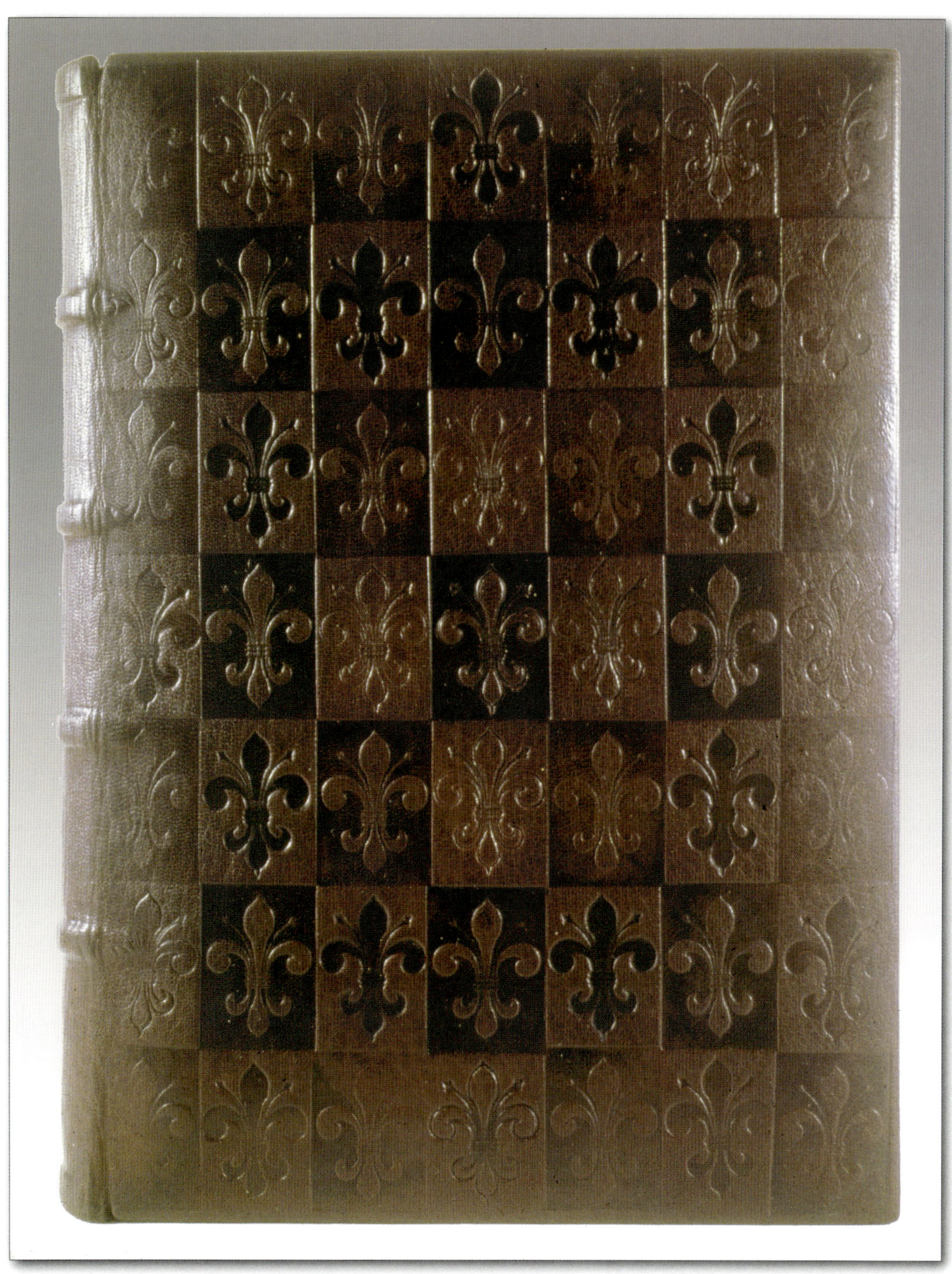

Blank Book for Tom Phillips' translation of Dante's Inferno.
Whatman paper. Binding by Minsky, 1979. 9⅝ x 7 x 1
Nigerian goat sumac tanned and dyed [see p. 48], blind tooled with Florentine lily design drawn by Phillips, made into intaglio, relief and outline tools.
Hinges of the same skin, with doublures of the same skin reversed.
Collection of the Sackner Archive of Concrete and Visual Poetry, Miami, FL

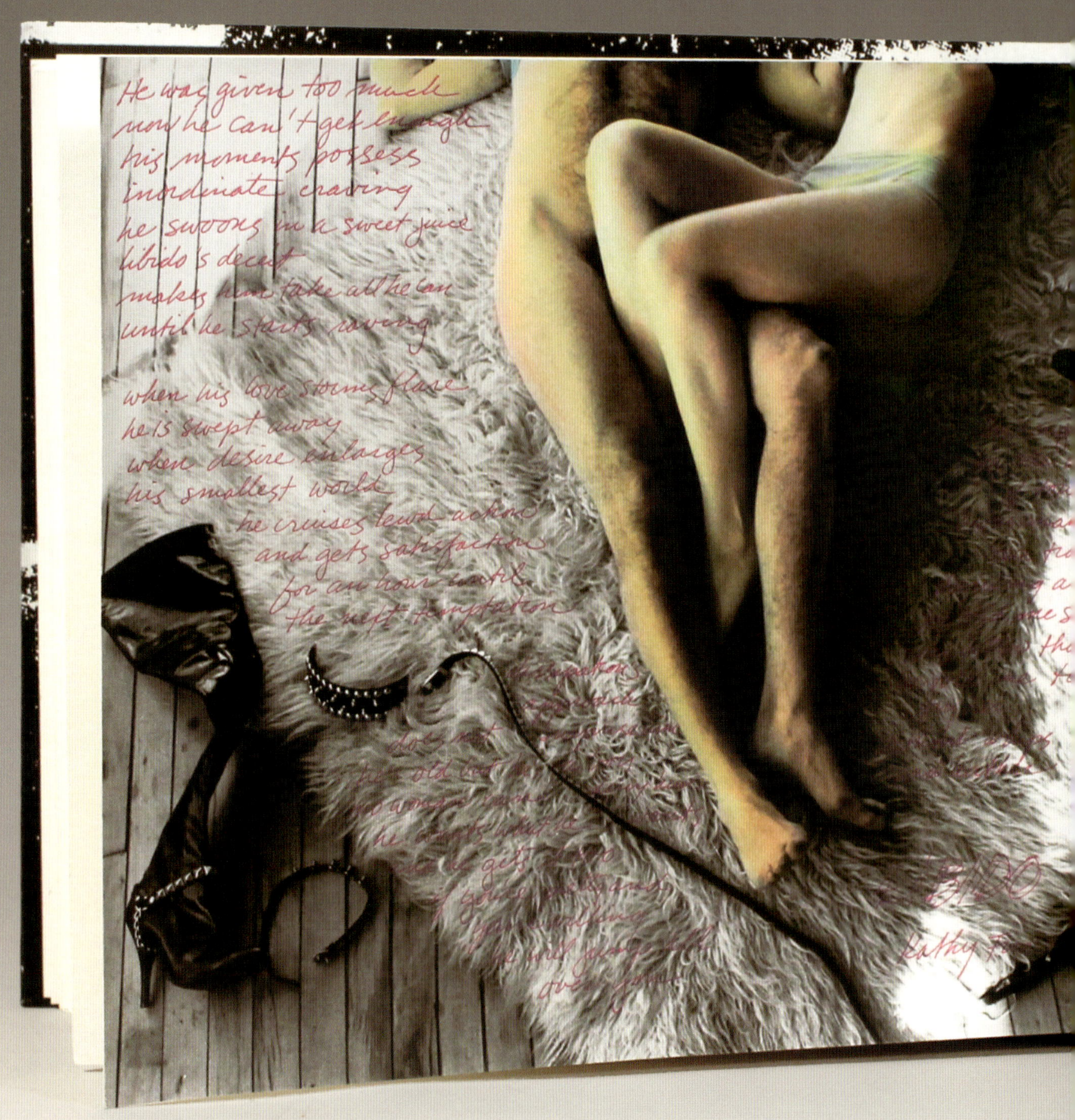

Minsky in London
Back endpaper, design and photo of Minsky and partner by Pat Gorman, 1978. Lyrics of *Libido* by Kathy Fire, performed on the 45 rpm vinyl recording by Kathy Fire and Reverse.

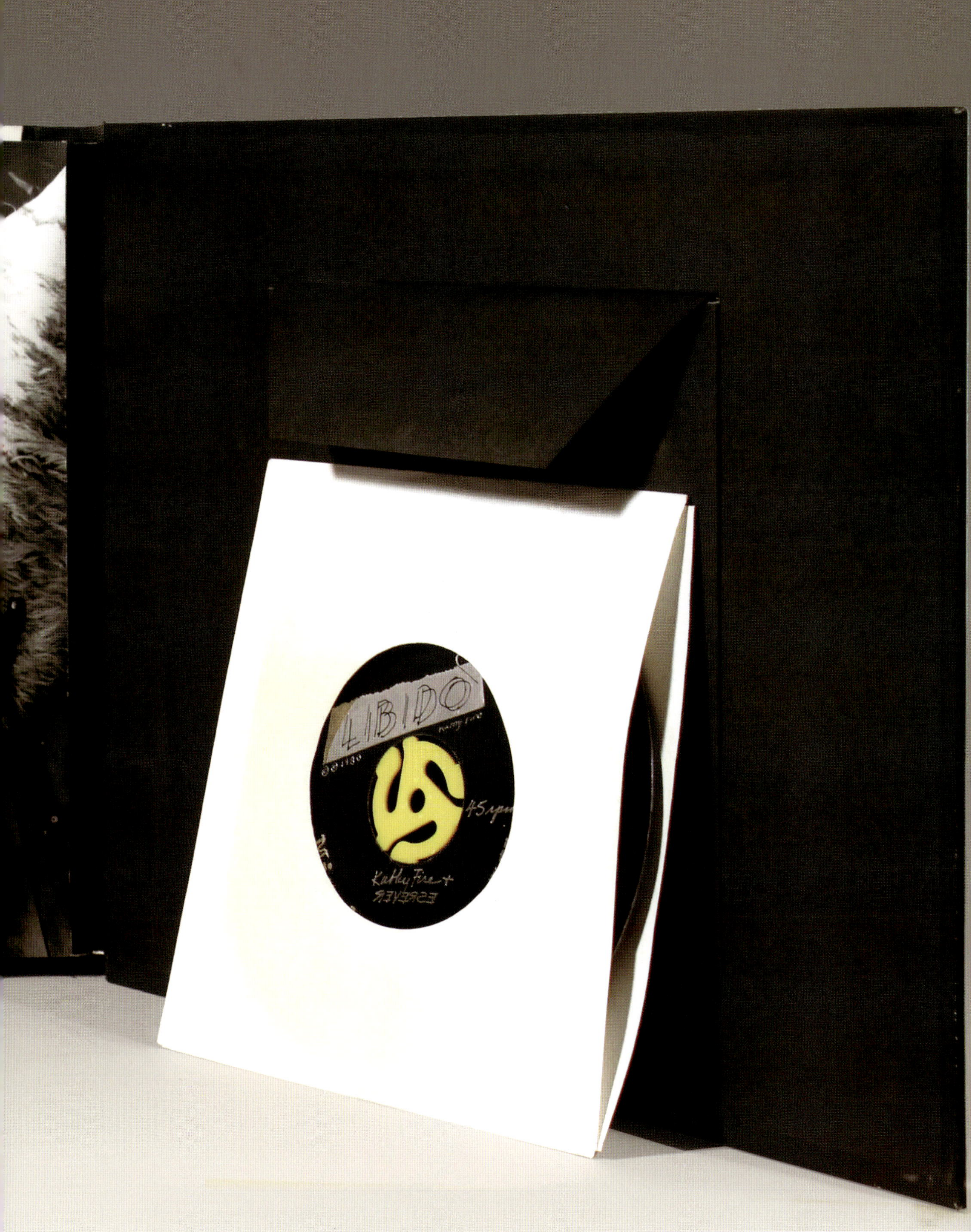
LIBIDO
Kathy Fire +

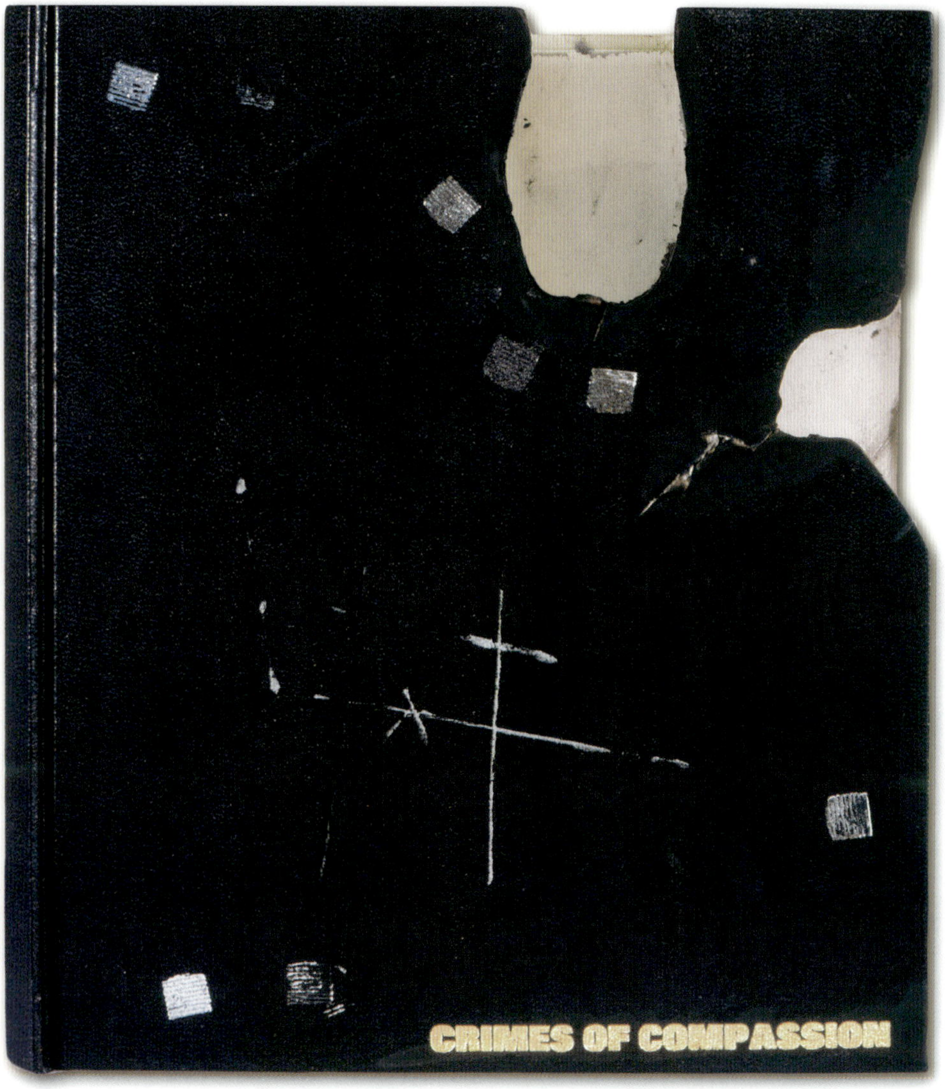

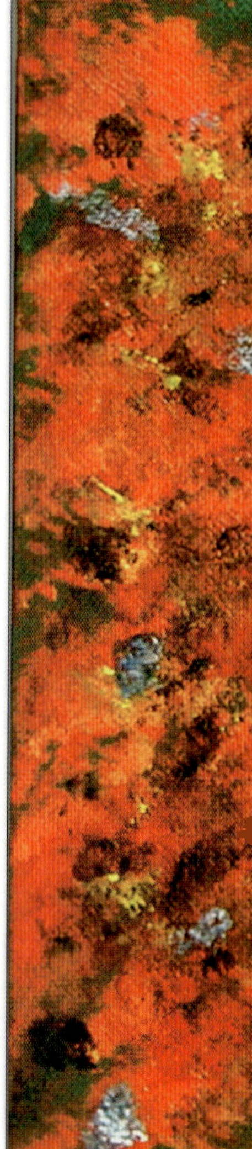

Crimes of Compassion
by Thomas W. Styron. Chrysler Museum, Norfolk, Virginia, April 16 – May 31 1981.
Reproductions of works in the exhibition interspersed with poems and song lyrics.
Binding by Minsky, 1981. 9 x 7½
Bookcloth on binders' board, cut and burned, hologram foil applied with hot pliers and screwdriver, gold stamped title.

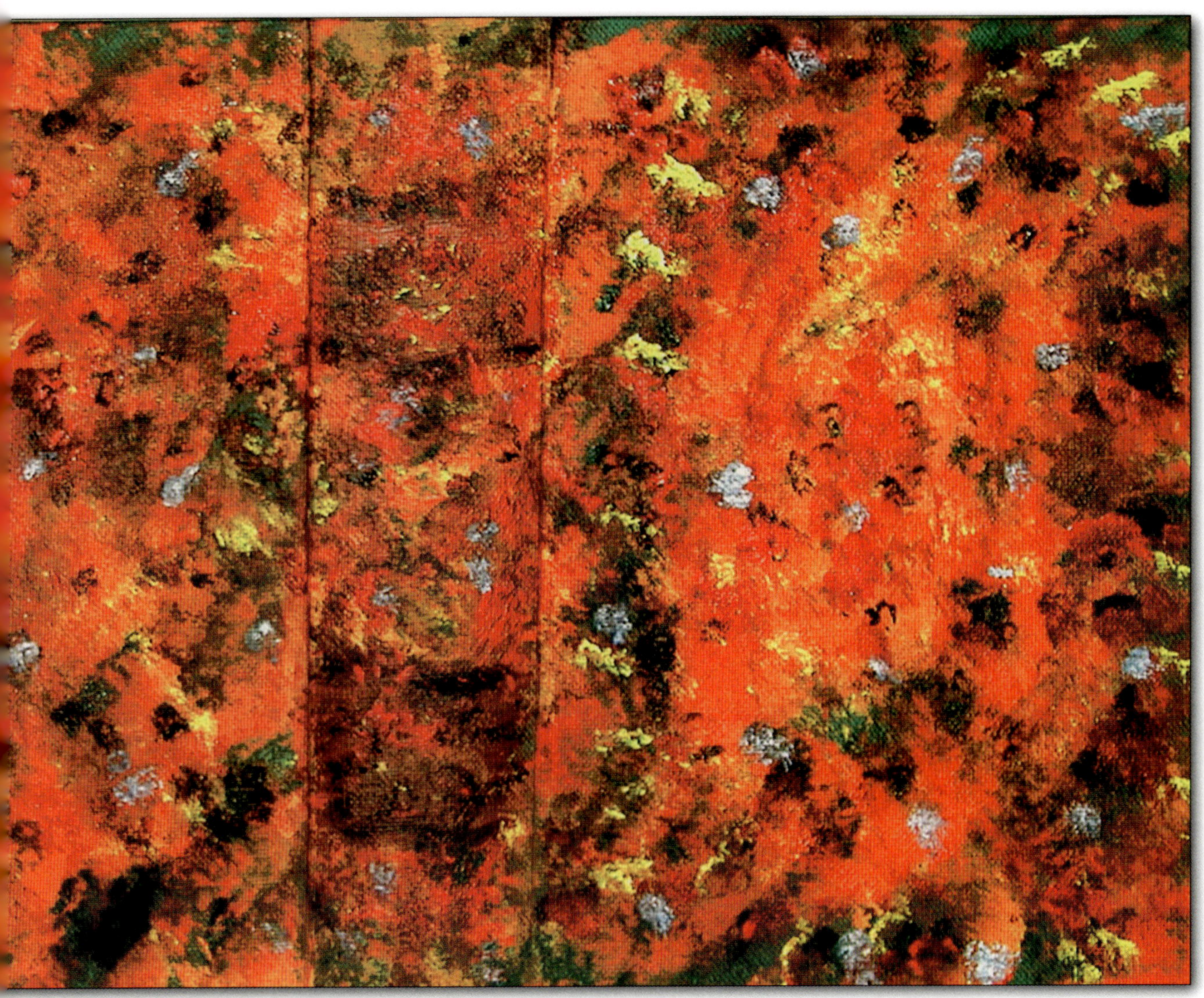

The Limits of Art:
Poetry and Prose Chosen by Ancient and Modern Critics
Collected and Edited by Huntington Cairns.
Bollingen Series XII, Pantheon Books, 1948.
Binding by Minsky, 1990. 9¼ x 6¾
Acrylic paint on existing book cover.
Collection of Clare Stone

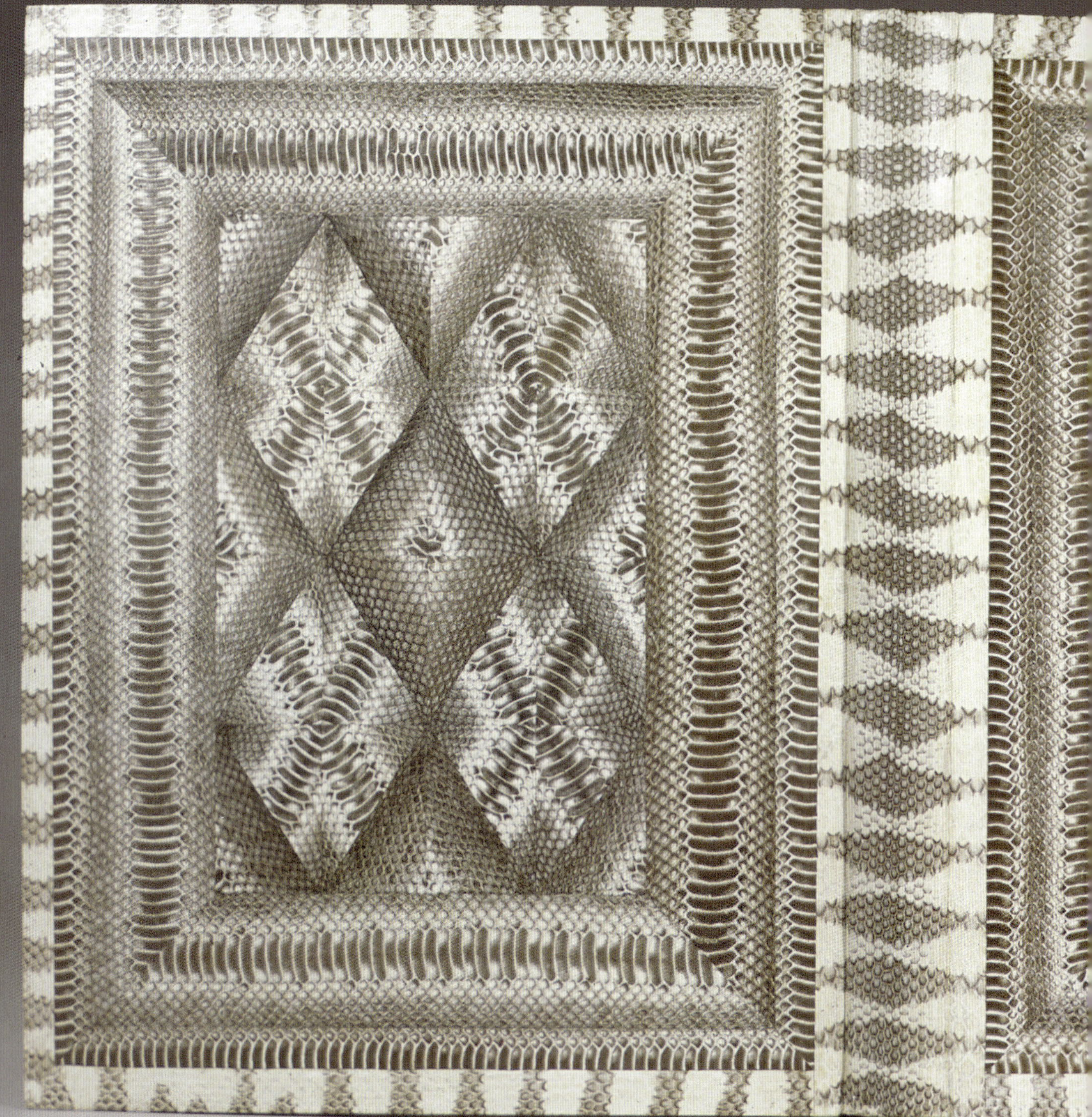

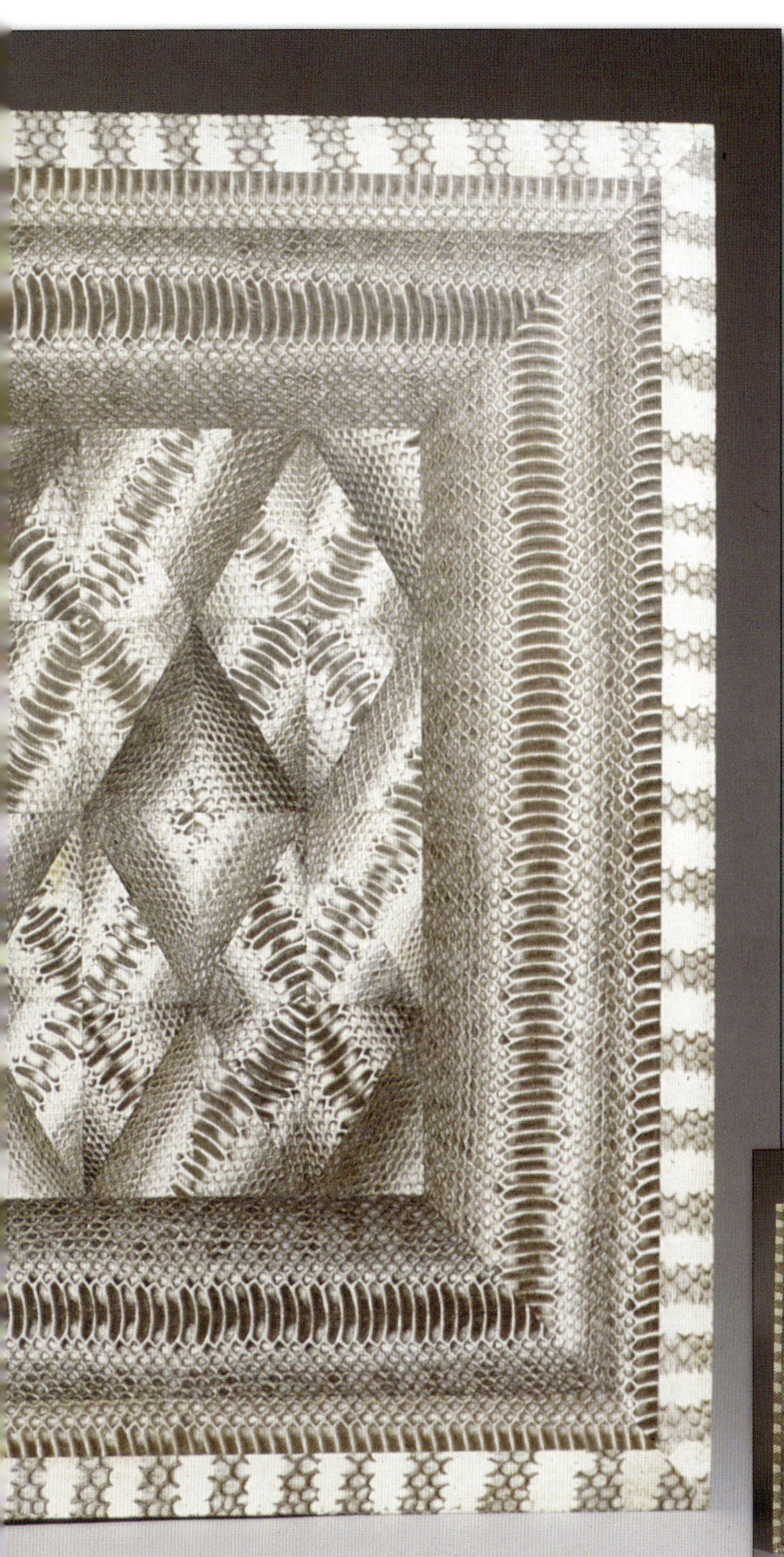

Blank Book
1988. 18 x 14
Inlaid snakeskin covers and doublures, handmade paper, linen endbands.
Below: the doublures are inlaid snakeskin.
Collection of Clare Stone, New York

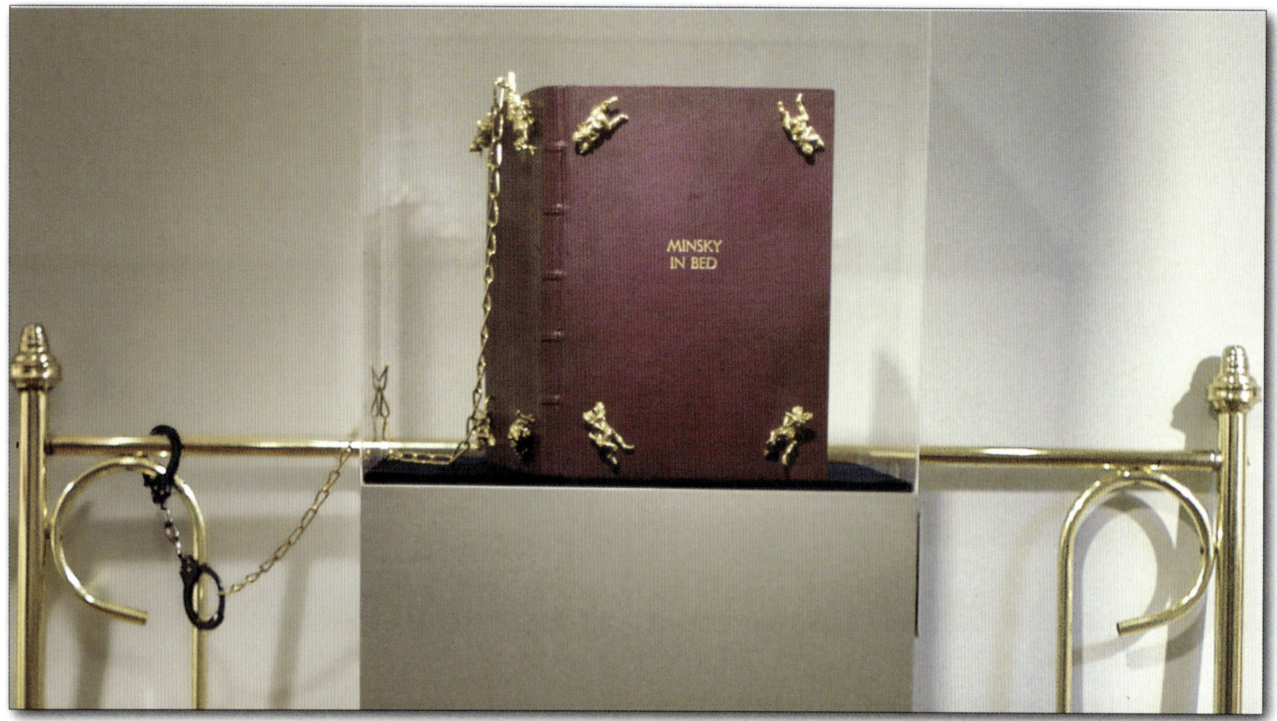

Minsky in Bed
1988. 15 x 10⅞ x 3
First prototype binding with one chapter printed letterpress, hand colored and gilded.
Installation at Zabriskie Gallery, New York, 1988.

Minsky in Bed

The story of my love life in the style of the incunabula

IN ADDITION TO BOOKS about the poisoning of America with toxic chemicals, the nuclear arms race, and world hunger, the prototype of *Minsky in Bed* was on view at the Zabriskie Gallery exhibition of 1988. This tome is an autobiographical excursion created in the format of incunabula, the printed books of the fifteenth century. Early books were so valuable they were sometimes chained to the bookshelf or lectern. They had brass knobs, known as bosses, attached to the covers, which kept the leather from coming in contact with the reading table.

The binding on *Minsky in Bed* was chained with handcuffs to a brass bedrail. For the bosses on the prototype I sculpted a copulating couple in wax and had it cast in bronze. A latex mould of the casting was used to reproduce copies in brass. The little sculpture was the same height in four rotations so it could be attached in a different position at each corner of the leather cover.

The sample chapter on display had a text written in the first person past and a commentary in the third person present, with historiated, inhabited, and illuminated initials [p. 60]. That chapter told of an amorous incident that occurred while I was a graduate student. The concept of the book was to be the story of my love life, from the earliest memories through the present. At the time of the exhibition I had four girlfriends, but that was soon to change.

A few weeks after the 1988 exhibition I met Barbara Slate at a croquet party. It was love at first sight and we have been together for 23 years. She is known as "the Queen of Comics," having written several hundred of them, including one in which Barbie® teaches bookbinding at The Center for Book Arts. Barbara became the copy editor of *Minsky in Bed.* It took eight more years of writing before the book was done.

In 1988 Canon announced the BJ-130 wide-carriage inkjet printer. I called and asked if I could try printing thick, rough sheets of handmade paper on it. They said yes, and the next day I did the first experiments. The Richard de

Bas (French) handmade paper printed beautifully. The print was 360 dpi, with water soluble black ink. I was able to hand color the image by spraying the printed sheet with an acrylic sealant. That first sample is now in the Richard Minsky archive at Yale, and was selected by the curator, Jae Rossman, for inclusion in the 2010 exhibition *Material Meets Metaphor: A Half Century of Book Art by Richard Minsky.*

I resolved to abandon letterpress for *Minsky in Bed* and produce the work digitally. I bought the printer and a software program named Ventura Publisher, which included the Digital Research GEM (Graphical Environment Manager), which ran in DOS on my 386 computer. This enabled me to see the page on screen as it would appear in print. The output was a Postscript file, and Canon provided a Postscript interpreter for the BJ-130.

The BJ-130 printed in black ink only. This book was now a true computer incunabulum, using the newest printing technology. As was done in Gutenberg's day, the initial letters are hand colored and gilded.

In 1989 I took the first inkjet chapter to London, and Jan van der Wateren, the curator of the National Art Library at the Victoria & Albert Museum, ordered Copy No. 1 of *Minsky in Bed.* The V&A already had Copy No. 1 of *Minsky in London.*

Each chapter of the book was sent to the three subscribers as it was completed. In 1997 they sent back all the fascicles for binding. The V&A purchase order specified that they wanted it "bound in Minsky's stained bedsheets." The British sense of humor. But they got their way, and I made the cover into a little bed out of the actual sheet and blanket that some of the episodes in the book took place on.

Ruth and Marvin Sackner ordered a binding like the handcuffed prototype, with the copulating couples gold plated. But when they saw the V&A copy, they ordered a box for it with a bed made from the same sheets and blanket.

There were so many changes in hardware and software over the years that the files I had used for the earlier chapters were obsolete. Even though I had announced an edition of ten copies, only the three that were begun in 1989 were able to be printed.

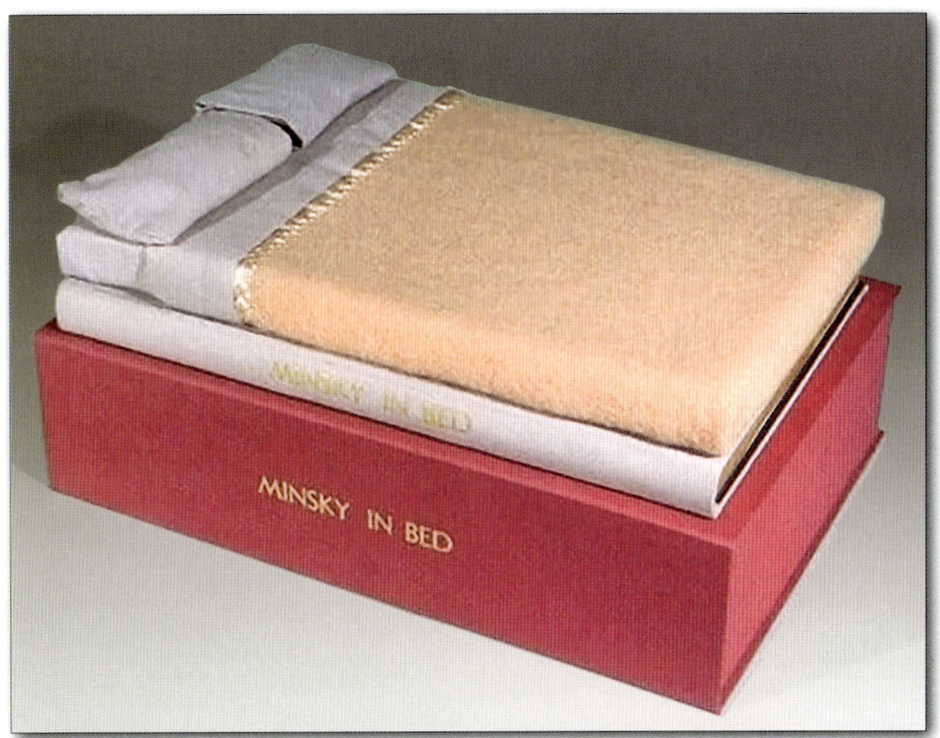

Minsky in Bed
Copy Number 1
1997. 15 x 10½ x 2
Bound in Minsky's bedsheets and blanket. Cloth box and wrapper.
Collection of The Victoria and Albert Museum, London, England

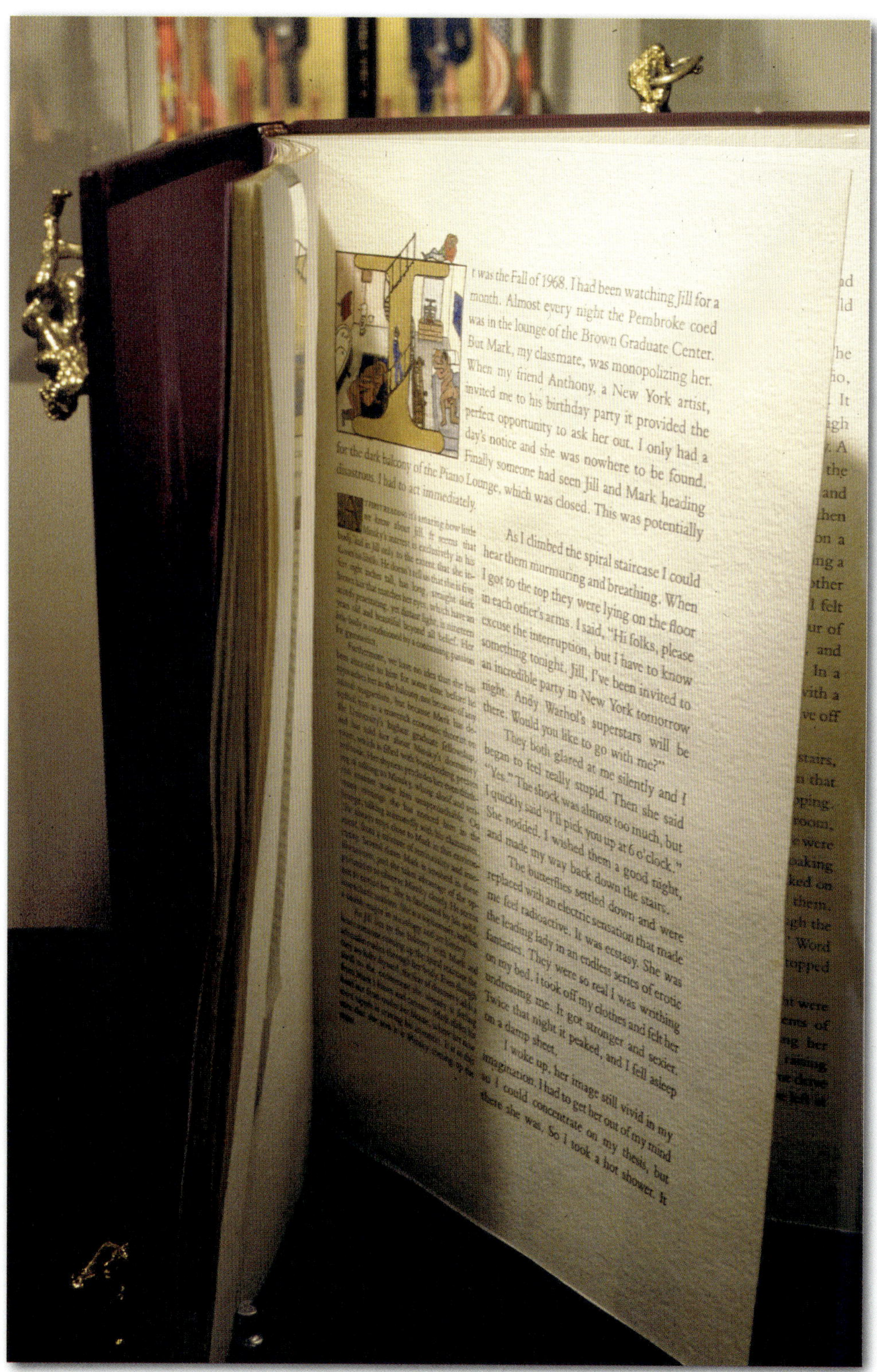

Minsky in Bed
1988. 15 x 10⅞ x 3
First prototype binding with one chapter printed letterpress, hand colored and gilded.
Installation at Zabriskie Gallery, New York, 1988.

Shortly after this pleasant occasion Sheryl moved into my large apartment in Queens. I always had at least two friends as roommates there, since my grandmother Edna's death five years earlier. Sheryl set up her loft bed in the large room that had been my grandmother's. We both worked long hours and enjoyed our rare moments of leisure together. The months quickly passed.

One evening, about a year after she moved in, Sheryl came out of her room with a strange look on her face. "Your grandmother just tried to come into my body and talk through me," she said. Edna had always promised she would come back and talk to us from the other side if it were possible.

"What happened?" I inquired. "I was lying there," she began, "when I felt a presence in the room. The initials E.E. came to me. I knew your grandmother's name was Edna, so I figured it must be her." "Go on," I said. "I felt she wanted to enter my body and speak through me. I was beginning to think to myself, 'that might be OK,' when I felt this powerful force rushing into me." Sheryl paused. "So what stopped it?" I prompted. "She came too fast. I got scared and blocked it off. It was too strange."

During the next bookbinding class Sheryl is careful not to act in any way that would alert the other students about her extracurricular activities. She is aware that Minsky has a hard enough job without having to expose his private life to the other students. She is just slow to finish her headband, being sure she is the last to leave. Actually, she leaves the next morning.

A few weeks later Sheryl has lunch with her friend Cheryl, and tells her about the new turn in her love life. Sheryl and Cheryl were students together at Buffalo, and kept up their friendship when both moved to New York. They are both of a literary persuasion, and Sheryl charms her friend with the story of her seduction of her teacher. As the months go by, Cheryl learns more about Minsky from her friend, who has told her about the Center and his grandiose notions of changing the way people look at books. When Cheryl arranges her little dinner party her only plan is to have a nice social evening and maybe get some new ideas for her graduate thesis.

She loves to cook, and designs a dinner that is easy to prepare, so she can relax with her guests. By the end of the meal Cheryl feels she has a new topic for her thesis and a new friend. The high intellectual level of the conversation makes her want to extend the evening. As they sit on the couch she loosens up, and starts touching Minsky's arm as they talk.

He continues the conversation as though this is perfectly normal. She glances at Sheryl to see if there is any negative reaction to this gesture, but her friend's response to the look is to smile and stroke Minsky's head. He appears oblivious to this exchange between the women. Taking this as approval, Cheryl moves closer and gets more physical, putting her arm around Minsky's shoulder and laying her hand on Sheryl's arm as it strokes his head. Nobody flinches, and the Sheryls, seeing the opportunity for a delicious adventure, make sure events progress to a pleasurable conclusion.

Sheryl had no way of knowing that Edna's middle name was Elsie. And that was not the last time my grandmother paid a visit.

Page from Minsky in Bed

c. 1990. 14½ x 10½

Inkjet and watercolor on handmade paper.

The Crisis of Democracy

IN 1980 THE POLITICAL SCENE was changing. I had heard about a book titled *The Crisis of Democracy.* It was written for an organization named The Trilateral Commission, established by Zbigniew Brzezinski and David Rockefeller in 1973 to supplant the Bilderberg group, which Prince Bernhard had run since 1954. In this text the authors propose that there is too much freedom in contemporary democracies, and that it is necessary to curtail personal freedoms in order to preserve the governability of democracies.

In order to learn more about the group I ordered some material from them. Jimmy Carter was a member of the Trilateral Commission. What surprised me was that in the forthcoming Presidential election each team from the two major parties and the "independent" party included at least one member of this club. I bound the book in sheep, gold, and barbed wire to reflect the metaphor of the text, and exhibited this book as a political commentary at my exhibition *Ten Conversation Pieces* at the Allan Stone Gallery in May, 1981 [p. 6].

The book is more relevant today than when I bound it. Since 1980, the Presidents of the United States, members of this not-for-profit organization before their nomination, worked toward consolidating power in the Executive branch. George H. W. Bush and Bill Clinton were members, and Brzezinski was Barack Obama's mentor at Harvard. The terror attack of Sept. 11, 2001 precipitated the passage of the USA PATRIOT Act, which had failed to pass during the Clinton administration, but was on hand for the (George W.) Bush administration to speed through Congress [see also p. 69].

This book was originally purchased as a paperback. The surface-dyed, glazed sheepskin is abraded by the barbed wire every time the book is opened and closed, exposing the inner flesh that contrasts with the grain of the leather. The action is not so extreme as to cause the book to disintegrate rapidly, but slowly erodes the decorative surface of the skin. The 23K gold title remains bright. The barbed wire springs back to form a reading stand when the book is opened [photo below, after 25 years].

In 2007 I created an updated version of this work to reflect the development of geopolitical realities, with the tougher skin of a goat being constrained by the more dangerous razor ribbon [facing page].

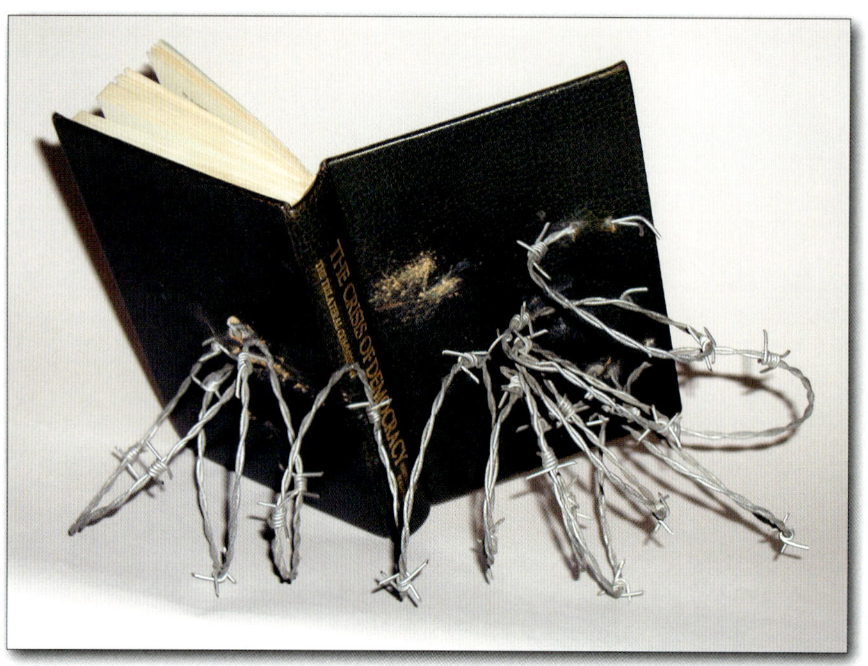

The Crisis of Democracy
by Crozier, Huntington and Watanuki for the Trilateral Commission.
New York University Press, 1975.
Binding by Minsky, 1980. 8¾ x 6 x 11
Sheep, gold, barbed wire. Photo: 2005.
Collection of the Haas Family Arts Library, Yale University

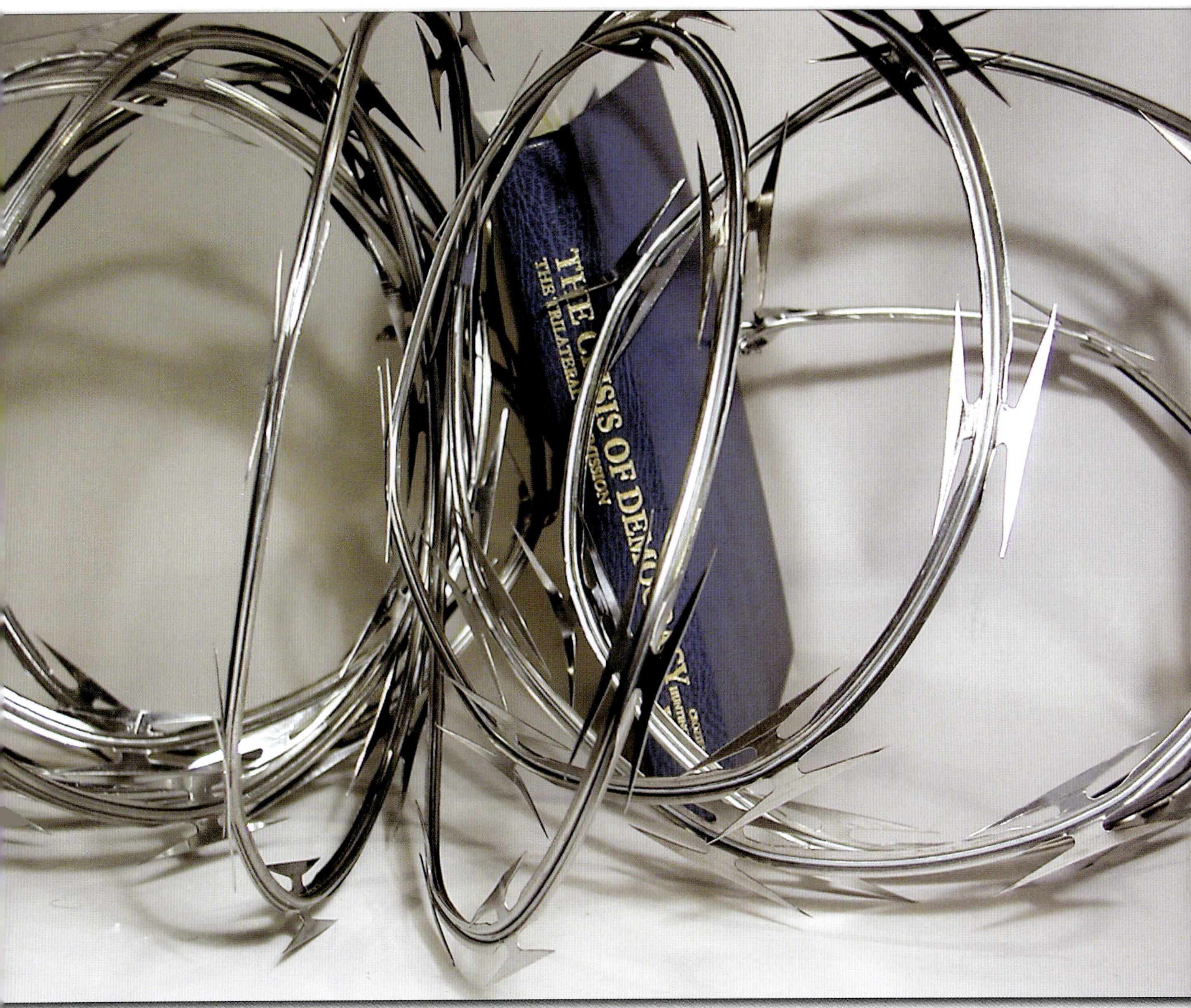

The Crisis of Democracy
by Crozier, Huntington and Watanuki for the Trilateral Commission. New York University Press, 1975.
Binding by Minsky, 2007. Goat, gold, razor ribbon. 15 x 17 x 17
Jack Ginsberg Artists Book Collection of Johannesburg, South Africa

The Bill of Rights

IN 1993, AS A CULMINATION of the bookworks on social and political themes that began with *The Crisis of Democracy,* I started work on a series about the United States Constitution, beginning with books exemplifying aspects of The Bill of Rights. It began when Salman Rushdie's *Satanic Verses* made headlines around the world. A fatwah put a price on his head, and there were book burnings in radical Islamic countries. With a single publication he lost the four freedoms guaranteed by the First Amendment to the United States Constitution. I made a book burning kit titled *The First Amendment: Reliquary for the Ashes of Salman Rushdie's Satanic Verses* [p. 66], which was exhibited at the Elaine Benson Gallery in Bridgehampton, Long Island, NY.

That year I gave a lecture in Washington, DC for the American Society of Journalists and Authors. A man who had been sitting in the back of the room came to me with a book in his hand. Larry Sullivan, Curator of Rare Books at the Library of Congress, asked if I would bind his book, *The Prison Reform Movement.* I welcomed the commission, and adopted it as *The Eighth Amendment* [p. 67]. It took three years to conceive and execute the work.

The Second Amendment was more complex, with seven books on the rights of gun owners and the militia movement that developed after Ruby Ridge and Waco, in a snakeskin cabinet with a MAK-90 rifle and a thousand rounds of ammunition. I had never fired a gun before starting this project, and had to practice marksmanship in order to shoot the endpapers, which are inkjet prints representing the targets of the racist, anti-semitic, and anti-governmental militias that grew from the Aryan Nation and the Ku Klux Klan [p. 68].

In 2000 I got a call from Marty Shepard, a friend from Sag Harbor with whom I had played music since the 70s. Marty and his wife, Judy, are publishers, under the imprint Permanent Press. Marty said he had a book titled *Branches,* that was an epic poem, and thought it would be a good choice for a limited edition binding. I expected it would be pastoral, and had thoughts about binding it in bark paper. When it arrived, the first page was bucolic, but it turned quickly into a gripping text as the narrator described throwing his stepson down a well and lamenting that because he didn't die in the fall like the others, he had to shoot him.

This is the story of Sheriff Branches, a West Texas lawman who acts as judge, jury, and executioner. As the story progresses, one can almost sympathize with his motives. The boy had joined a neo-Nazi group and was practicing marksmanship on man-size targets behind the barn with a 9 mm pistol. I bound the book in khaki shirt-cloth with a pocket, a Sheriff's badge, and nametag, and produced an edition of 100 copies for Marty, shooting each copy through the cover several times with a 9mm pistol. I had to get a pistol permit, which involved being fingerprinted, an FBI background check, and a lieutenant coming to our home to interview us.

As I was binding this edition it struck me that this, with a little tweaking, could be the Fifth Amendment [p. 75]. It also suggested that *The Bill of Rights* should be an edition. Allan Stone had already bought the Reliquary, and Larry Sullivan owned *Forlorn Hope: The Prison Reform Movement.* Putting together an exhibition of The Bill of Rights based on the unique works would be an administrative challenge at best. As an editioned set of 10 works it would stay together, and also could be in several places. I asked Marty to send me 25 more copies of *Branches.* To make it part of *The Bill of Rights* I added a box with a black leather holster with the text of the Fifth Amendment stamped on it. Perhaps, if the sheriff had thought about due process of law every time he took his gun from the holster, things would be different.

I then selected books for all ten amendments. In some cases this was easy, for others, which were long out of print, it was daunting. For two of them I printed small editions just for this set.

In January of 2001 Louis K. Meisel suggested that this be an exhibition, which he scheduled in his SOHO gallery for the following spring.

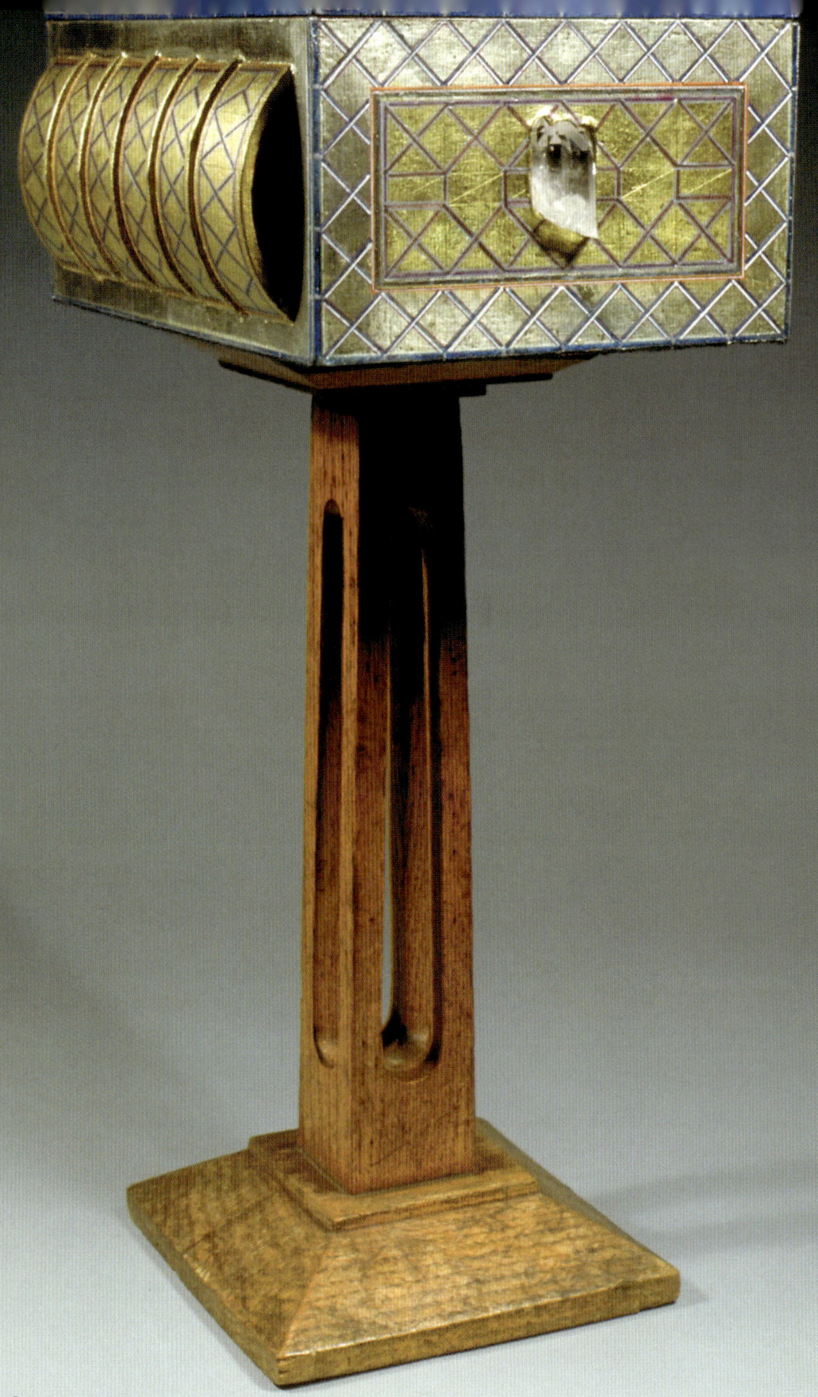

The First Amendment
Reliquary for the Ashes of Salman Rushdie's *Satanic Verses*
1993. 19 x 8 x 11
A Book Burning Kit, containing a copy of the First American Edition of the book, incense and matches. Lemon Gold leaf, White Gold leaf, ink and lacquer over bookbinders' board; Crystal Quartz, cut and polished Agate, emerald cut Citrine; wood base.
Missing.

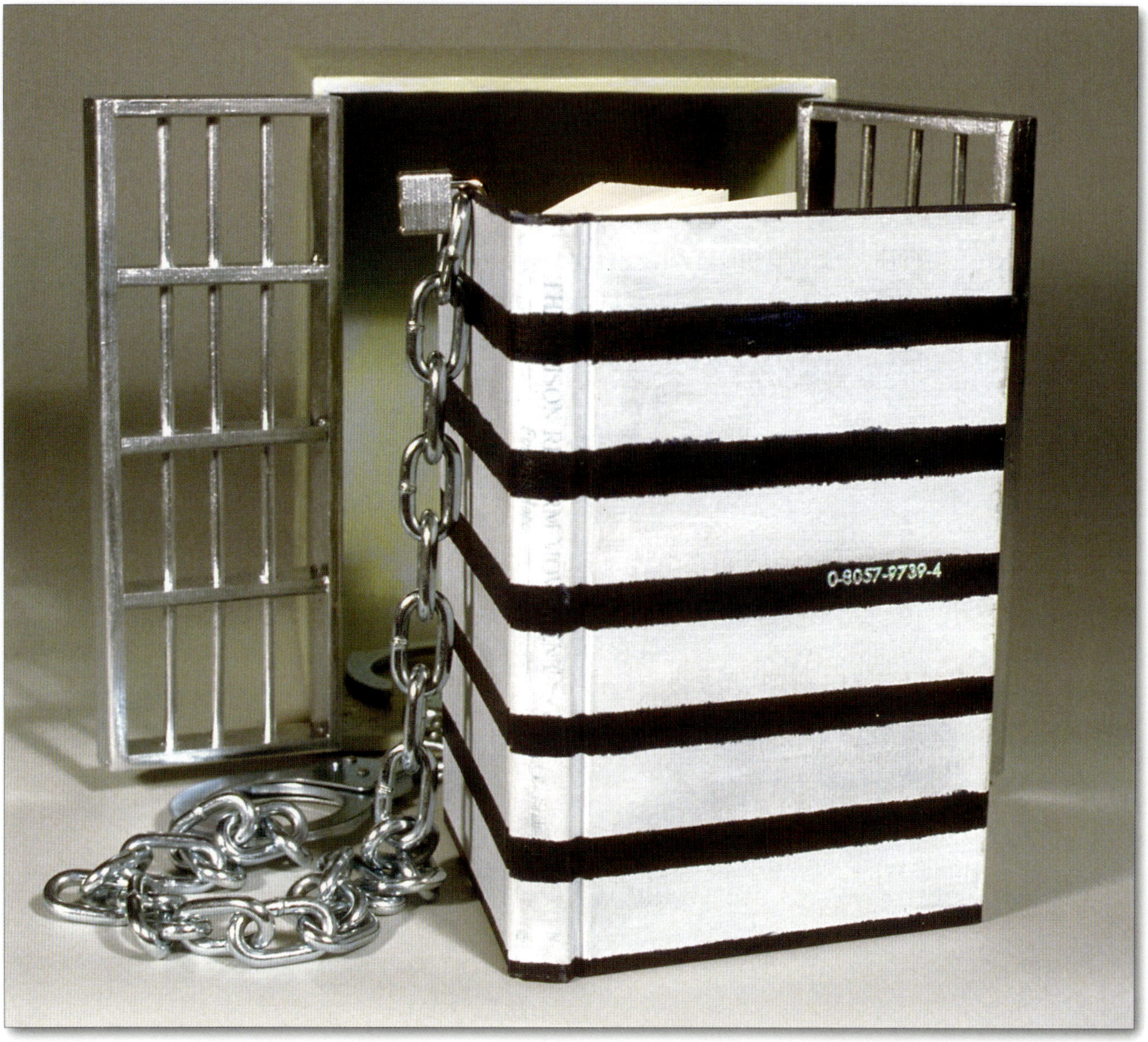

Forlorn Hope
The Prison Reform Movement
The Eighth Amendment
by Larry E. Sullivan. G.K. Hall, New York, 1990
Binding by Minsky, 1996. 10 x 8 x 7
Chain binding with handcuffs and padlock, painted in acrylic prison stripes over publisher's binding, with ISBN stamped in hologram foil, in a case with jail doors. Acrylic/latex over wood.
Collection of Larry E. Sullivan, New York

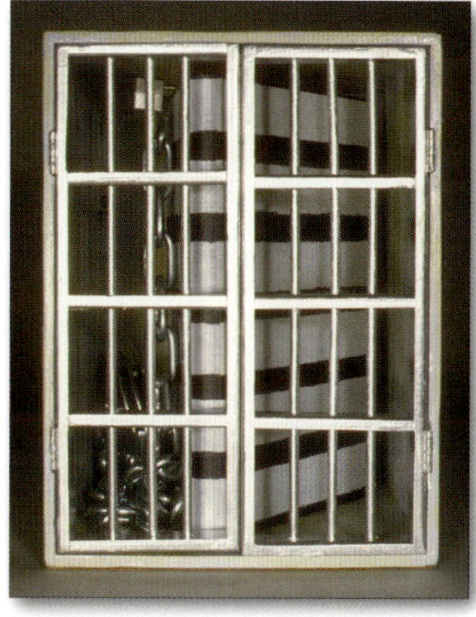

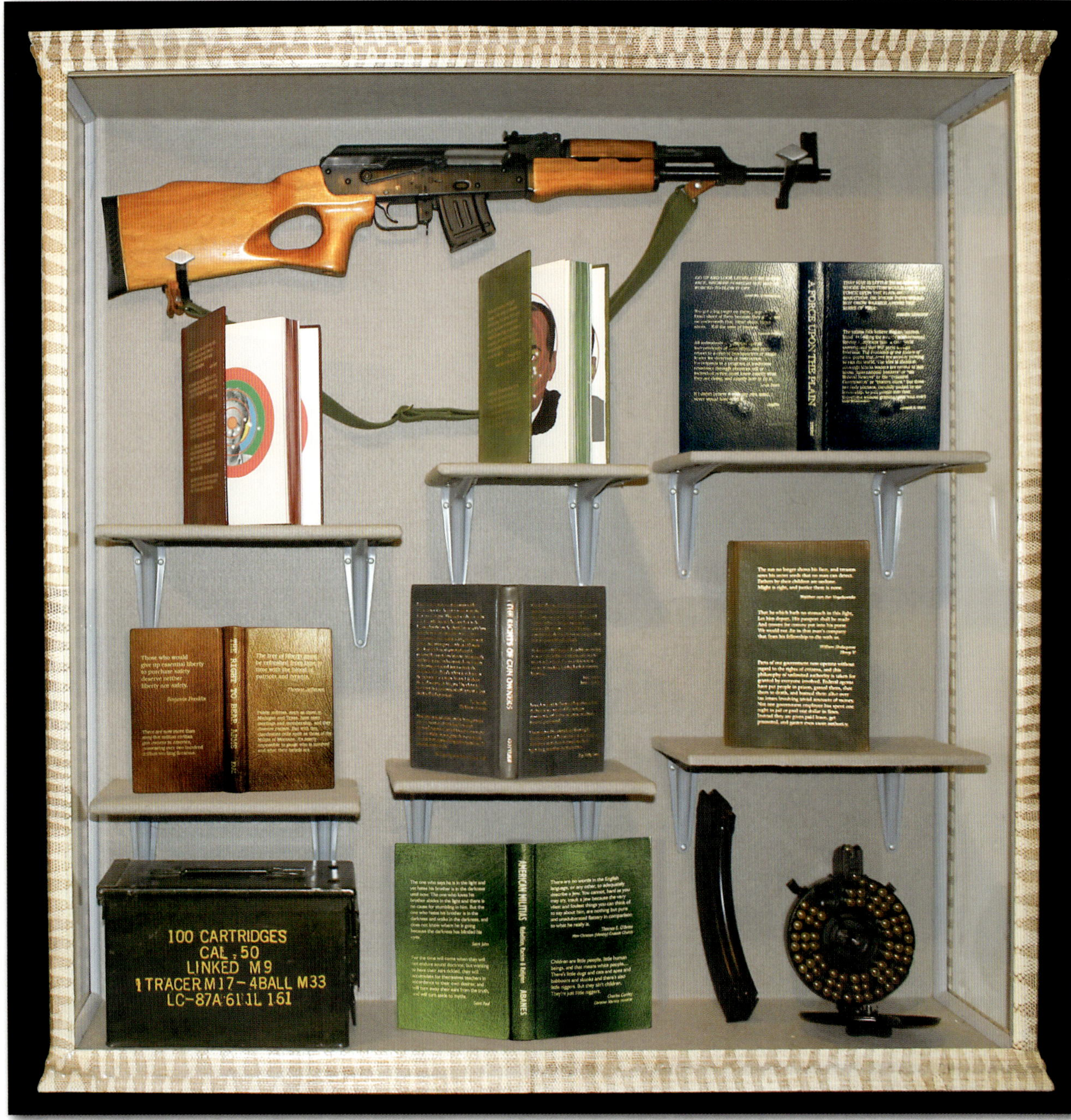

The Right to Bear Arms
The Second Amendment
1996-98. 45 x 45 x 11
Seven books on American gun culture [see p. 65] in goatskin bindings stamped with gold quotes from each book. Above the books is a Norinco MAK-90 Sporter, a semiautomatic version of the AK-47 assault rifle. Also in the case are 1,000 rounds of ammunition, two five-round hunting clips, a loaded 40-round "banana" magazine, and a loaded 75-round drum magazine.

The endpapers of each book are targets made of images representing the subject of that volume, printed inkjet on Rives BFK or handmade paper. The targets were shot with the MAK-90, an Enfield 2A-1, and a Ruger 10-22, at distances of 50 feet to 100 yards. Two of the books are shot through the covers.

The Bill of Rights Ten Volume Set

Thofe who would give up ESSENTIAL LIBERTY to purchafe a little TEMPORARY SAFETY, deferve neither LIBERTY nor SAFETY.

This motto is reproduced from the title page of *An Historical Review of the Constitution and Government of Pensylvania*, an anonymous book published in 1759 that has been attributed to Benjamin Franklin. The above text occurs in a letter to the Governor from the Assembly dated Nov. 11, 1755, petitioning to raise funds to arm the Susquehanna Indians, to keep them as allies against the French, who had armed the Delaware and Shawanese.

Essential Liberty
Inkjet On Paper. 13 X 40
Motto from the title page of *An Historical Review of the Constitution and Government of Pensylvania,* an anonymous book published in 1759, attributed to Benjamin Franklin and Richard Jackson. A 40″ wide print is in the Bill of Rights limited edition set, inkjet on paper .

September 11, 2001

I WAS WORKING ON *The Bill of Rights* in my studio at 15 Bleecker Street, expecting my assistant, a young French woman who had studied bookbinding at the Ecole Estienne in Paris, when my neighbor John walked in. "Come out here, Richard, you've got to see this." We walked down the street toward the corner of Lafayette. It was a beautiful September day with a bright blue sky. "I was just sitting in the NOHO Star having breakfast," he continued, "when I saw a plane fly overhead, way too low. I ran outside, and it flew straight into the World Trade Center." By that time we were at the corner, looking at the sight of flames and smoke coming from a gaping hole in the top of one tower. "That was no accident," said John, "I watched it fly straight and under control."

People were walking by on their way to work, some coming out of the subway, and few even looked up and noticed what was going on. Maybe two or three minutes had passed since the plane hit. Clearly the world had just changed. This was not the first terrorist attack at the WTC, but it was a new paradigm.

I went back to the studio. My assistant arrived. She had to walk past that corner, with its clear view. "Did you see it?" I asked. "See what?" she replied. I said "Come with me. You are going to see something you will never want to see again." "You are scaring me," she said. "You should be scared." We walked to the corner, where a larger crowd was now looking up.

We returned to the studio. I turned on the TV. They were calling it an accident, then the second plane hit. We got back to work. It seemed the only reasonable response to terrorism. We were in the new normal.

The bridges and tunnels were closed. The National Guard would not let me north of 14th street. It was three days before I could get home to Barbara and Samantha, who was now four years old. Although the phone lines stopped working minutes after the event, I was able to keep in touch by e-mail.

September 19 the first version of the USA PATRIOT Act was introduced to Congress, and with some adjustments it became law on October 26, despite objections to its assaults on civil liberties. It was convenient for the administration that such a complex piece of legislation just happened to be handy a few days after the September 11 attack.

Suddenly there was a lot of interest in *The Bill of Rights.* The exhibition reception on May 2 was packed. *The New York Times* review ran across six columns. Requests to show the set came from colleges and art centers, and it became a focus of commentary. I posted a page of Bill of Rights teaching aids at minsky.com, with projects and assignments from elementary school through college.

Seeing responses to this artwork blogged by 11th grade students in an American History class was among life's most rewarding moments.

The First Amendment

Congress shall make no law respecting an establishment of religion, or prohibiting the free exercise thereof; or abridging the freedom of speech, or of the press; or the right of the people peaceably to assemble, and to petition the government for a redress of grievances.

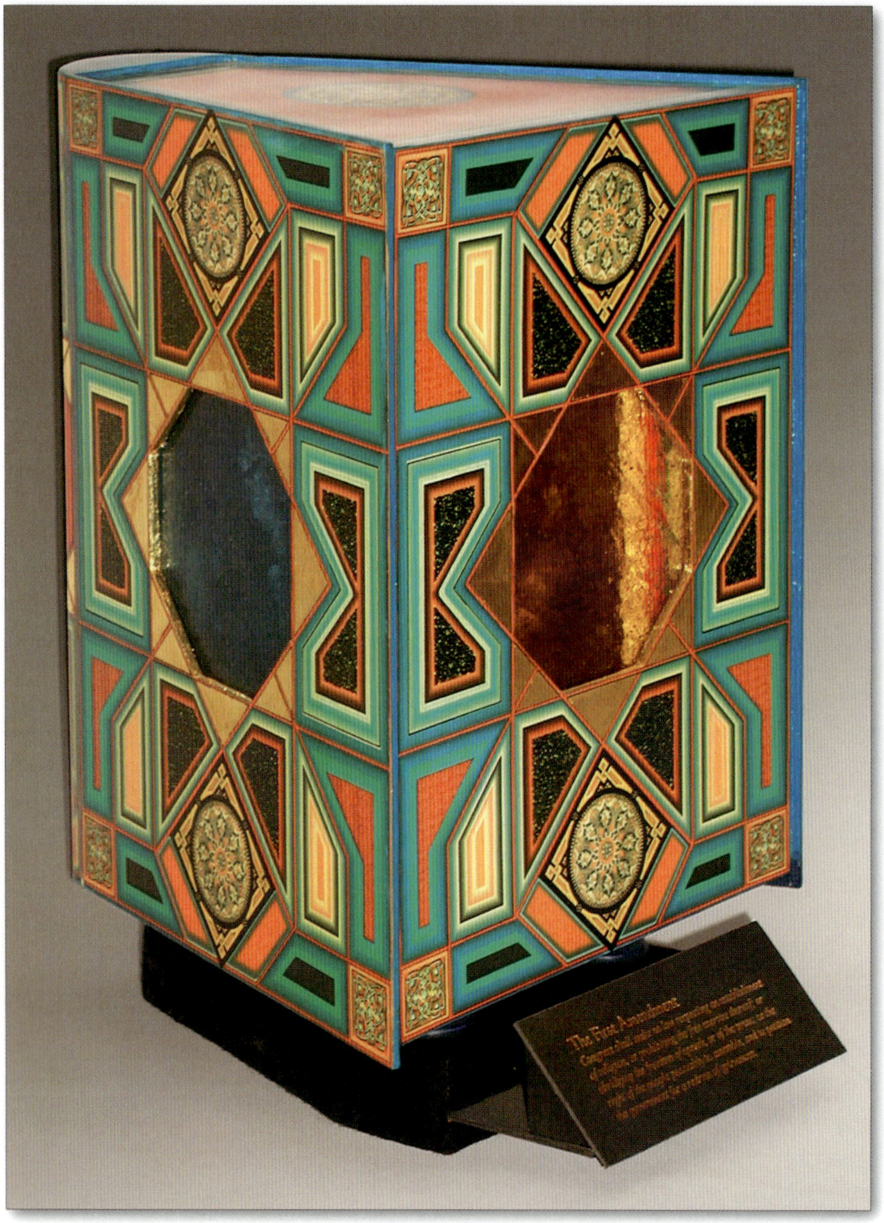

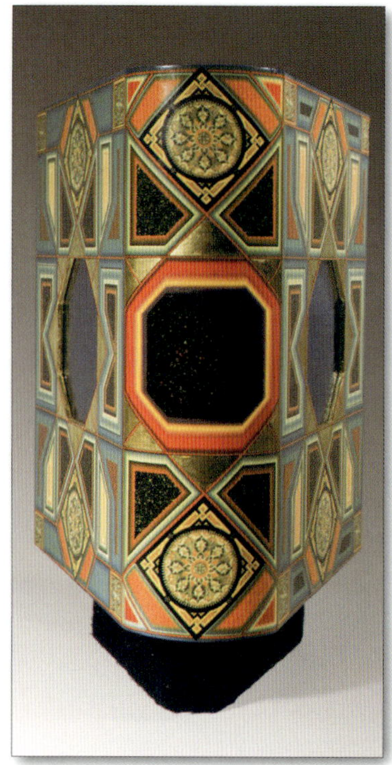

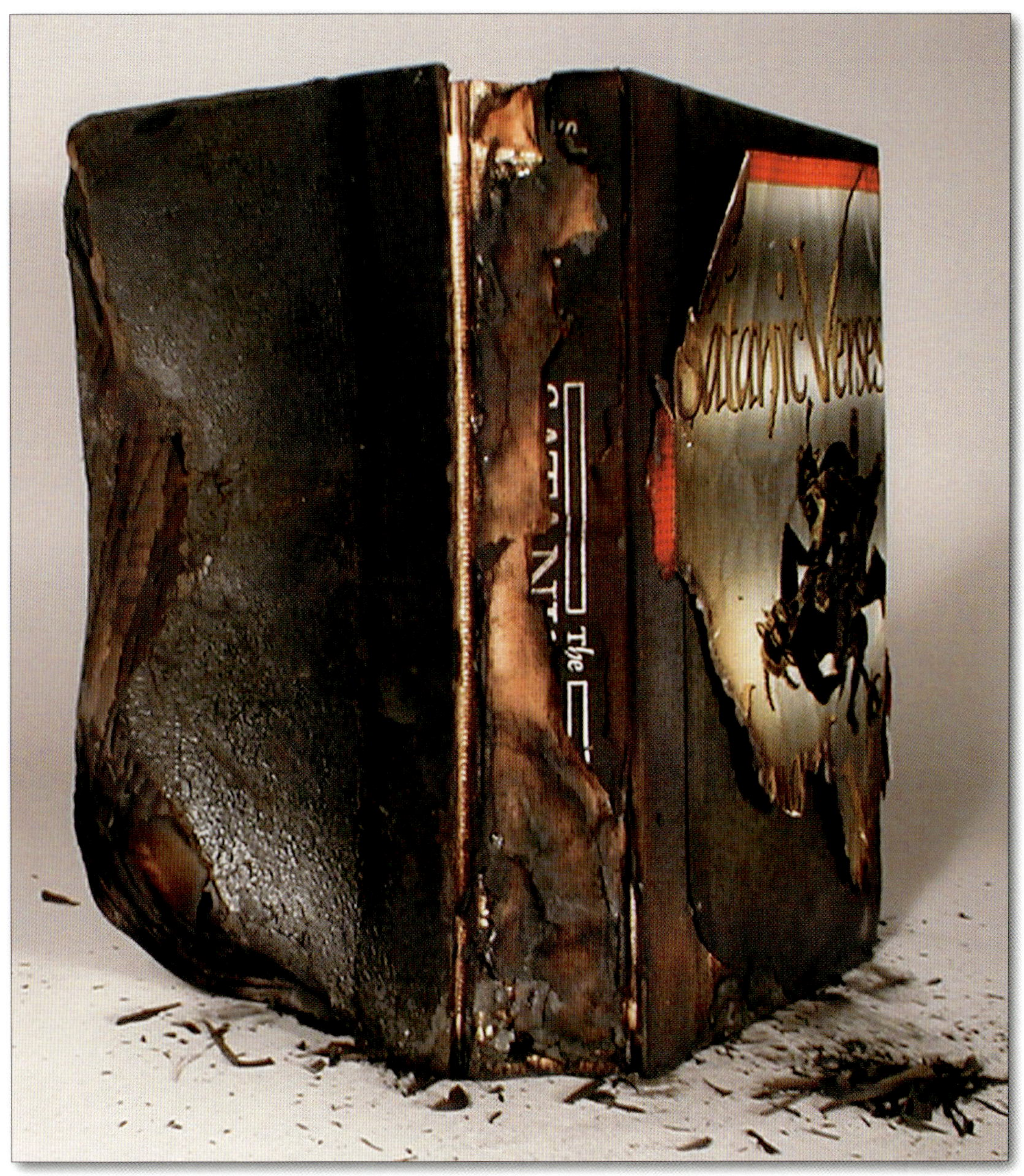

Reliquary for the Ashes of Salman Rushdie's *Satanic Verses*
Ink-jet on paper laminated to binder's board, with polyurethane and UV filter coatings, stained glass, 23K gold leaf, felt covered wood base with 23K gold stamped text of The First Amendment. 12 x 12 x 12

Upon publication the author lost the freedoms of Press, Religion, Speech and Assembly in some countries. The Fatwah issued on Rushdie and the book-burnings made headlines around the world. This is exactly what the first amendment protects us from. This is a sealed book-shaped reliquary containing the burned book. Above is the book for copy No. 1, after burning on January 1, 2001, before being placed in the reliquary.

The Second Amendment

A well regulated militia, being necessary to the security of a free state, the right of the people to keep and bear arms, shall not be infringed.

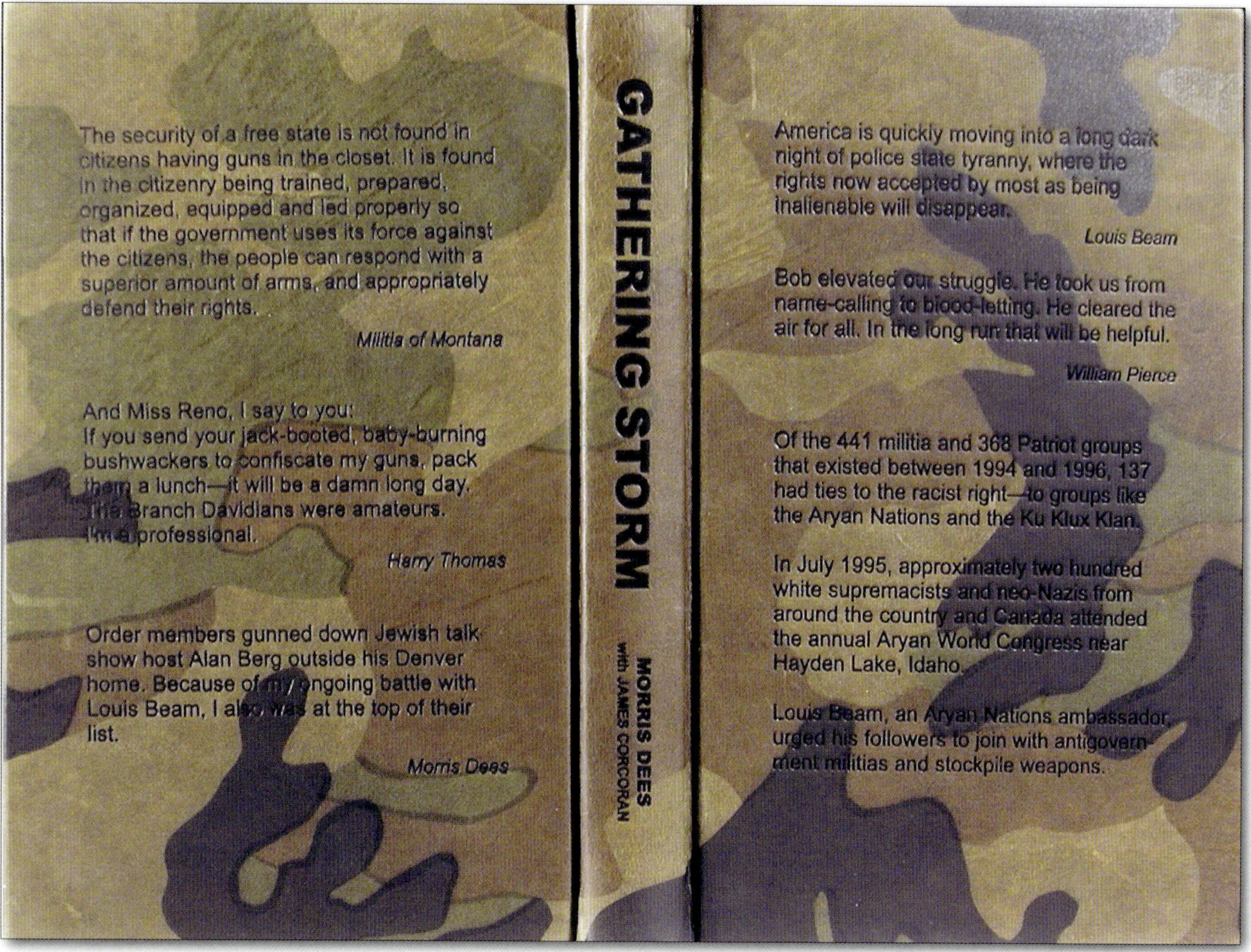

Gathering Storm: America's Militia Threat
by Morris Dees with James Corcoran.
HarperCollins, New York, 1996.
Camouflage leather, foil stamped in black with quotes from the text on the front and back covers. Protective enclosure of camouflage cotton cloth with the text of the second amendment printed inkjet on khaki cloth. The front endpaper is the author as a target and saint, with a halo of gold leaf, as in medieval and Renaissance icons.

The Militia movement in the United States expanded dramatically in the mid 1990's. Spurred by the Randy Weaver incident at Ruby Ridge and the catastrophe at Waco, fear of government abuse led to militia organizations in every State. Many then broke into small cells of about five members, a strategy followed by the Al Qaeda network. Dees is intimately familiar with the players. Militia spokesman and former Ku Klux Klan Grand Dragon Louis Beam was prosecuted by Dees when he led the KKK intimidation of Vietnamese fishermen in Texas. Dees' office was firebombed.

The Third Amendment

No soldier shall, in time of peace be quartered in any house, without the consent of the owner, nor in time of war, but in a manner to be prescribed by law.

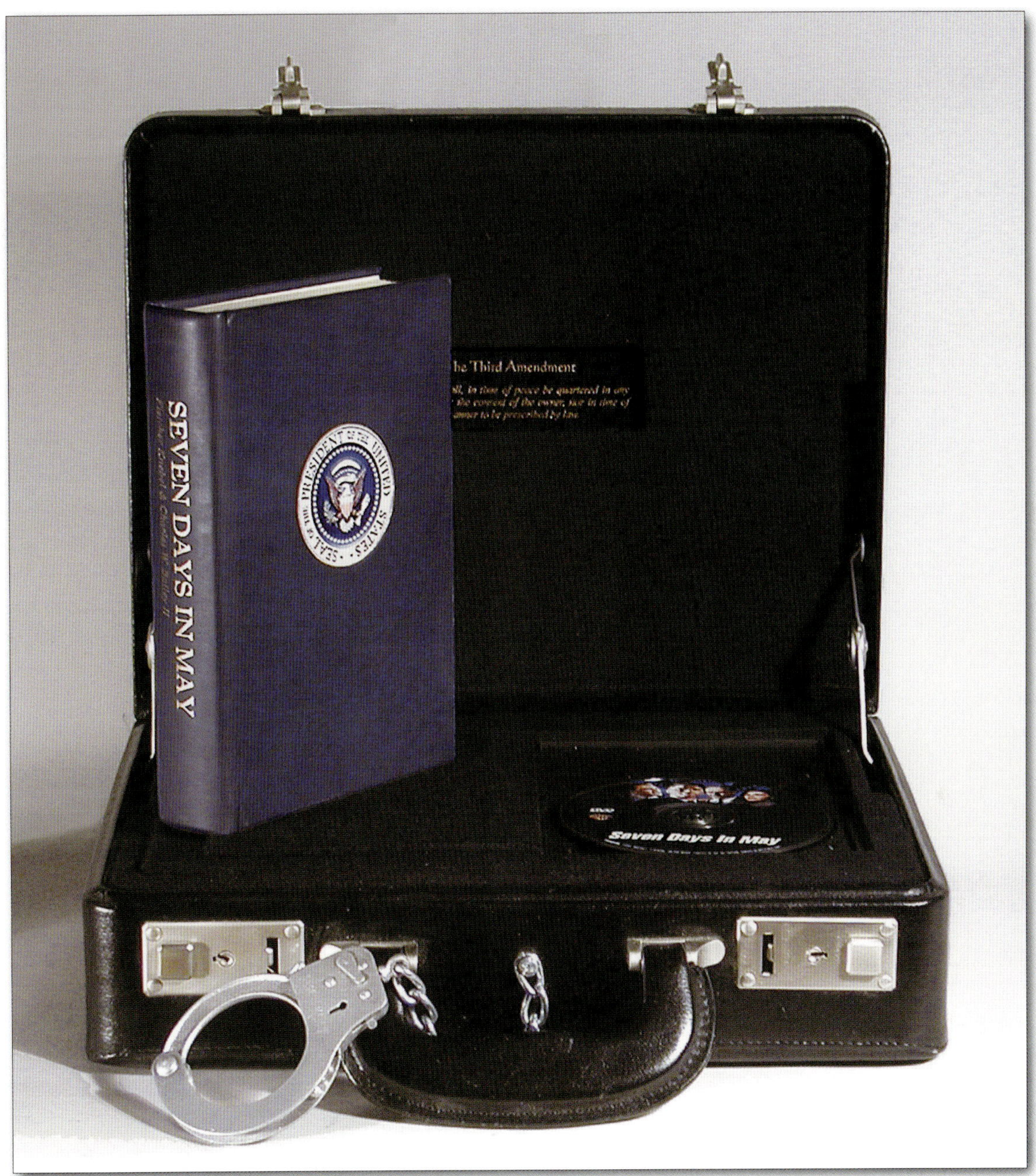

Seven Days in May
by Fletcher Knebel and Charles W. Bailey. Harper & Row, New York, 1962; with a dvd of the 1964 film starring Burt Lancaster and Kirk Douglas, directed by John Frankenheimer; screenplay by Rod Serling. The text of the third amendment is stamped in 23k gold on black board, in a recessed panel inside the case cover. Calf binding with gold title; inlaid seal of lacquered inkjet on Rives BFK mounted on 2-ply museum board; attaché case and handcuffs.

The Fourth Amendment

The right of the people to be secure in their persons, houses, papers, and effects, against unreasonable searches and seizures, shall not be violated, and no warrants shall issue, but upon probable cause, supported by oath or affirmation, and particularly describing the place to be searched, and the persons or things to be seized.

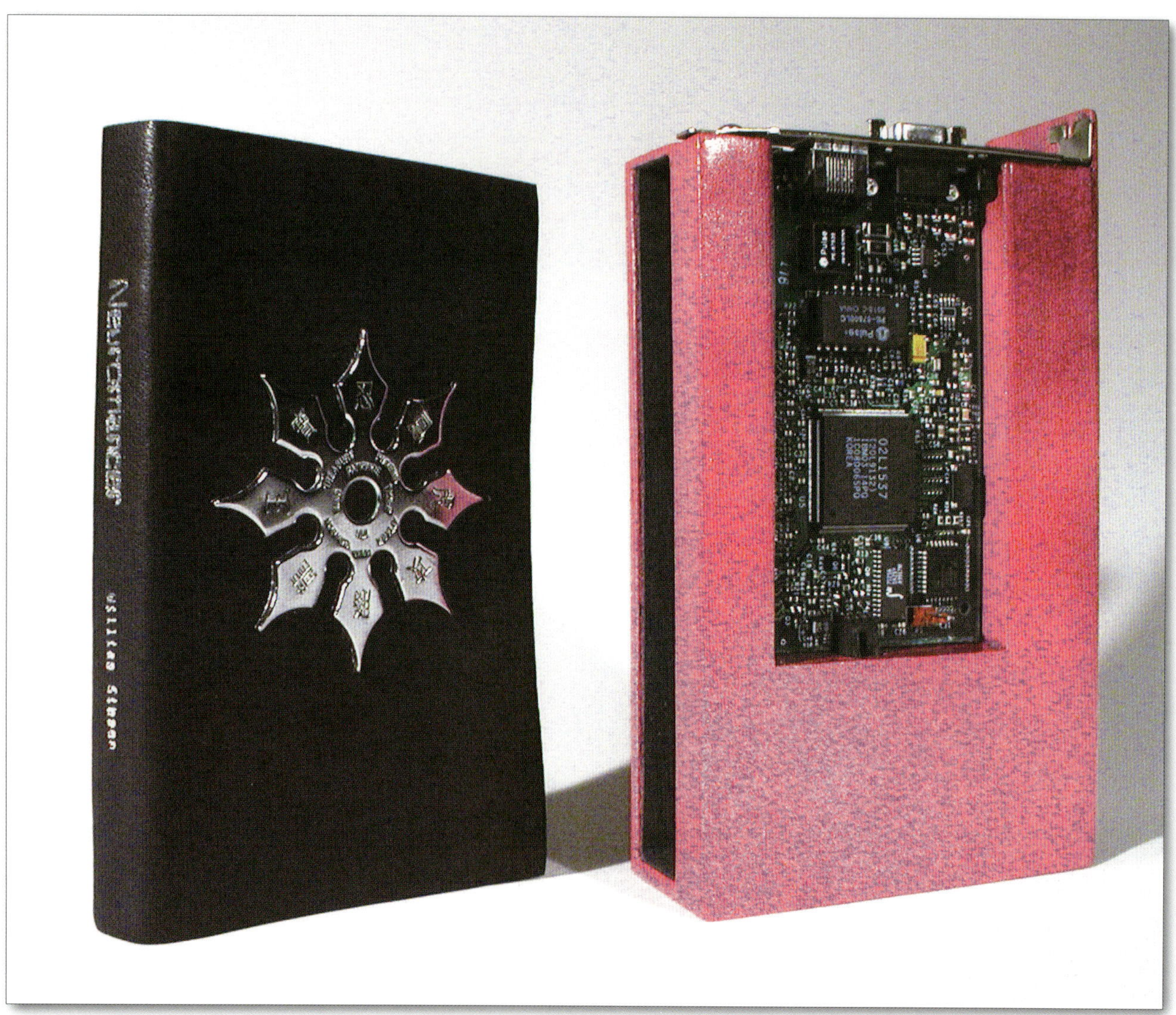

Neuromancer
by William Gibson. Ace, New York, 1984.
Limp black leather, shuriken (Ninja throwing star). The pink slipcase has the text of the fourth amendment stamped in hologram foil on one side. On the other side of the case is an embedded Network Interface Card.

The Fifth Amendment

No person shall be held to answer for a capital, or otherwise infamous crime, unless on a presentment or indictment of a grand jury, except in cases arising in the land or naval forces, or in the militia, when in actual service in time of war or public danger; nor shall any person be subject for the same offense to be twice put in jeopardy of life or limb; nor shall be compelled in any criminal case to be a witness against himself, nor be deprived of life, liberty, or property, without due process of law; nor shall private property be taken for public use, without just compensation.

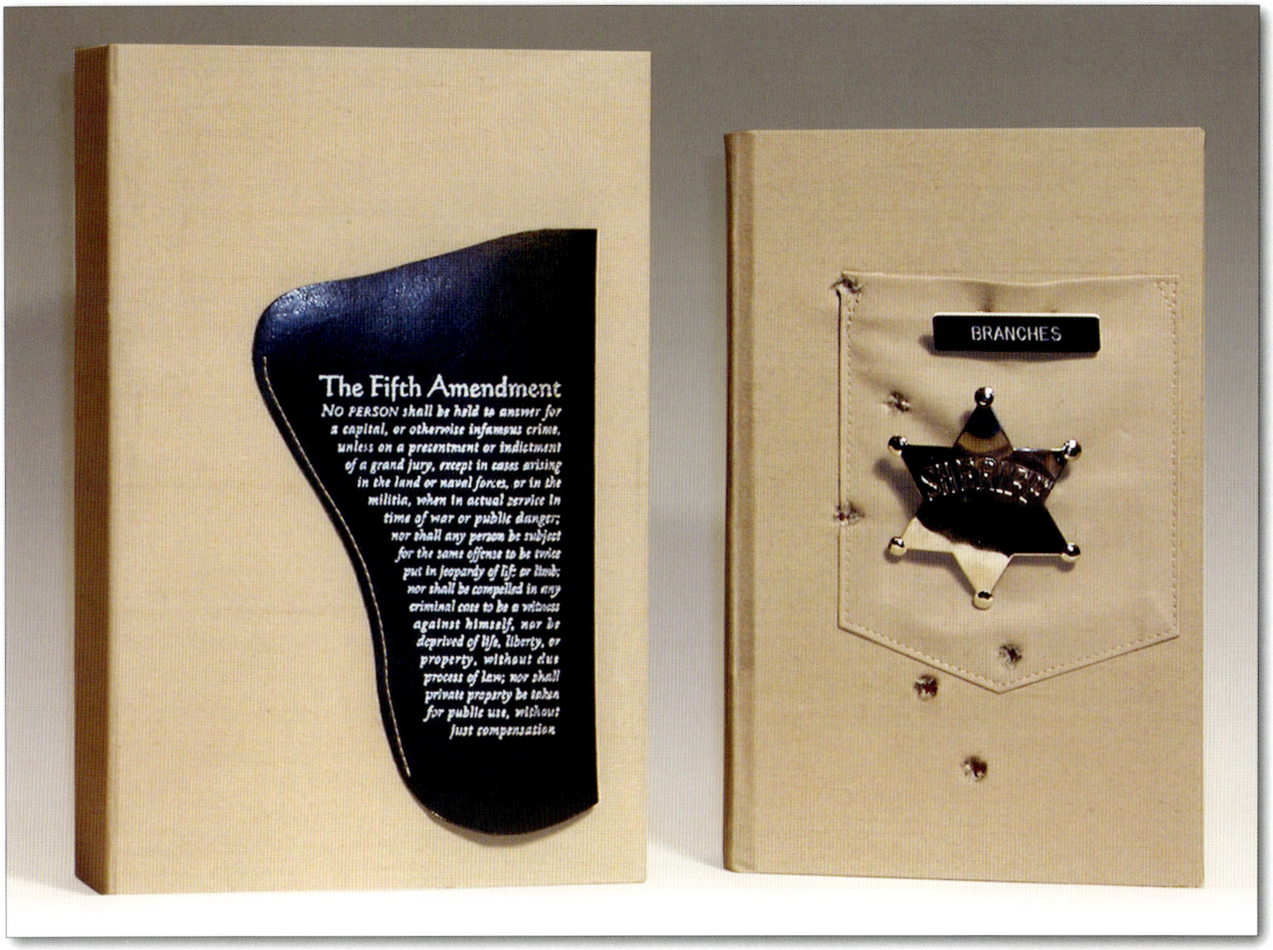

Branches
by Mitch Cullin. Illustrated by Ryuzo Kikushima. Permanent Press, Sag Harbor, New York, 2000. Shirtcloth, leather, foil stamping, badges, 9mm bullet holes shot through the cover by Minsky.

An epic poem written in the first person as the story of a Sheriff in Texas who is judge, jury, and executioner.

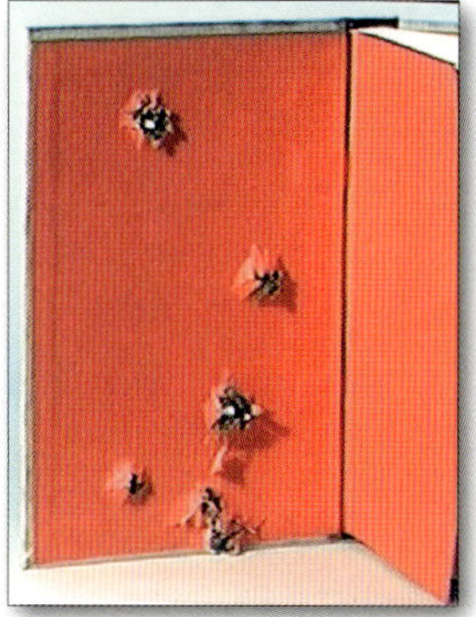

The Sixth Amendment

In all criminal prosecutions, the accused shall enjoy the right to a speedy and public trial, by an impartial jury of the state and district wherein the crime shall have been committed, which district shall have been previously ascertained by law, and to be informed of the nature and cause of the accusation; to be confronted with the witnesses against him; to have compulsory process for obtaining witnesses in his favor, and to have the assistance of counsel for his defense.

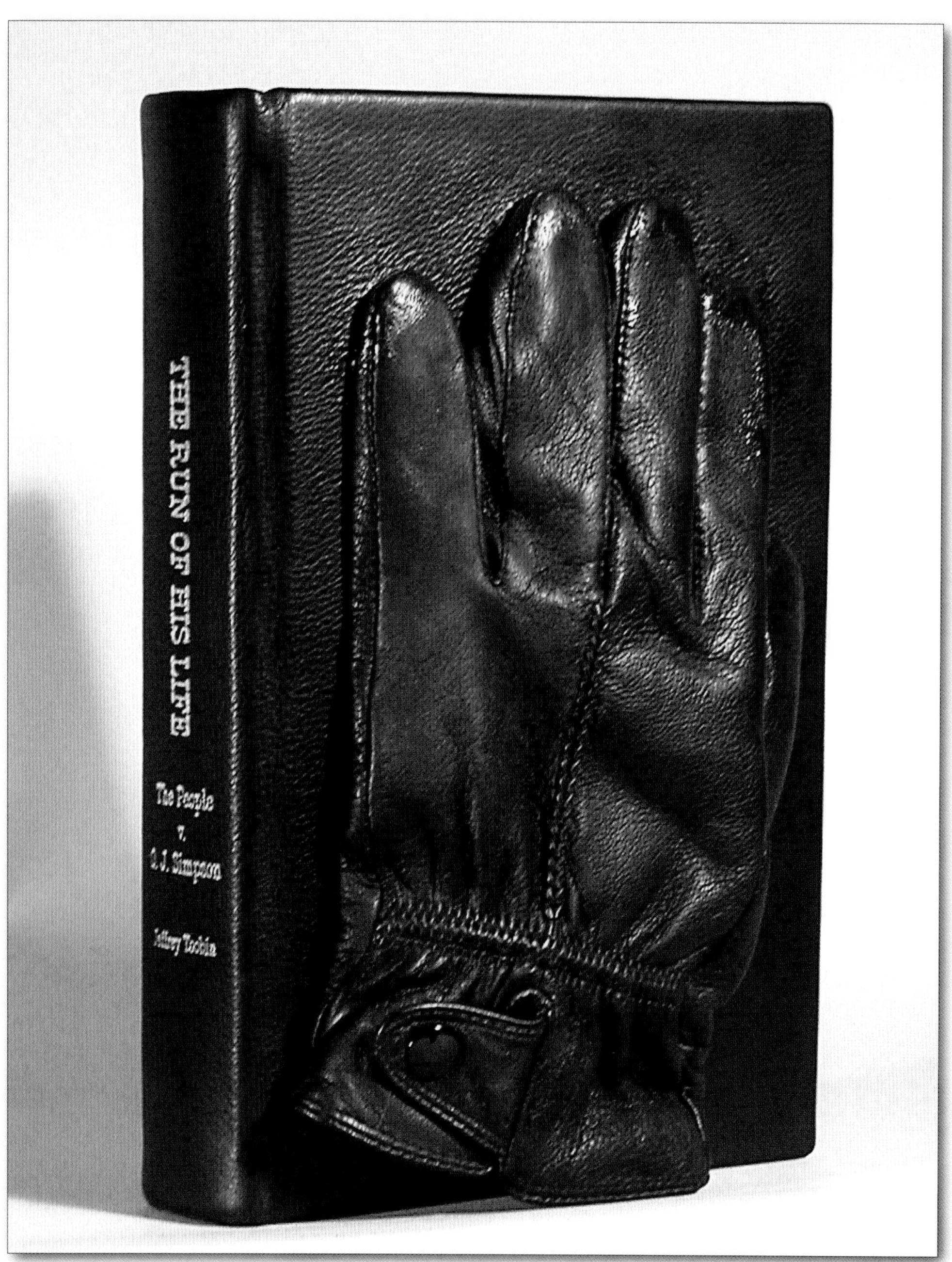

The Run of His Life: The People v. O. J. Simpson
by Jeffrey Toobin. Random House, New York, 1996.
Leather, leather glove, acrylic paint, foil-stamped title.

The Seventh Amendment

In suits at common law, where the value in controversy shall exceed twenty dollars, the right of trial by jury shall be preserved, and no fact tried by a jury, shall be otherwise reexamined in any court of the United States, than according to the rules of the common law.

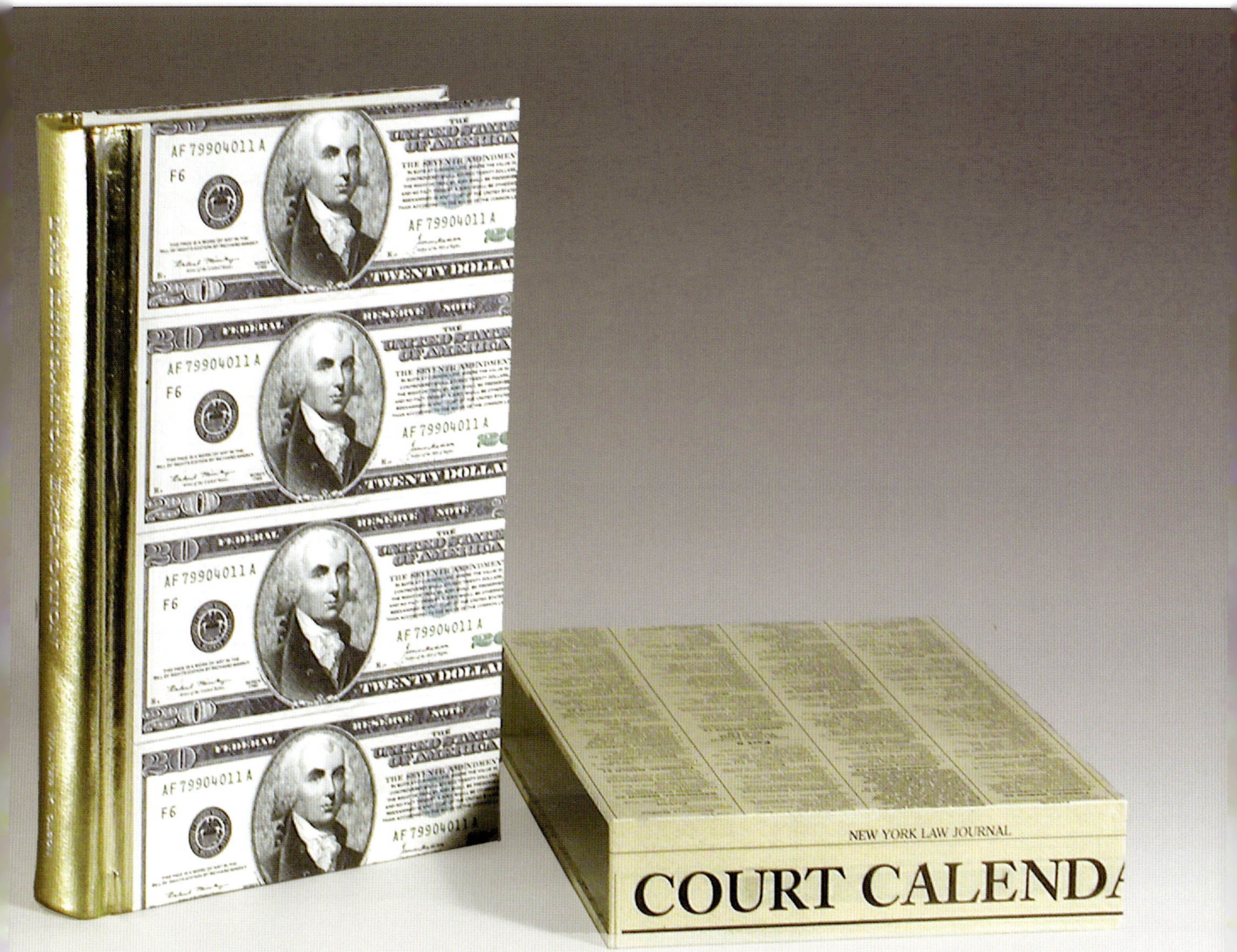

The Litigation Explosion: What Happened When America Unleashed the Lawsuit
by Walter K. Olson. Truman Talley Books, New York, 1991. Gold leather spine, title foil stamped in silver (neither is the genuine metal). The gold and silver make it hard to decipher. Slipcase covered with court calendar listings from the *New York Law Journal* coated with ultraviolet filter acrylic.

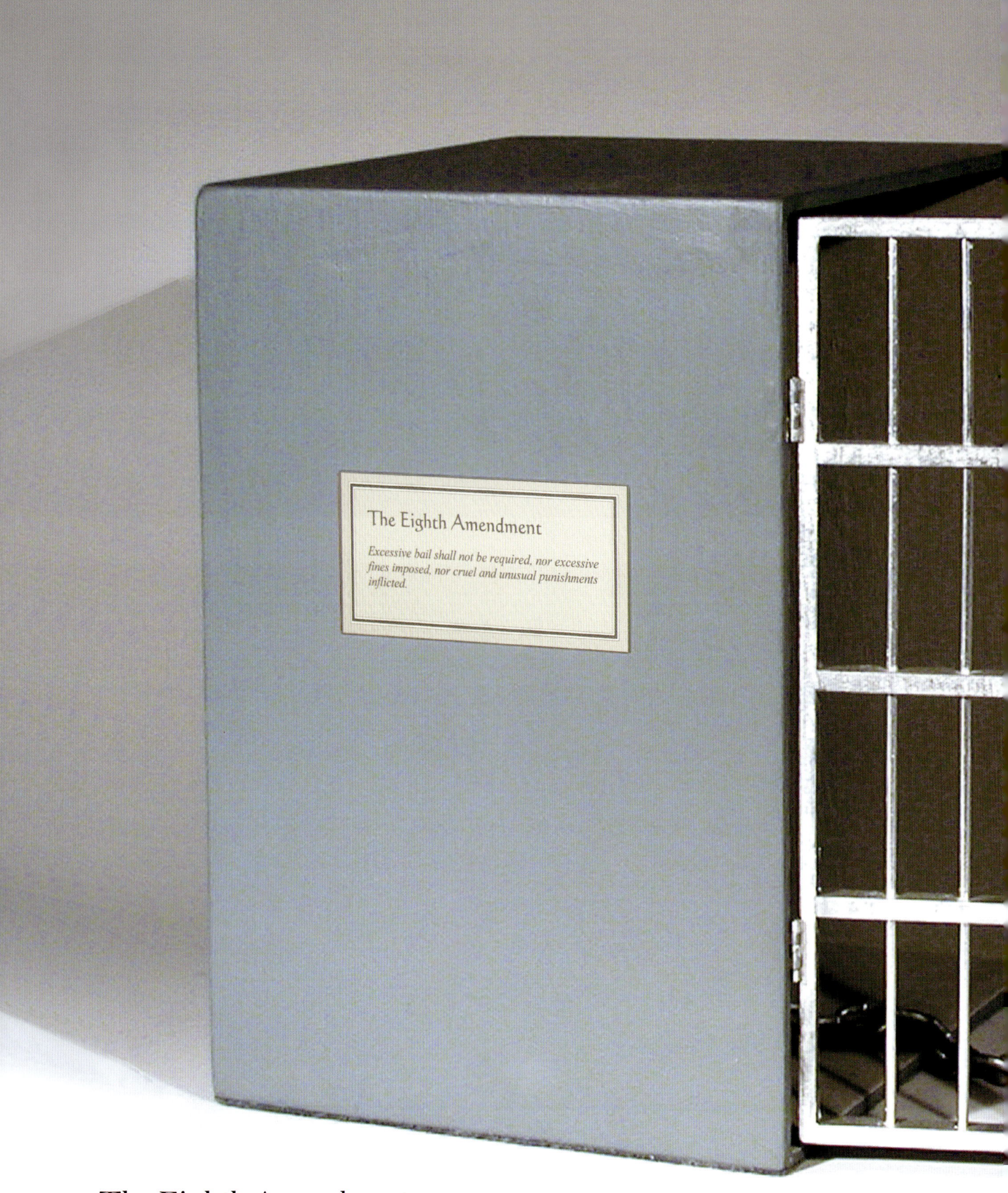

The Eighth Amendment

Excessive bail shall not be required, nor excessive fines imposed, nor cruel and unusual punishments inflicted.

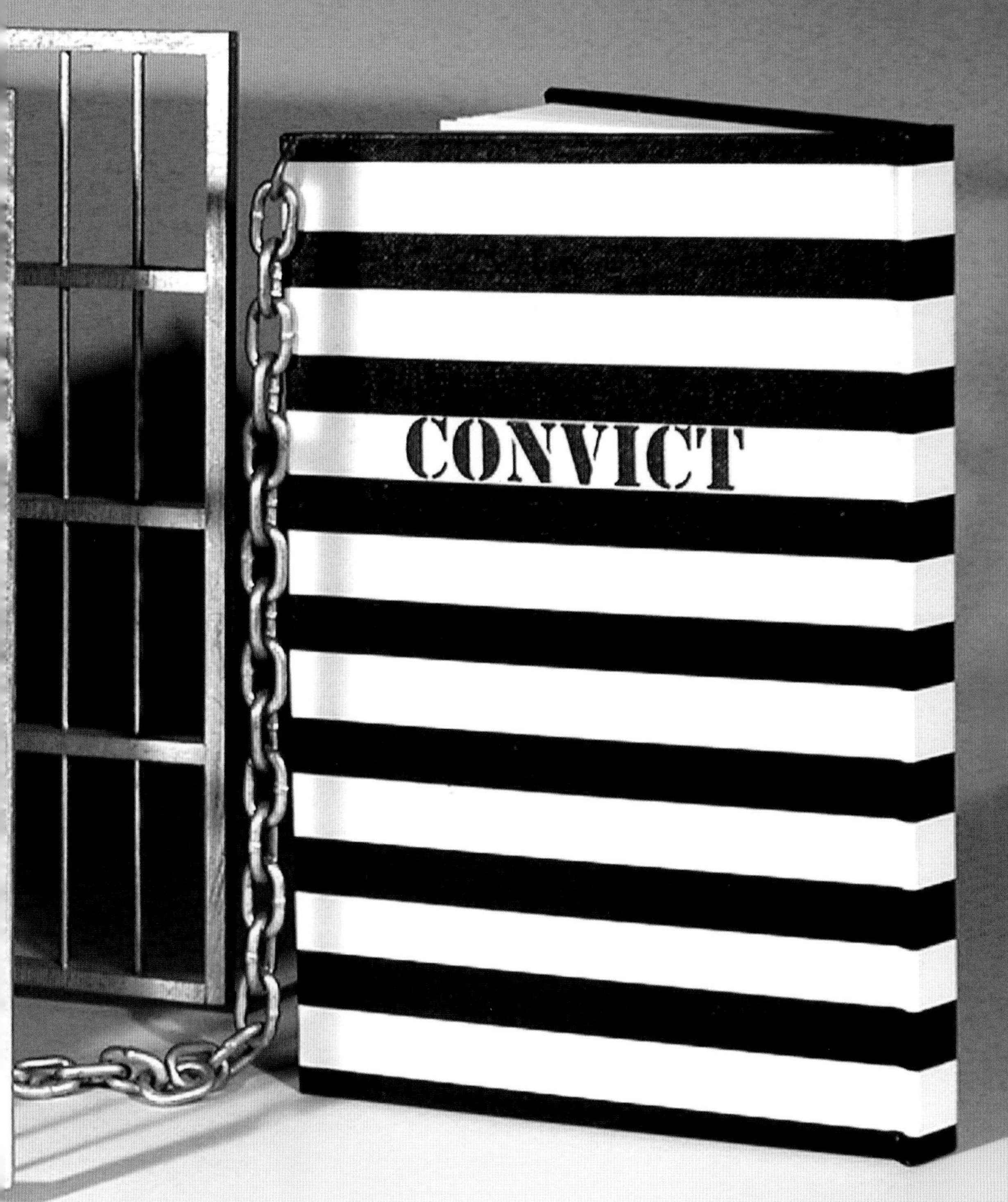

Forlorn Hope: The Prison Reform Movement
by Larry E. Sullivan. Richard Minsky, New York, 2002.
Inkjet on canvas chained to a miniature jail cell of painted wood.

The Ninth Amendment

The enumeration in the Constitution, of certain rights, shall not be construed to deny or disparage others retained by the people.

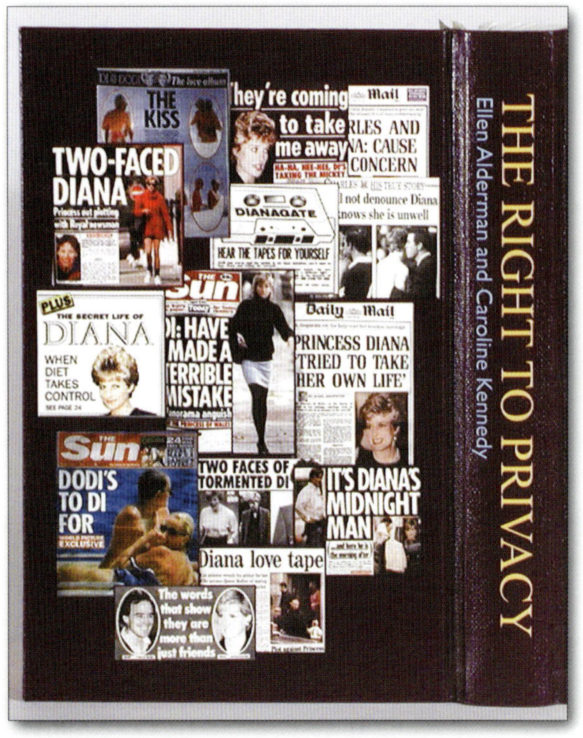

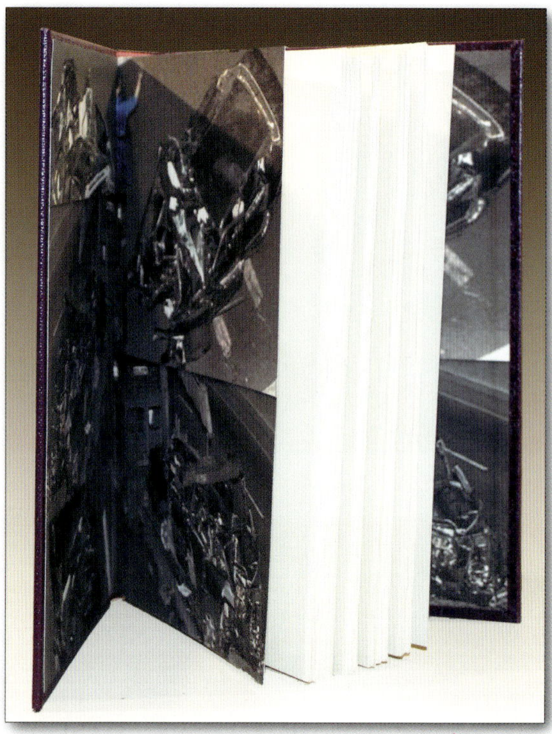

The Right to Privacy
by Ellen Alderman and Caroline Kennedy.
Alfred A. Knopf, New York, 1995.
Inkjet on canvas. The back cover is a montage of tabloid headlines. Endsheets are a montage of her crashed car, inkjet on paper. Trying to get some privacy killed her. It lies in a velour lined black cloth box with the text of the Ninth Amendment printed on a Fabriano Roma label.

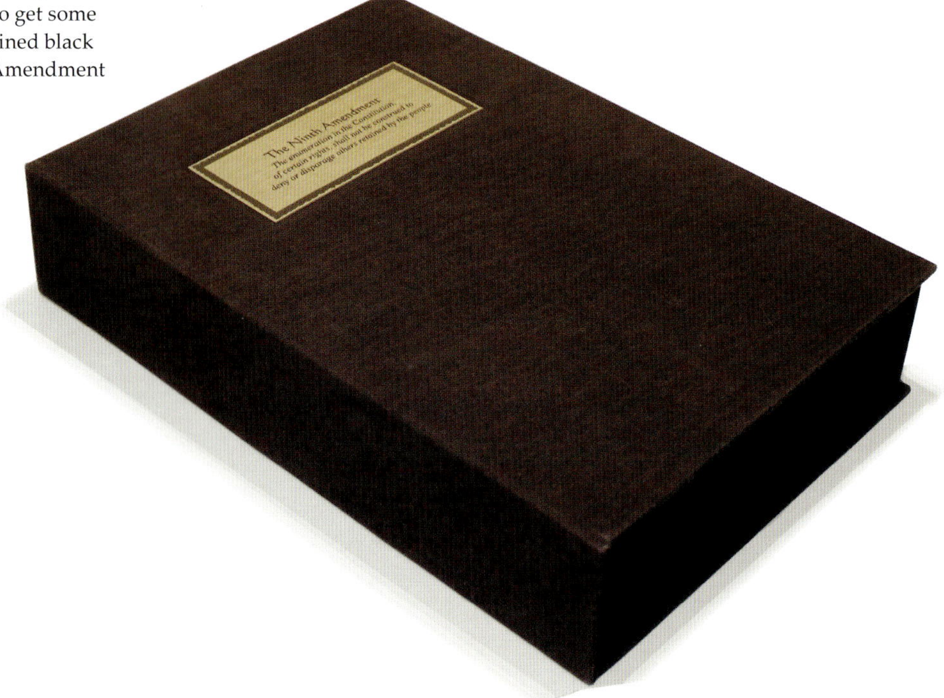

The Tenth Amendment

The powers not delegated to the United States by the Constitution, nor prohibited by it to the states, are reserved to the states respectively, or to the people.

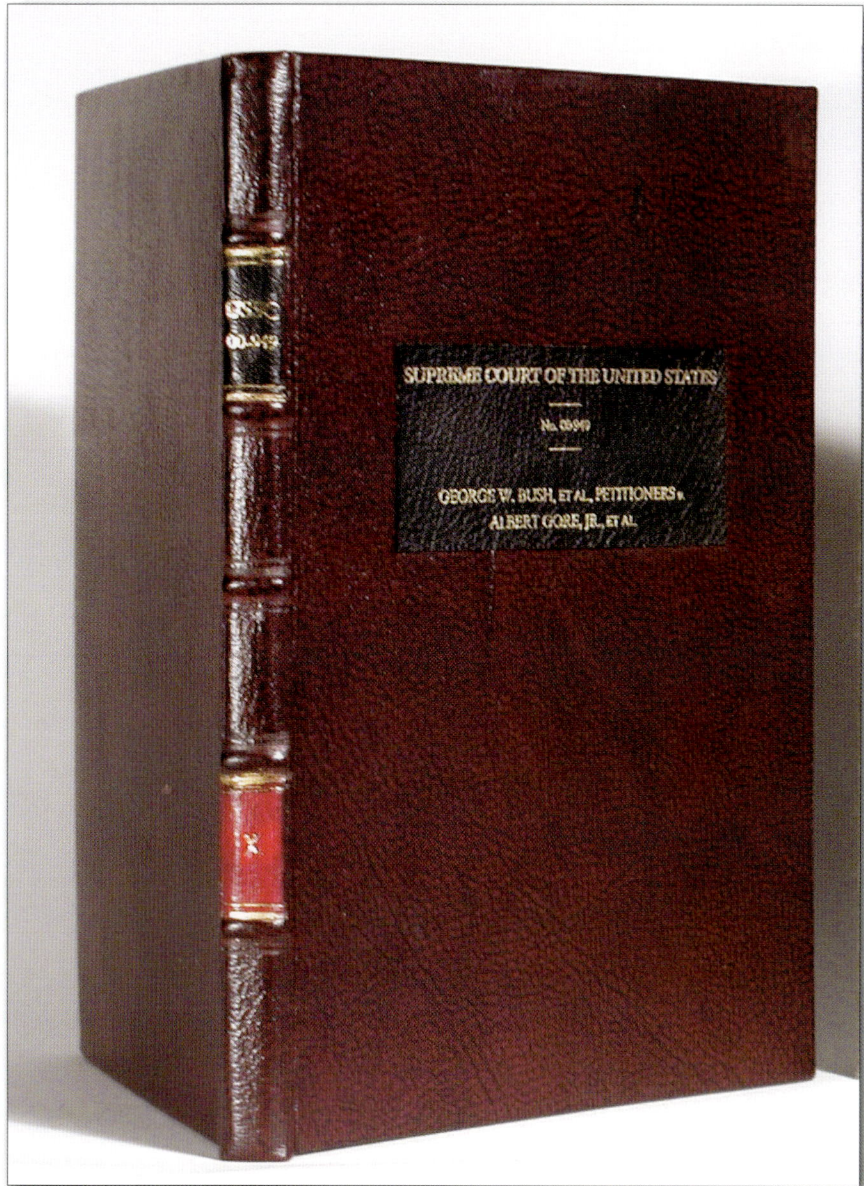

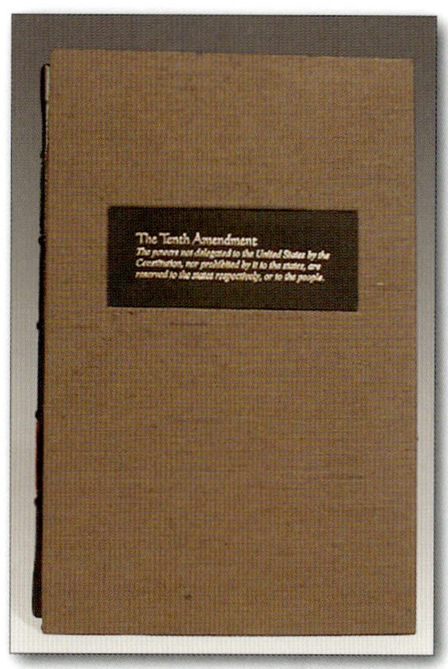

Text downloaded from the Supreme Court website the day it was issued, December 12, 2000. Normally we see the red label on top and the black one on the bottom, so there seems to be something subtly wrong. The title is also somewhat uneven and not exactly on the level. So at the same time as this volume looks like a classic law book from a distance, close inspection reveals this contemporary interpretation to be disturbing and somewhat tilted.

USSC No. 00-949
by The Supreme Court of The United States of America.
Richard Minsky, New York, 2001.
Photocopy on 100% cotton fiber paper. Two-tone grained cowhide, goatskin labels stamped in gold. Cloth slipcase with gold stamped paper label in recessed panel.

Geometric Studies

THE COVER FOR THIS CATALOG reflects elements of geometric composition used in the Art Deco era by the Hagenauer Workshop in Vienna. This commission inspired a decade of exploration in decorative design.

During a residency at Blue Mountain Center, an artist and writer's colony in the Adirondacks, I produced a miniature book of 70 painted studies [p. 85], some of which were executed as a series of works in leather and lacquer. They combined Constructivist and Deco elements within a space that owes much to Hans Hoffman's principles of push-pull on the picture plane.

Franz Kline's brushwork influenced the breaking up of space. The concept was to capture the feeling of movement and energy in a gestural brushstroke, using leather inlay [p. 94] or lacquer [p. 92]. This use of color and space keeps the eye moving in and out, and from one element to another. These decorative paradigms can also be used to evoke illusionistic or representational imagery, as in the book with two semicircular elements [p. 86]. The mind turns it into a horizon line and sees a view through the porthole on a ship, or through binoculars, or a periscope. Several covers were done by abstracting real landscapes into geometric patterns, like the river view on the Gracie Mansion guest book [p. 84].

This series included other miniature books of studies [pp. 91, 98], and culminated in a lacquer triptych in which the three volumes can be aligned in any sequence. These works focus on image and surface rather than metaphor. The absence of symbolism gives a universality that transcends the cultural literacy required for some of the political works. They are meditations on relationships of scale, position, and beauty.

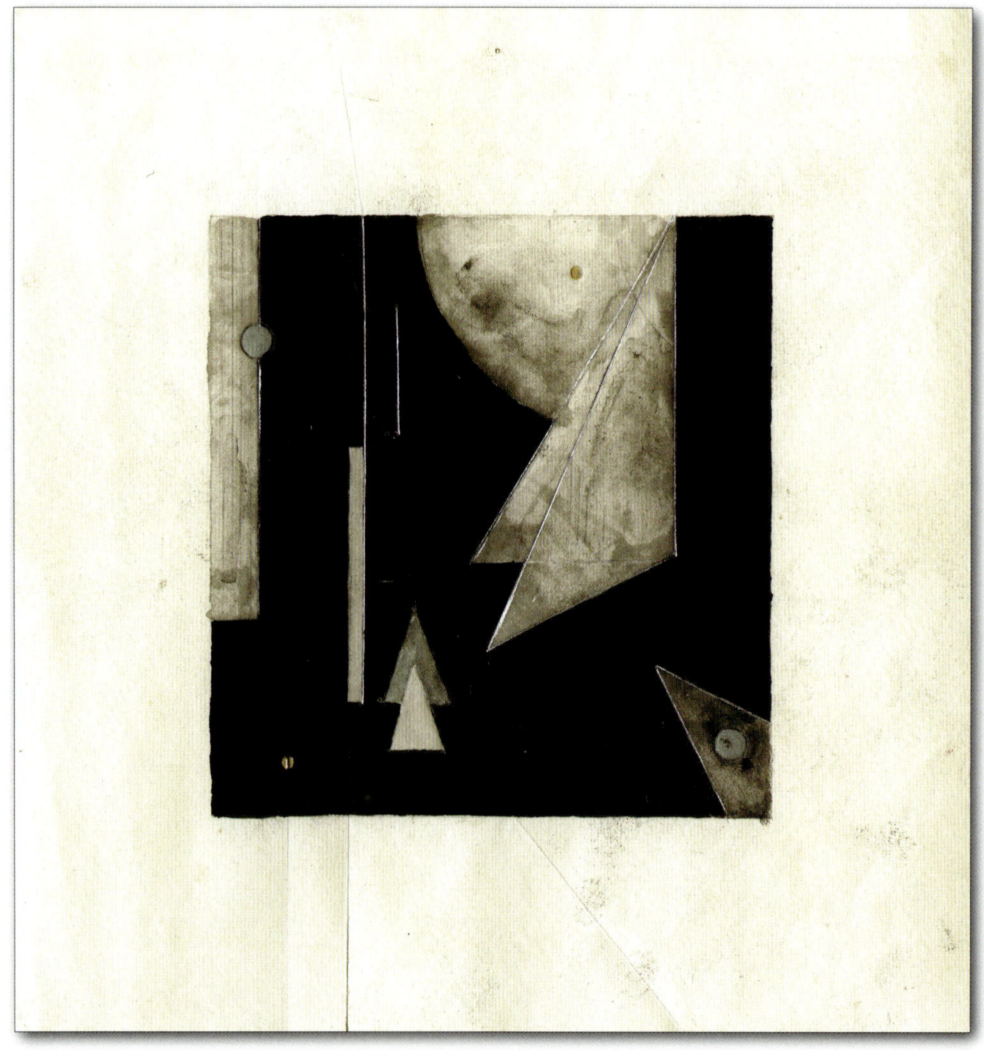

HAGENAUER-WIEN
1982. 9¾ x 9½
Binding of calf with hand tooled goatskin inlay panel, foil stamped spine. Catalog with photos mounted on handmade paper, letterpress descriptions and title page.
Collection of Vivian Milstein, New York

Opposite page: Study on paper for this binding; pencil, watercolor, and foil tooling.
Collection of the Haas Family Arts Library, Yale University

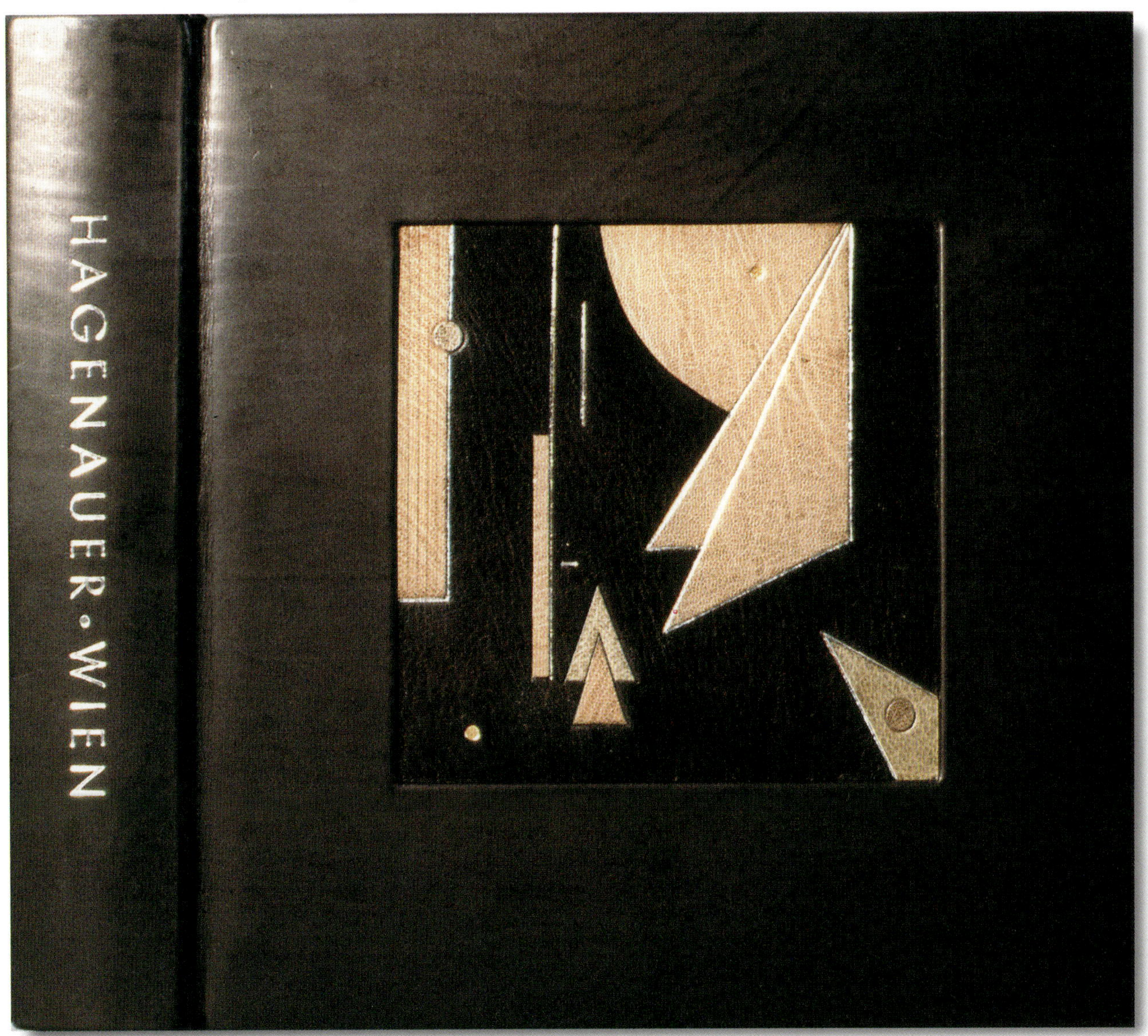

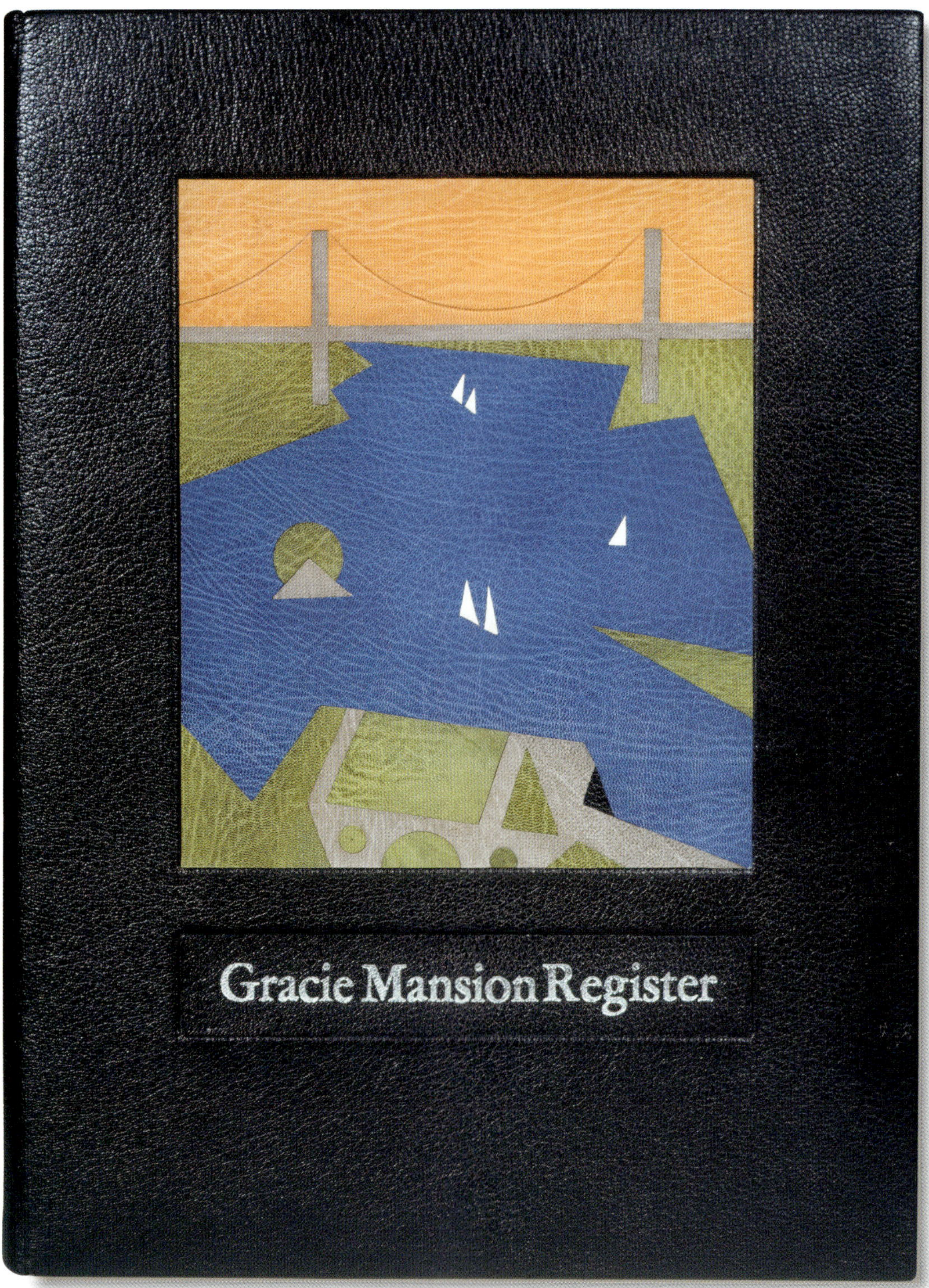

Gracie Mansion Register
1985. 13 x 10
Guest book for the official residence of the Mayor of New York City.
Black Chieftain goatskin, recessed pictorial inlay of goat and vellum, blind tooled, recessed panel with foil stamped title. Dieu Donné handmade paper, letterpress title page, dedication and colophon, linen endbands, chain ring embedded in head edge of back board.

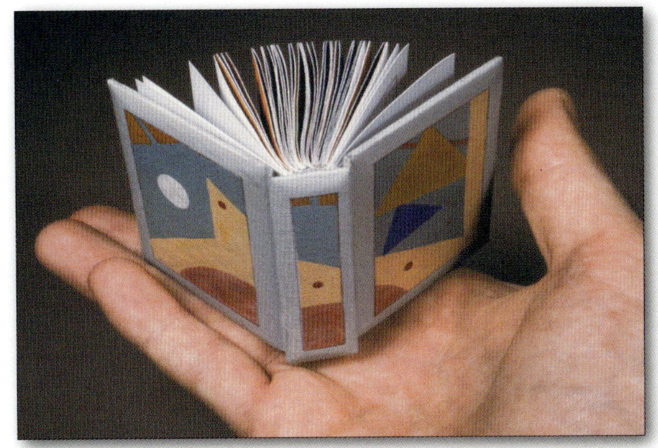

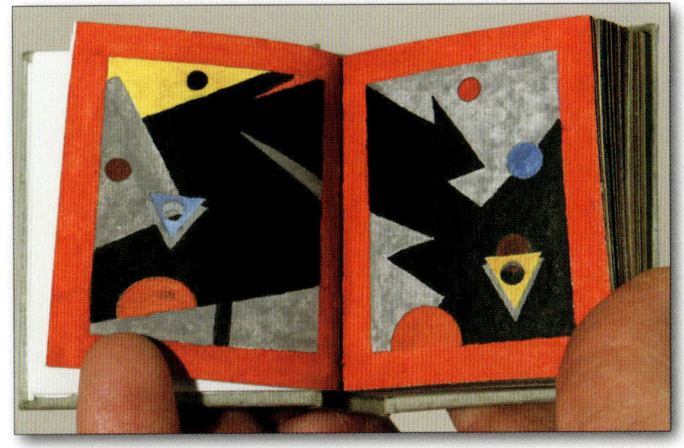

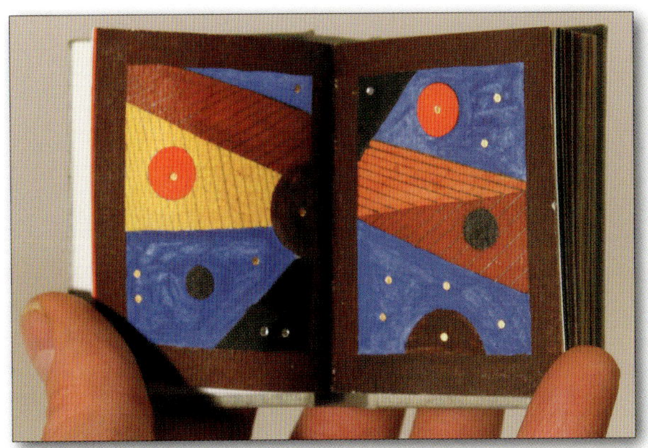

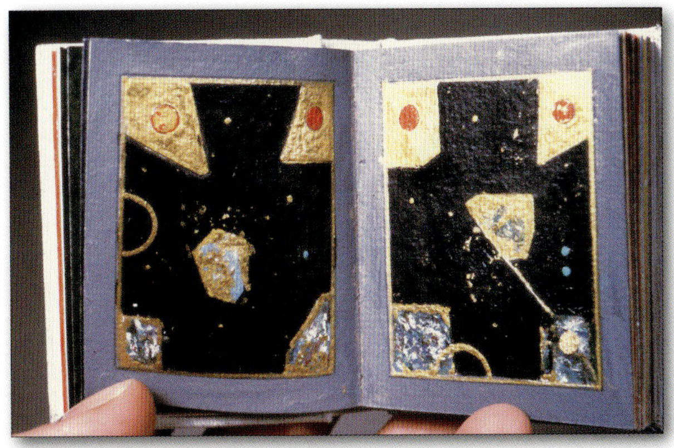

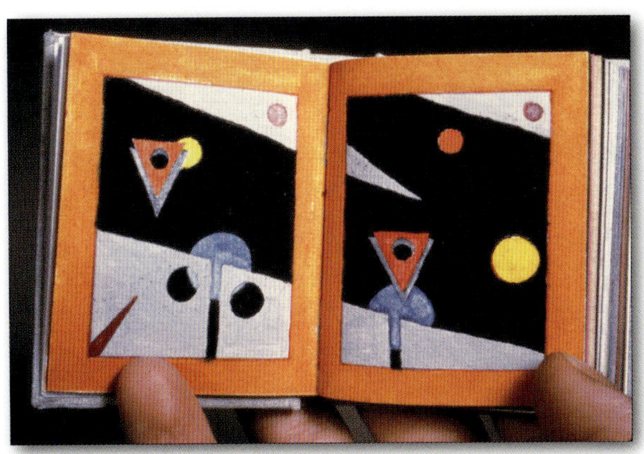

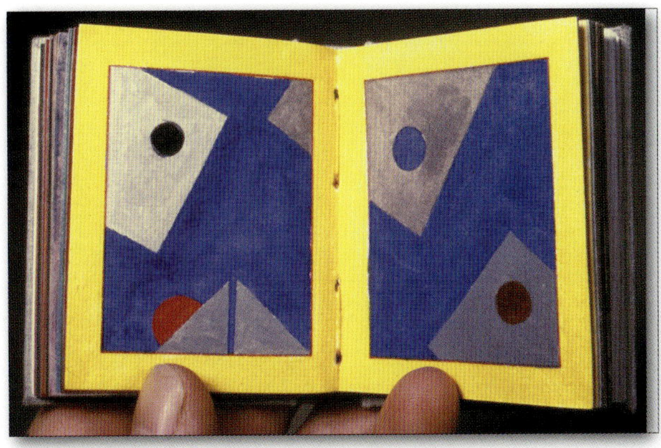

Seventy Studies
1985. 2⅞ x 2⅜
Original paintings by Richard Minsky, Letterpress title page, watercolor and acrylic paintings with pencil and gold leaf on paper. Flat-back case binding. Lacquered acrylic on bookcloth. Each two-page spread is a study for a bookbinding design.
Private Collection, New York

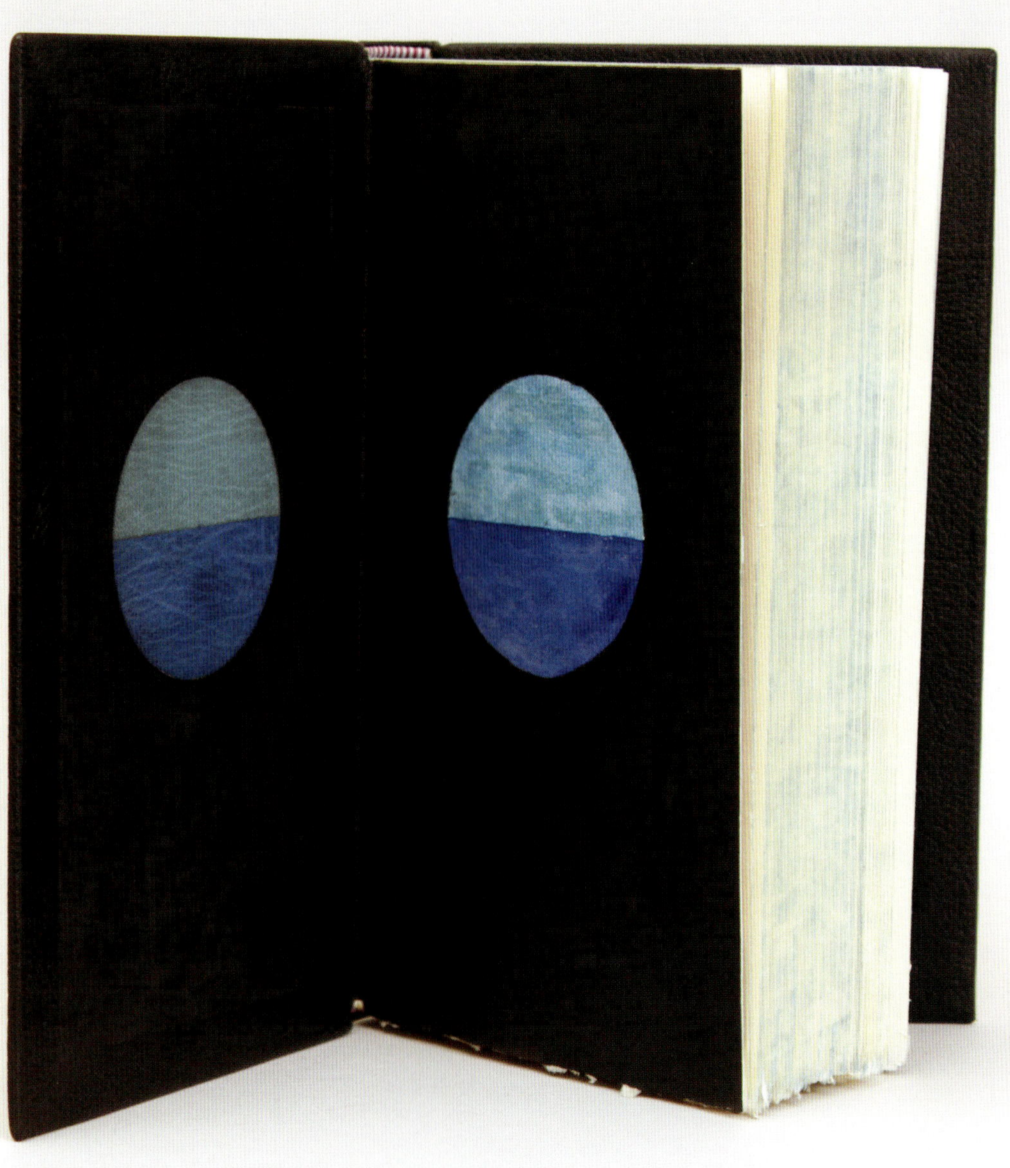

Blank Book
1985. 9¼ x 6¾
Goatskin with goatskin inlay on cover and doublure; watercolor endsheets.
Private Collection, New York

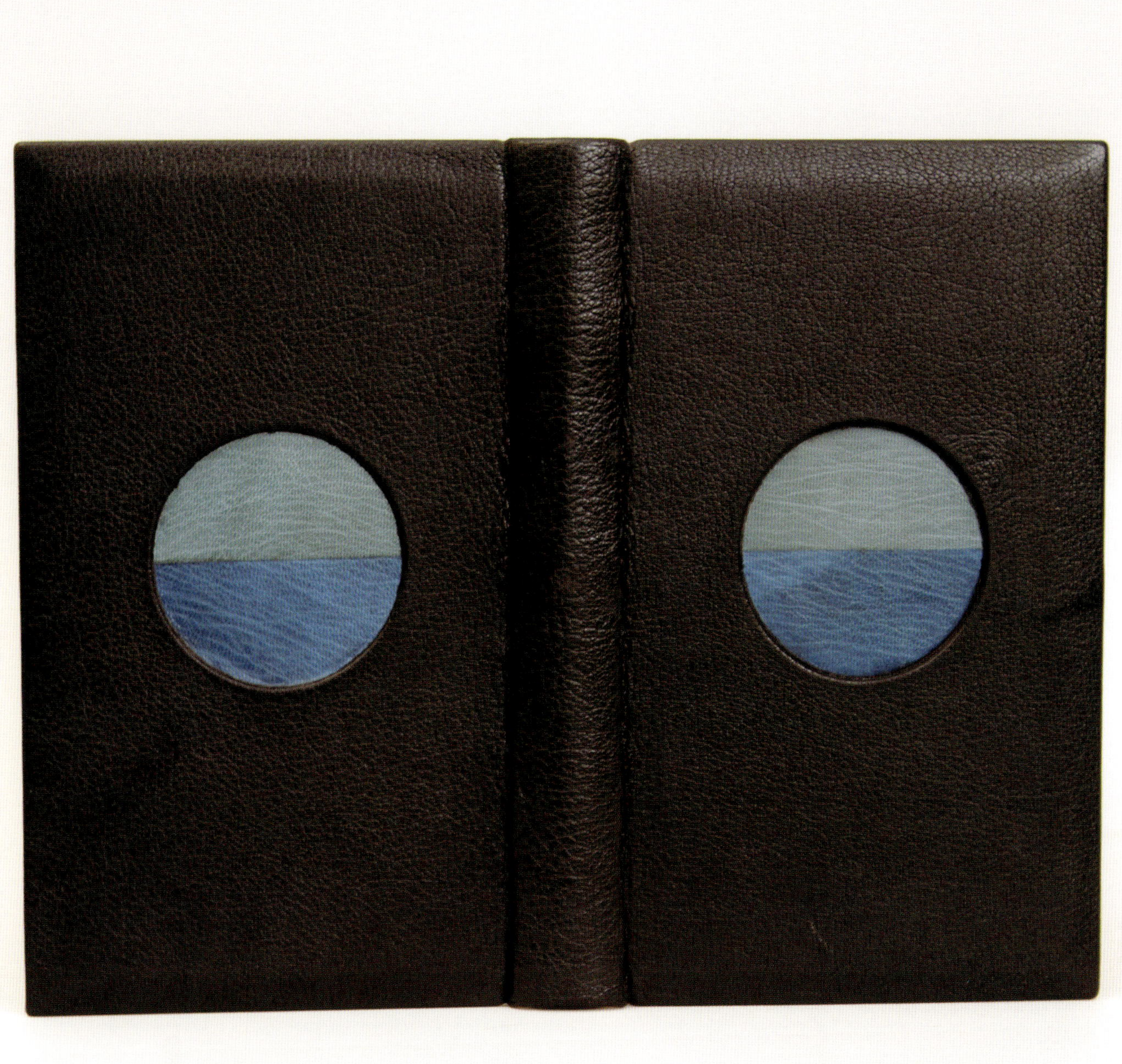

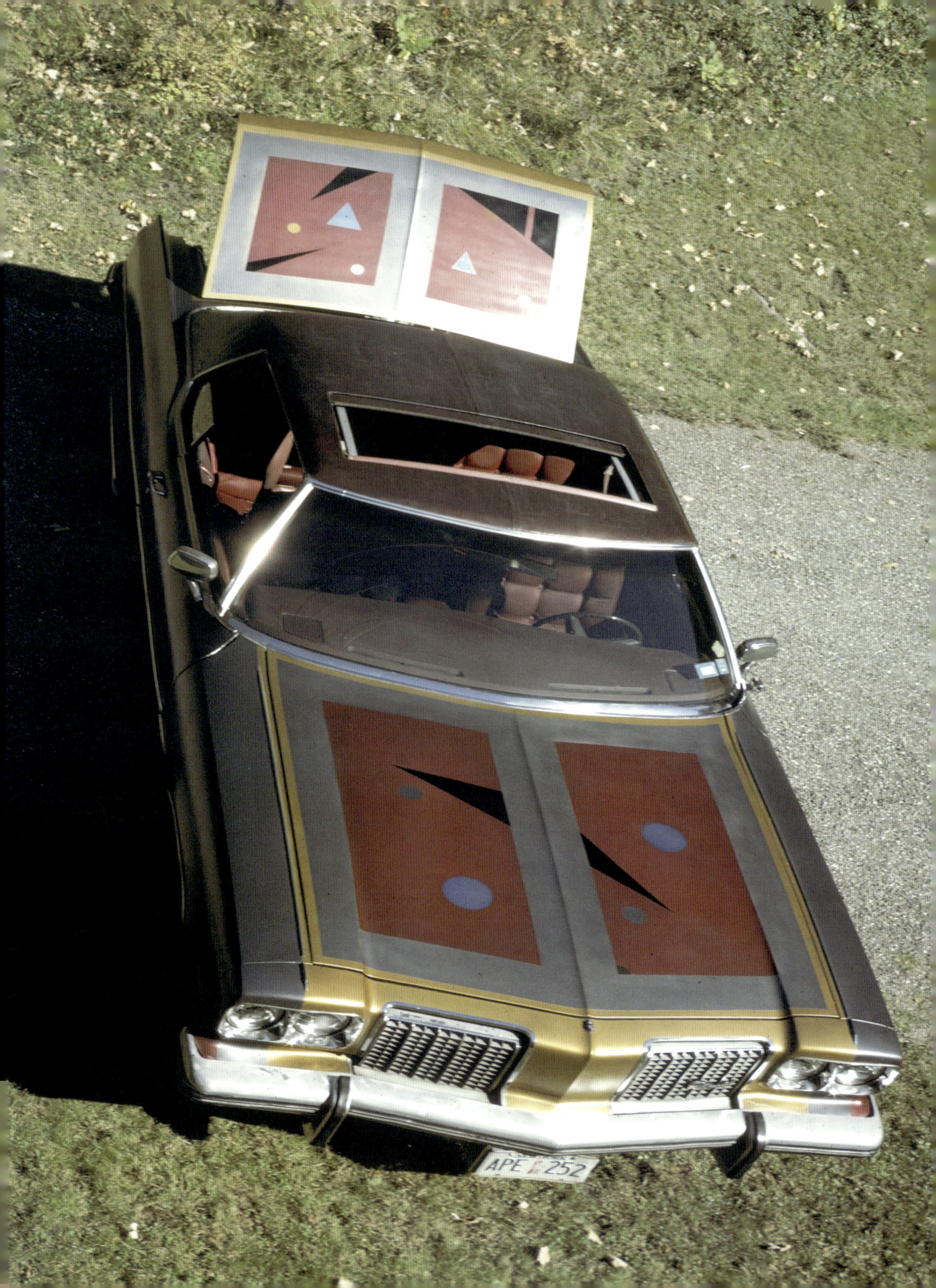
APE 252

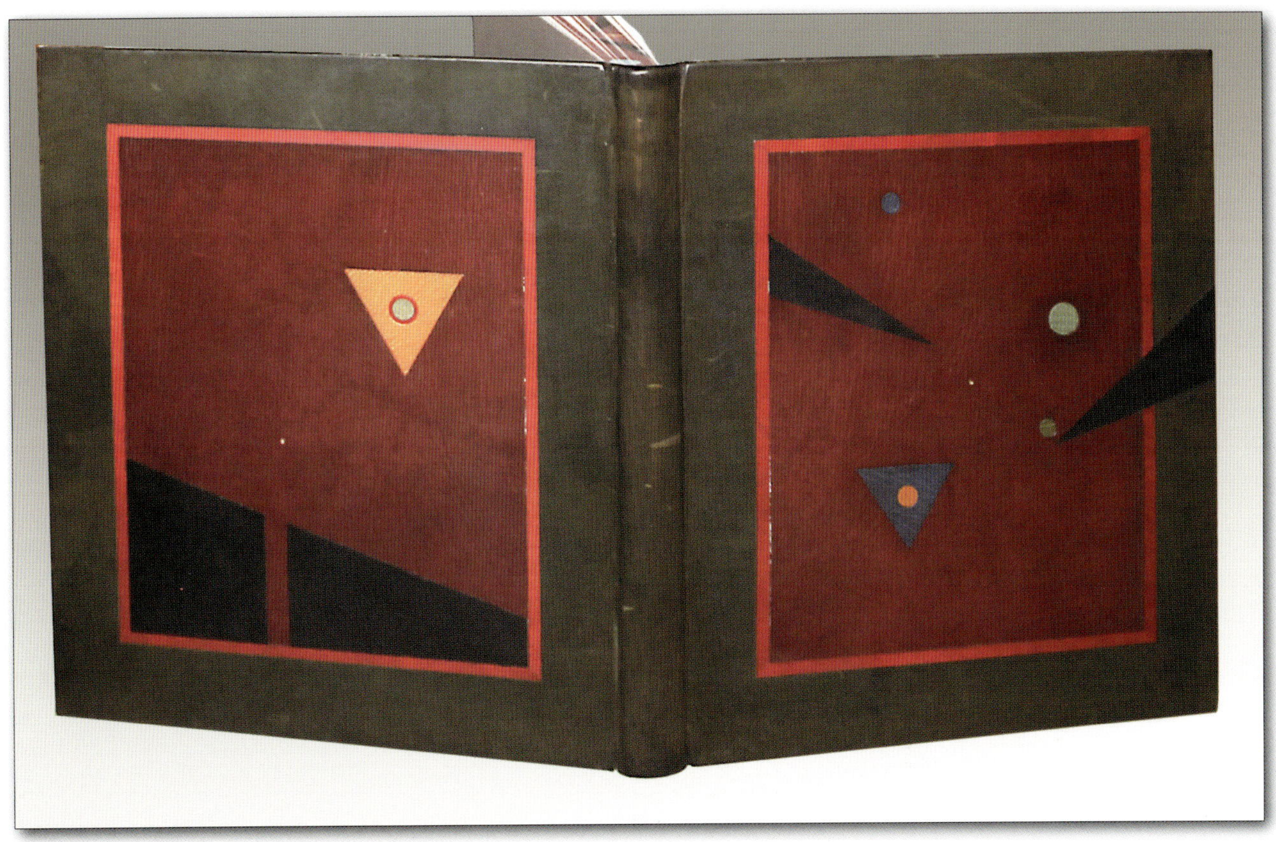

Travelog
1986. Log book 13½ x 9½
Calf with goatskin inlay, painted edges.
The design complements that of the car, which was the travel part of this set.
Book: Collection of Clare Stone, New York

1974 Oldsmobile 98 Regency automobile, lacquer.
The car was painted during a residency at the Blue Mountain Center. It no longer exists.

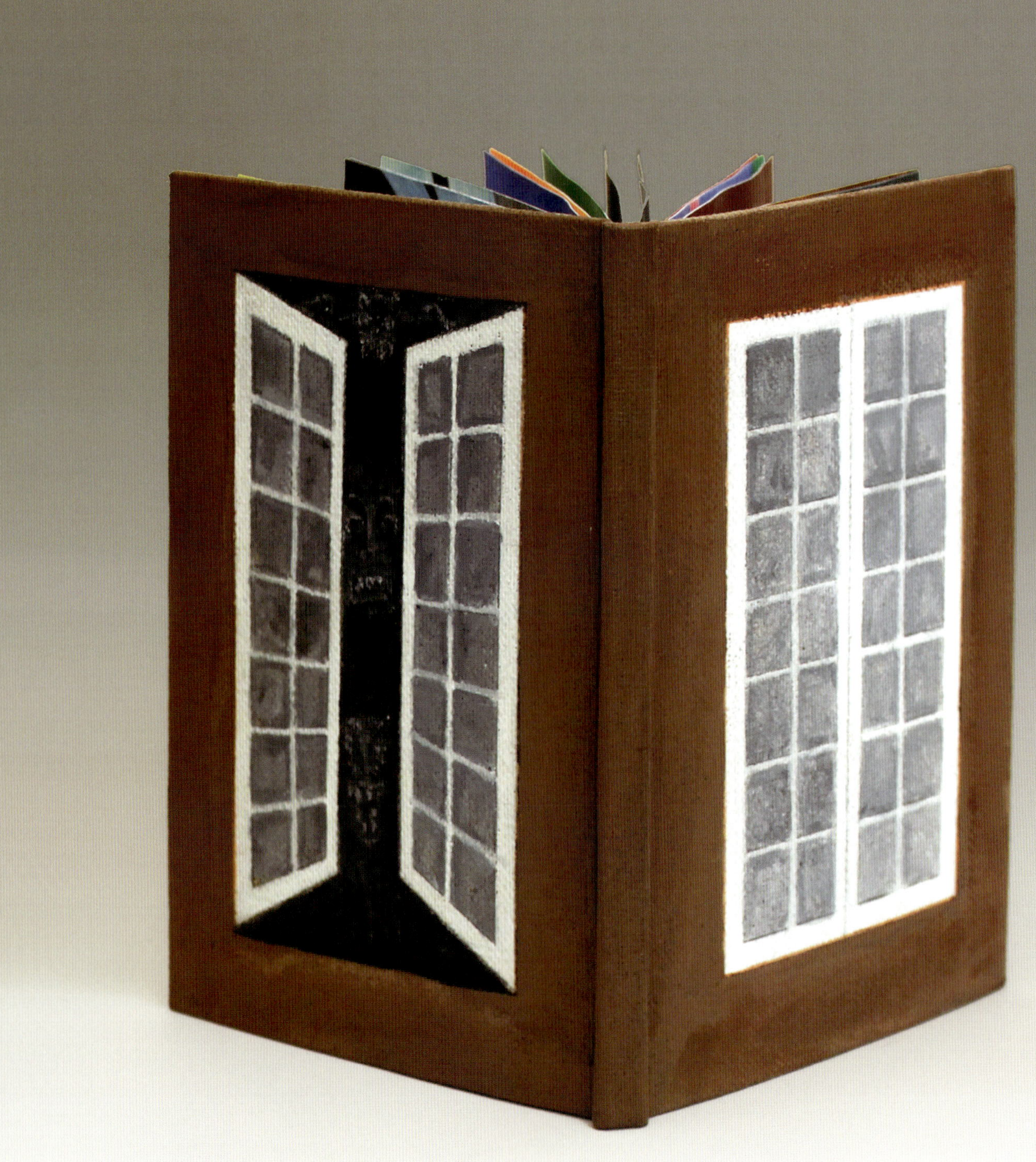

Untitled, 30 Studies
Undated, c. 1991. 5¾ x 3⅜
Acrylic on canvas cover, acrylic on paper pages. Facing page: three studies in this book that were adapted for a lacquer binding triptych [following pages].
Private collection, New York

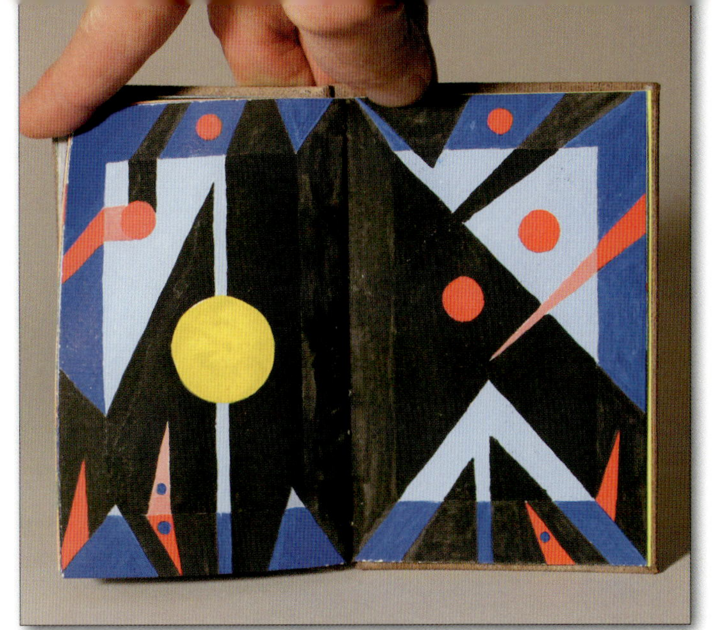

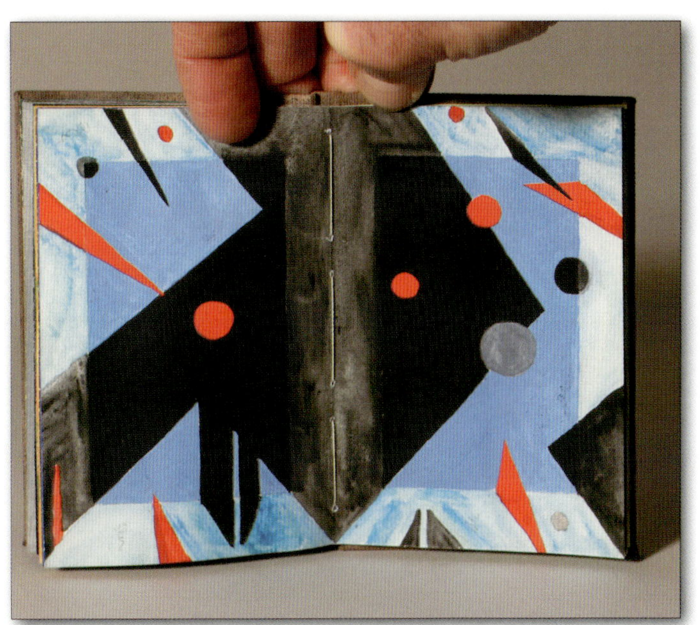

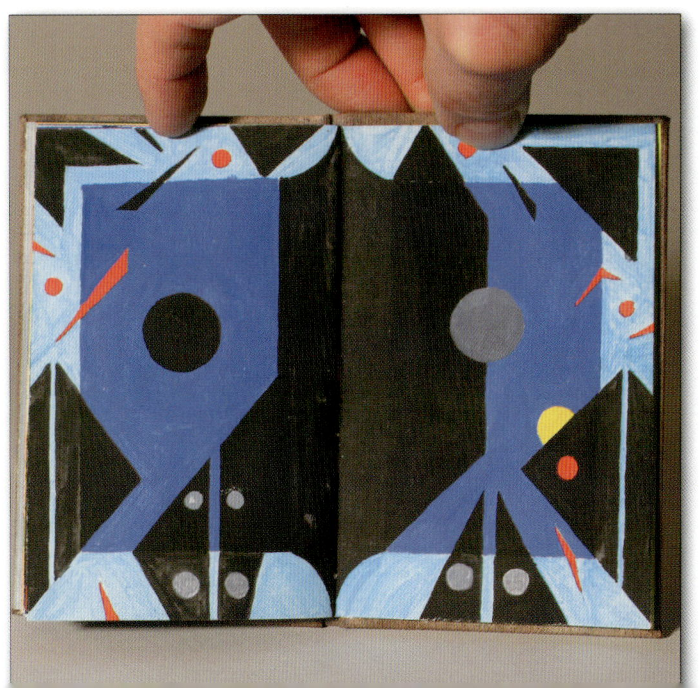

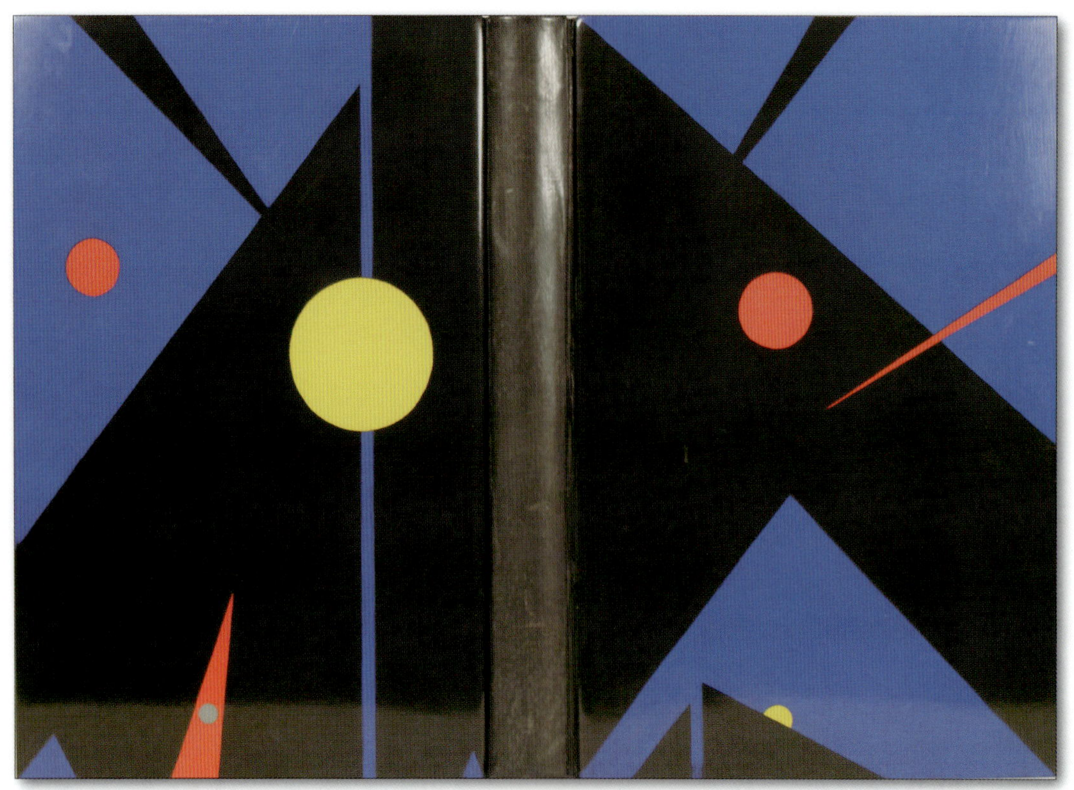

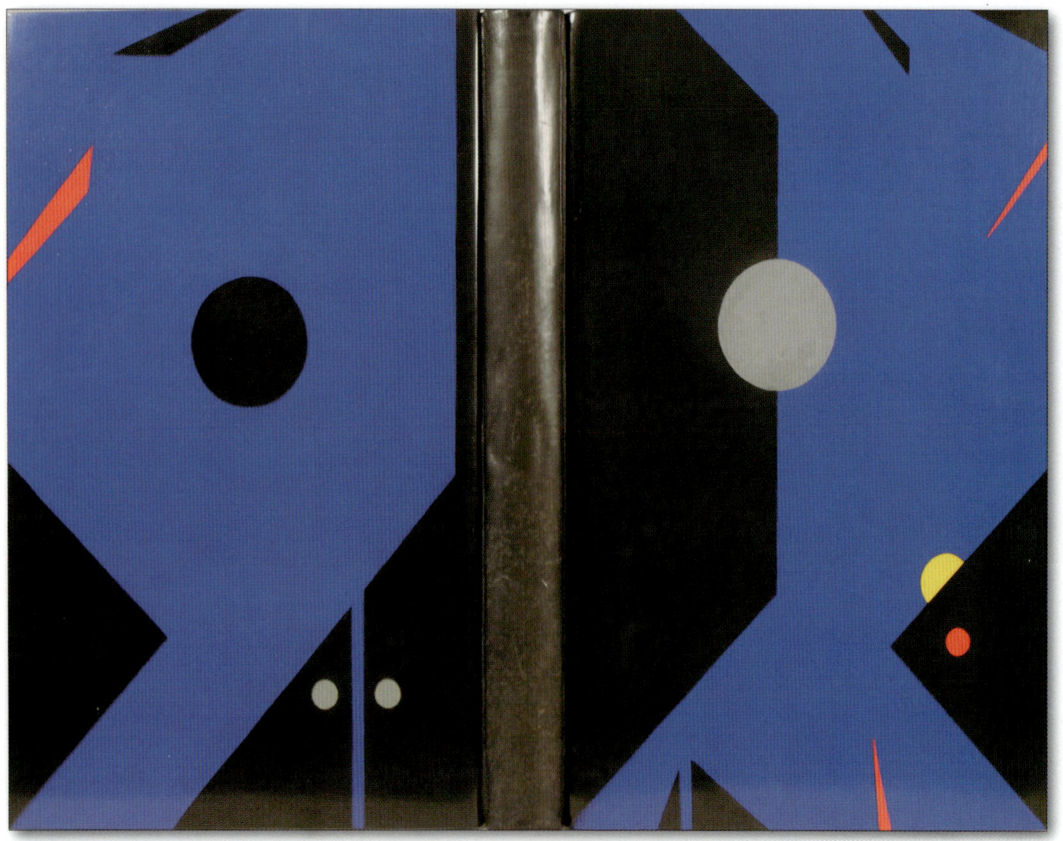

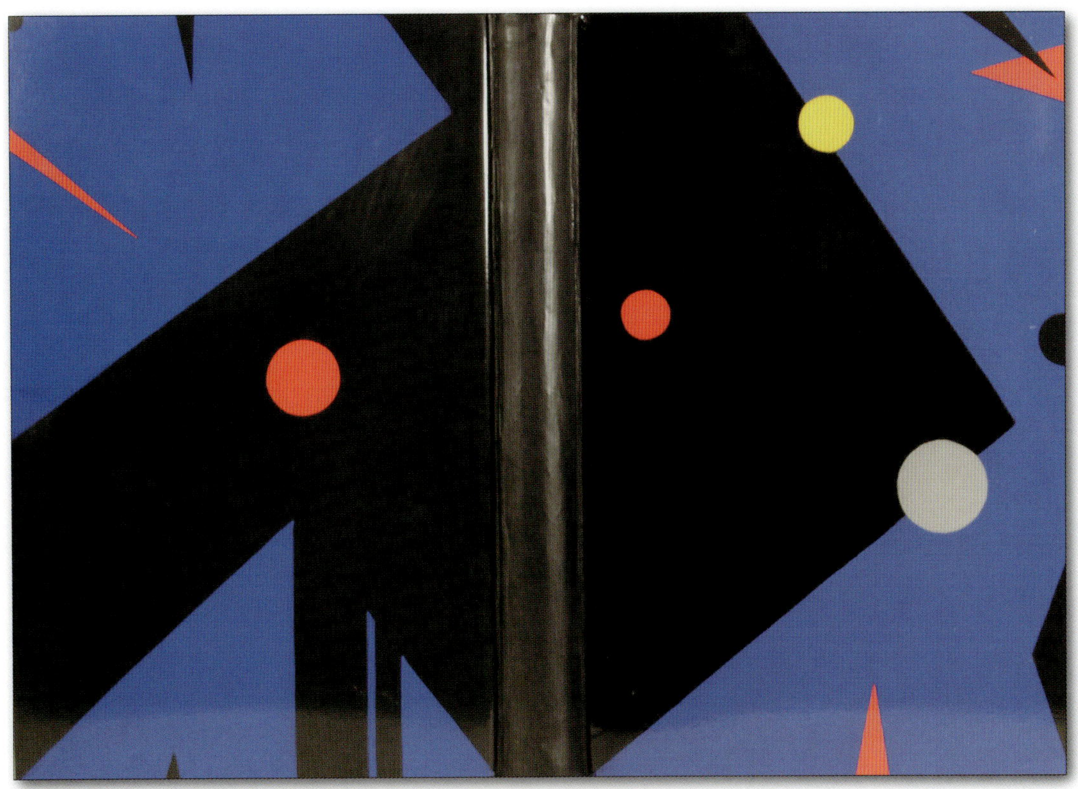

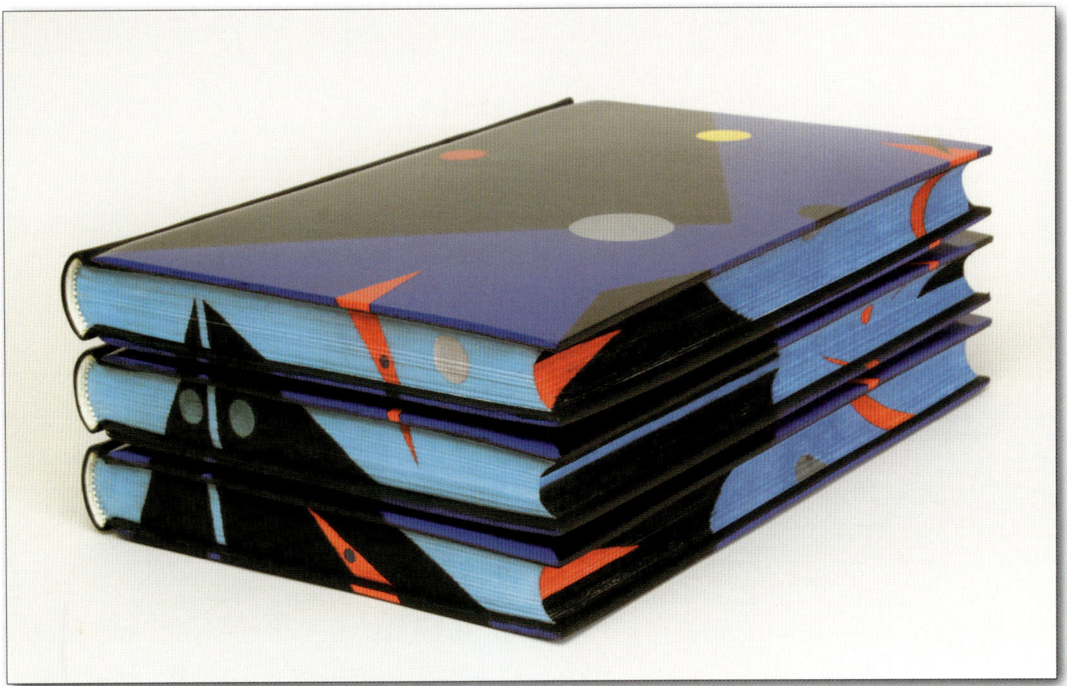

Triptych
Undated, c. 1991. Each volume 12¾ x 8¾, slipcase 13½ x 9¼ x 4
Three blank books of T. H. Saunders handmade paper, black calf spines, lacquer and acrylic on gessoed binders' board, all edges in watercolor and beeswax, linen endbands. Triple slipcase of black bookcloth.
Private collection, New York

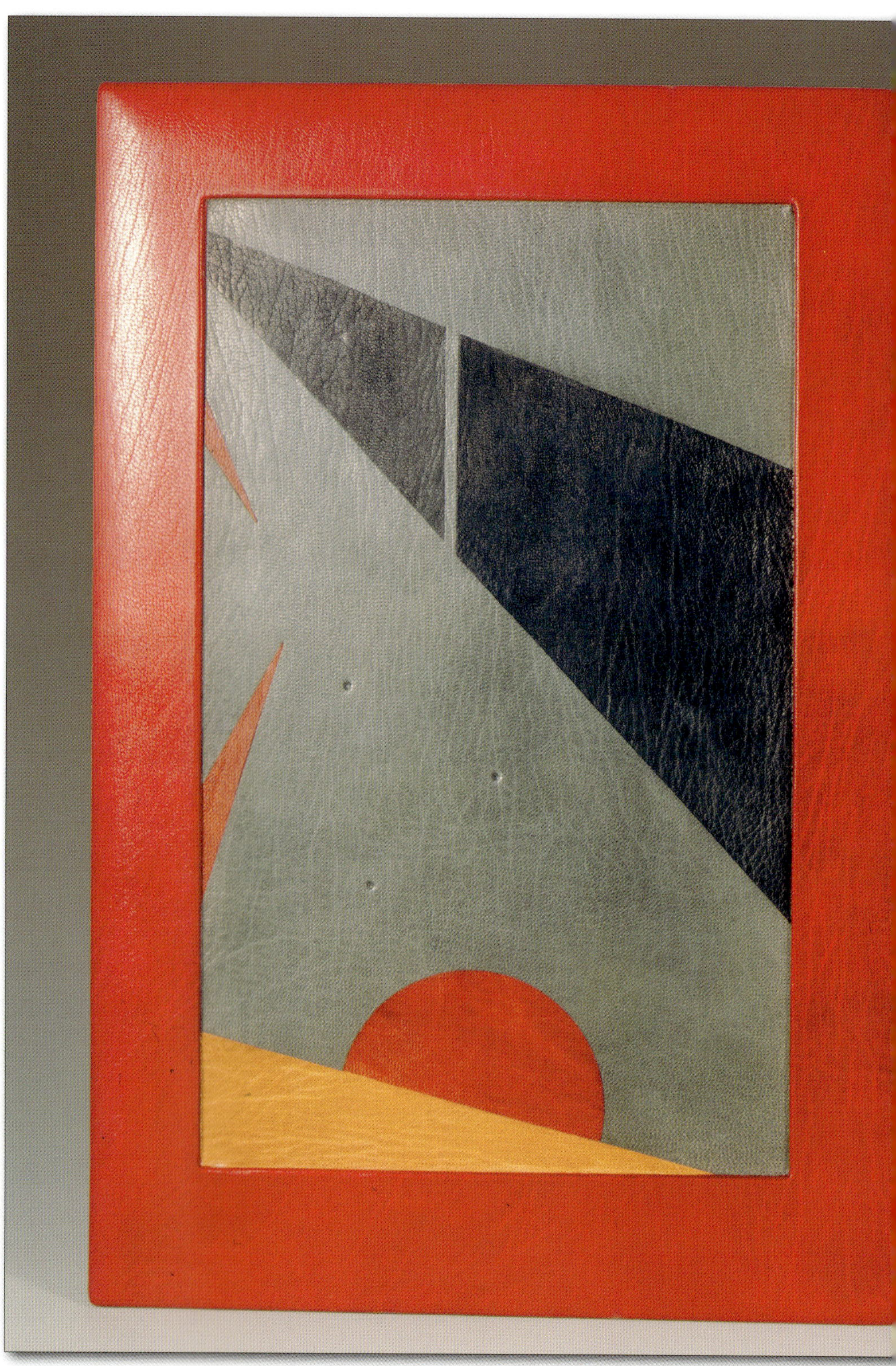

Inlaid Leather Guest Book
1983. 10 x 7
Red Nigerian Goatskin with inlay and onlay panels of a geometric design in both covers.
Collection of Louis K. and Susan P. Meisel

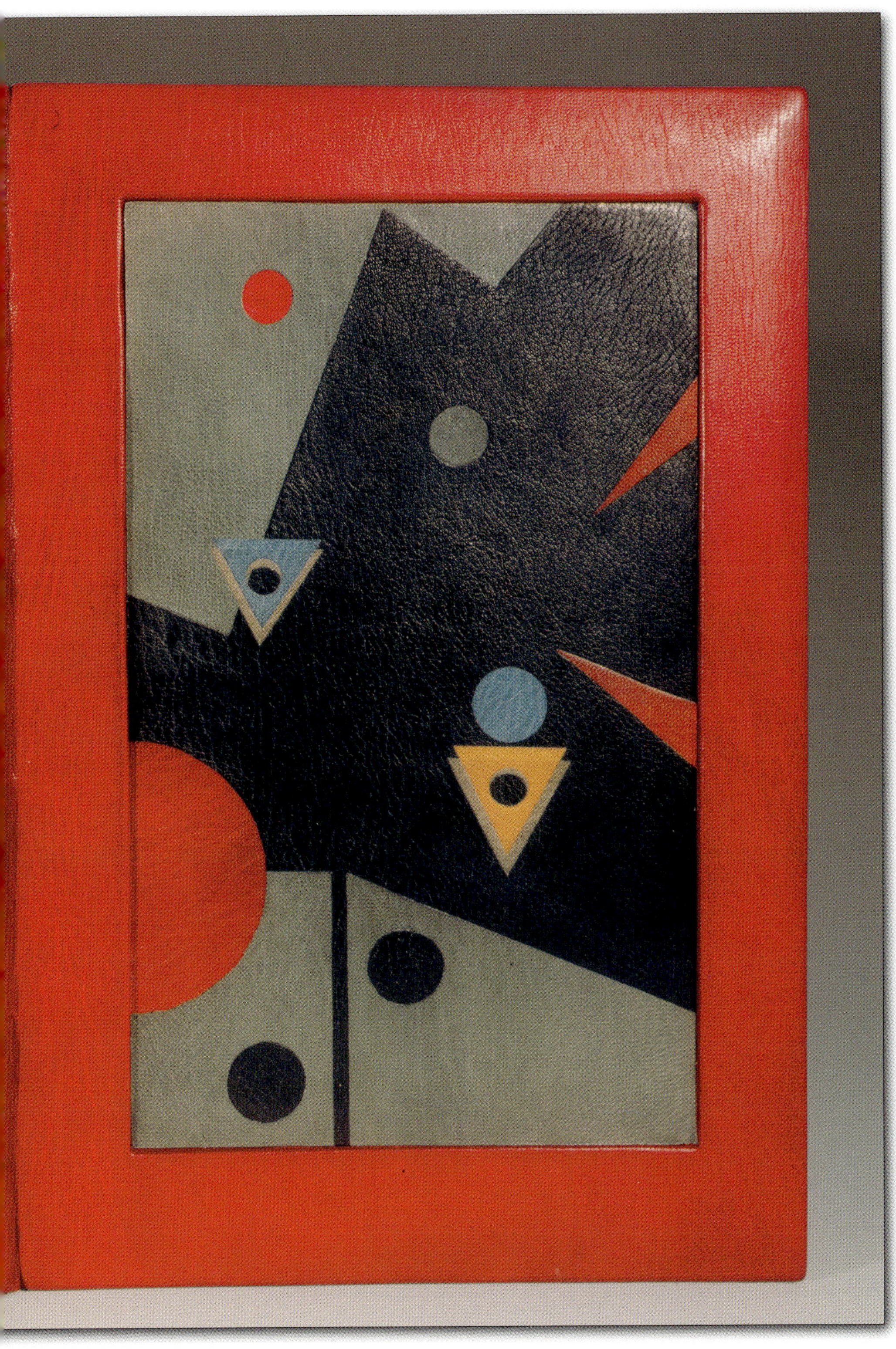

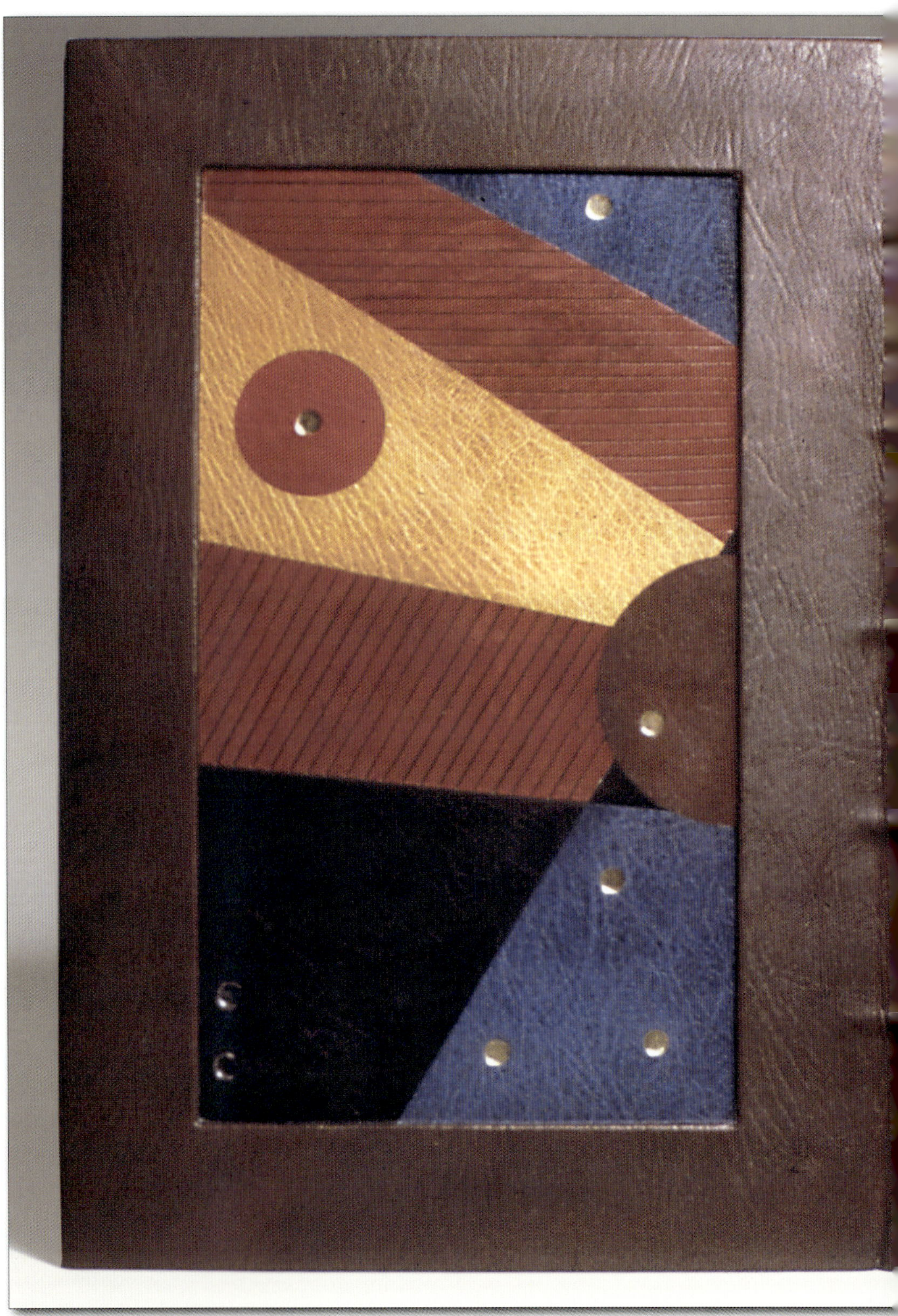

Inlaid Leather Blank Book

1983. 14¾ x 10

Brown Nigerian goatskin with recessed panels of inlaid goatskin, blind and gold tooled. Head edge in related pattern, watercolor and beeswax.

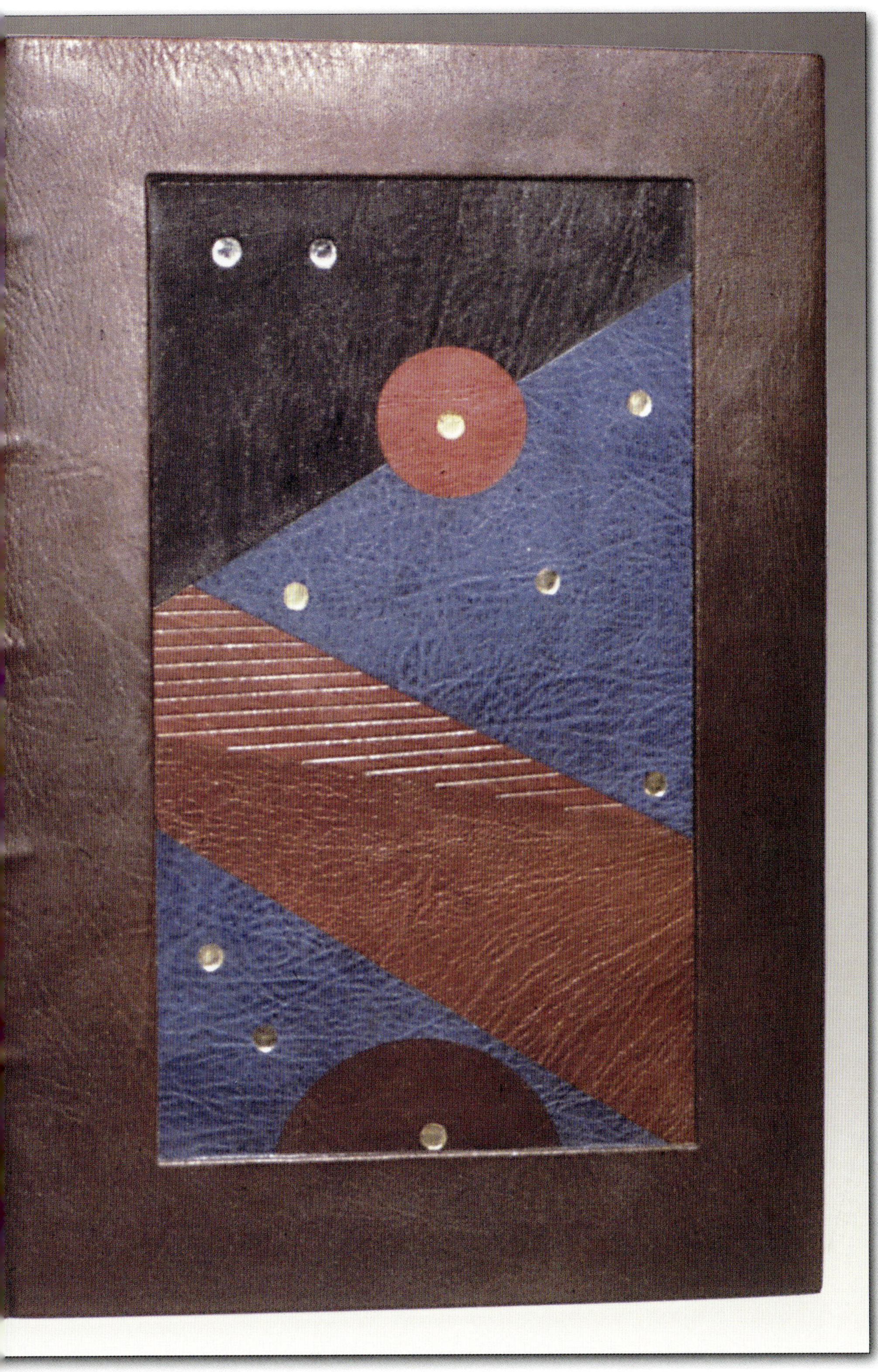

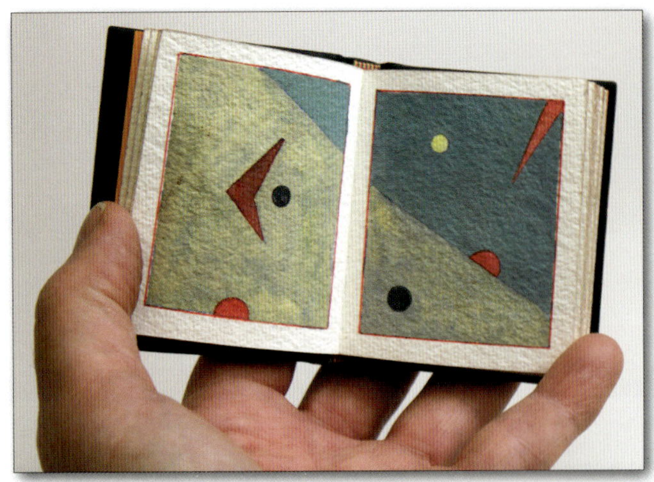
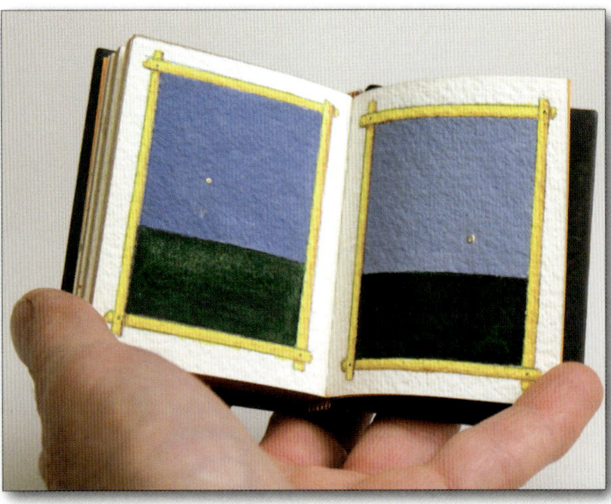
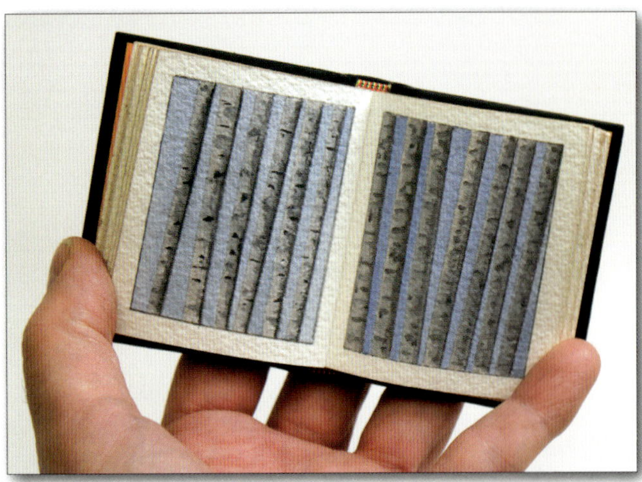
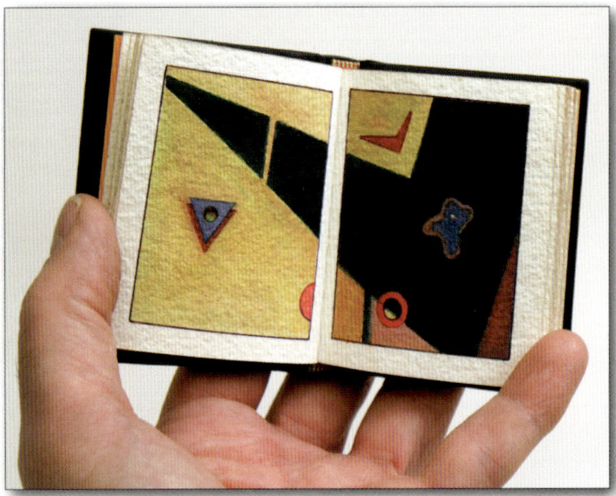

32 Studies
1991. 3⅛ x 2 ¾
Acrylic, watercolor, ink, and gold tooling on handmade paper.
Opposite page: Calf spine stamped in gold, acrylic and lacquer boards, three edges gilt.
Private Collection, New York

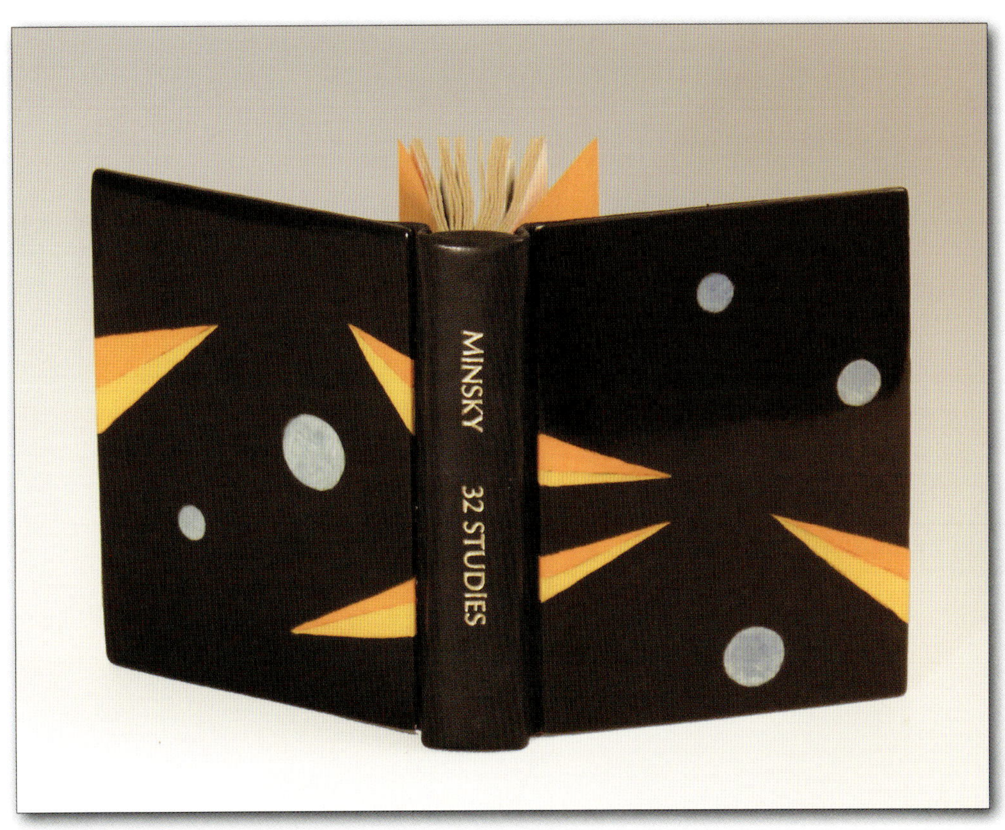
MINSKY 32 STUDIES

Commissioned Works

PEOPLE BRING all sorts of books to be bound. Some, like the Hagenauer catalog [p. 82], set off a series of visual explorations. Others require interpretations based on historical models. The 14th century girdle book is still a sensible solution for a monk's Breviary [below]. Ancient scrolls preserved in jars are evoked in the binding of Erica Jong's novel, *Sappho's Leap* [p. 104].

Material often meets metaphor in commissioned works, as in *The Hamptons* [pp. 107–109], which is bound in sand, shells and pebbles from a beach there. It bridges three decades, a reminder of the beach at Nice [p. 25].

Guest books provide the opportunity to work in a variety of media: photography [p. 110], painting [p. 111], and sculpture [p. 118].

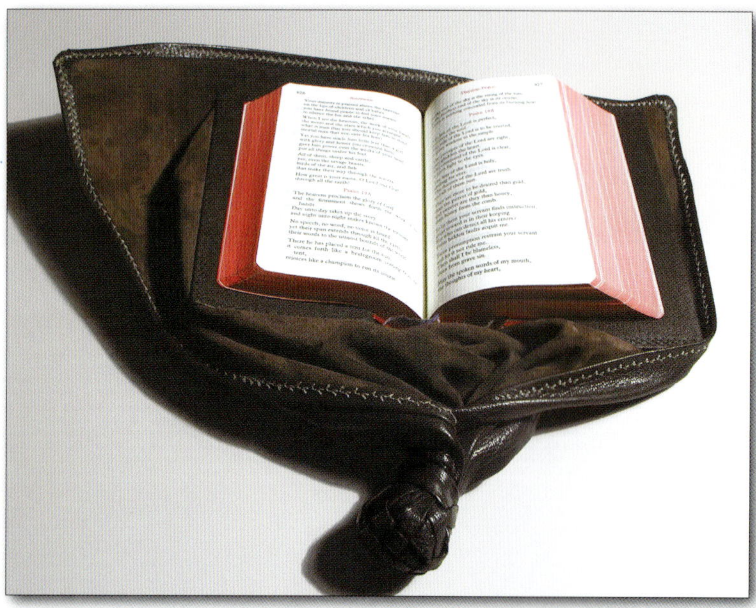

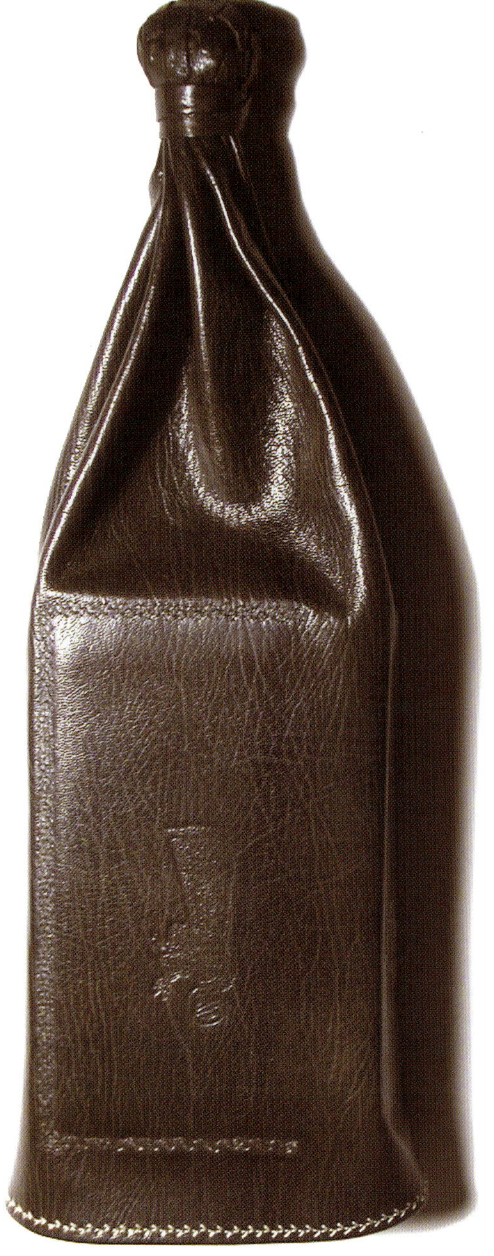

Girdle Book for Two Volumes
2004. 17 x 5½ x 2½
The Liturgy of the Hours
Catholic Book Publishing Co., New York, 1976
and
Proper Offices of Franciscan Saints
English-Speaking Conference of the Orders of Friars Minor, New York, 1976

A girdle book sleeve for the above two volumes, based on several historical models, made for daily use by a Franciscan Friar. Blind stamped on the exterior with images of the Cross of San Damiano, St. Francis [right], and the Arms of the Order of St. Francis. Stamped on the interior flaps with typographic abbreviations. Interior flaps also incorporate a prayer card and an image of Our Lady of Guadalupe. The books are removable, as each season requires a change of both volumes.
Private Collection

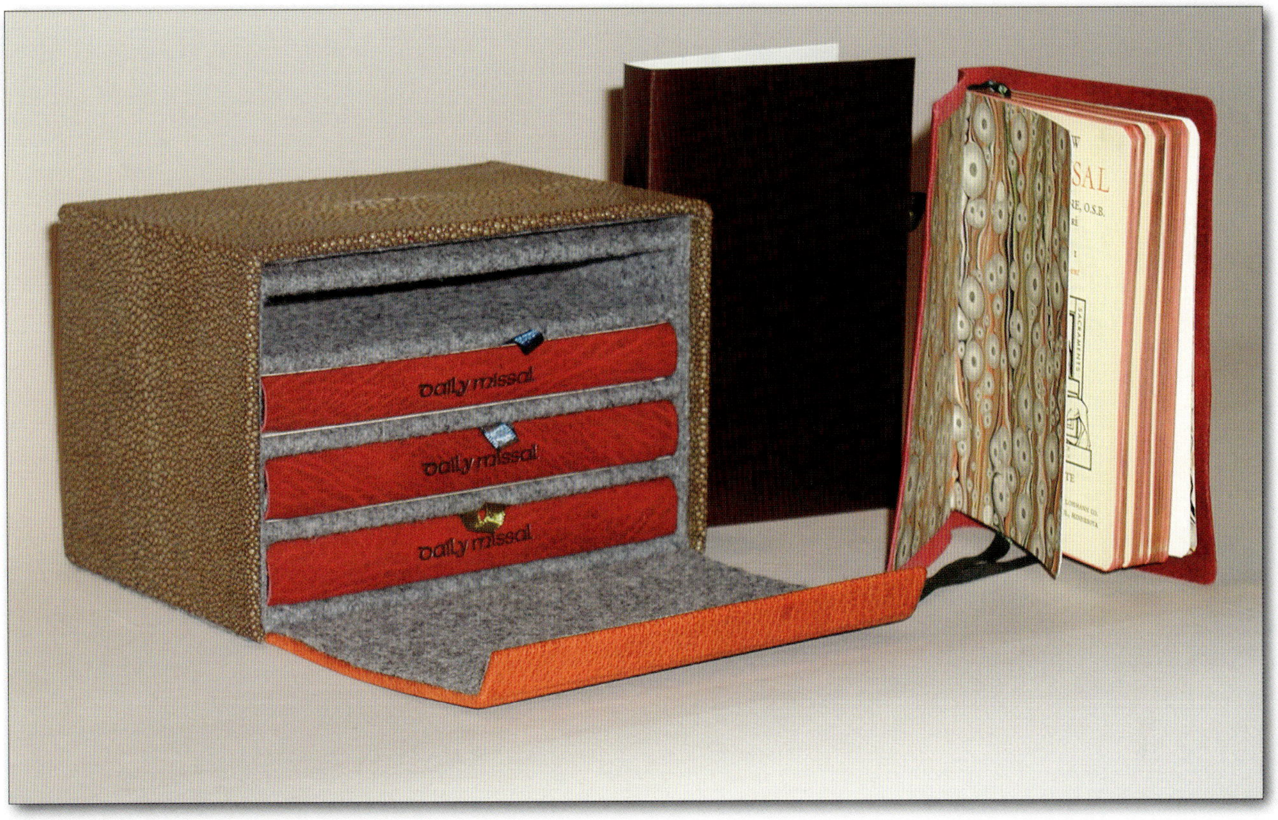

Daily Missal
Binding by Minsky, 2006. 4 volumes, each 4½ x 3
Goatskin over thin boards. Slipcase of olive shagreen (ray), felt lining, goatskin cover.
Private Collection

Francis Of Assisi: Early Documents
New City Press, New York, London, Manila, 2000
Binding by Minsky, 2004. Four Volumes 9 x 6
Issued as paperbacks, rebound in full goatskin with three modified yapp edges over thin boards. Page edges in 22K gold leaf over Armenian bole. Foil stamped title on spine, Cross of St. Damian on front cover, St. Francis on back cover with owner's name. Different marbled papers are used in each volume, and different colored ribbons. The volume number is blind stamped near the tail of the spine.
Private Collection

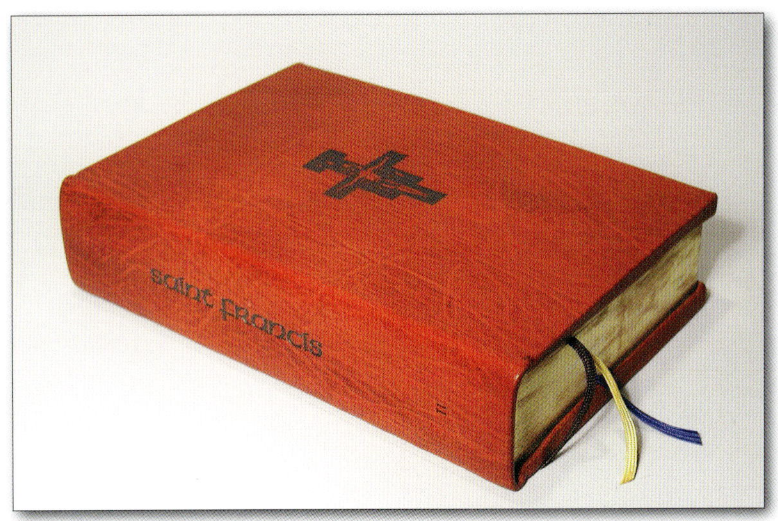

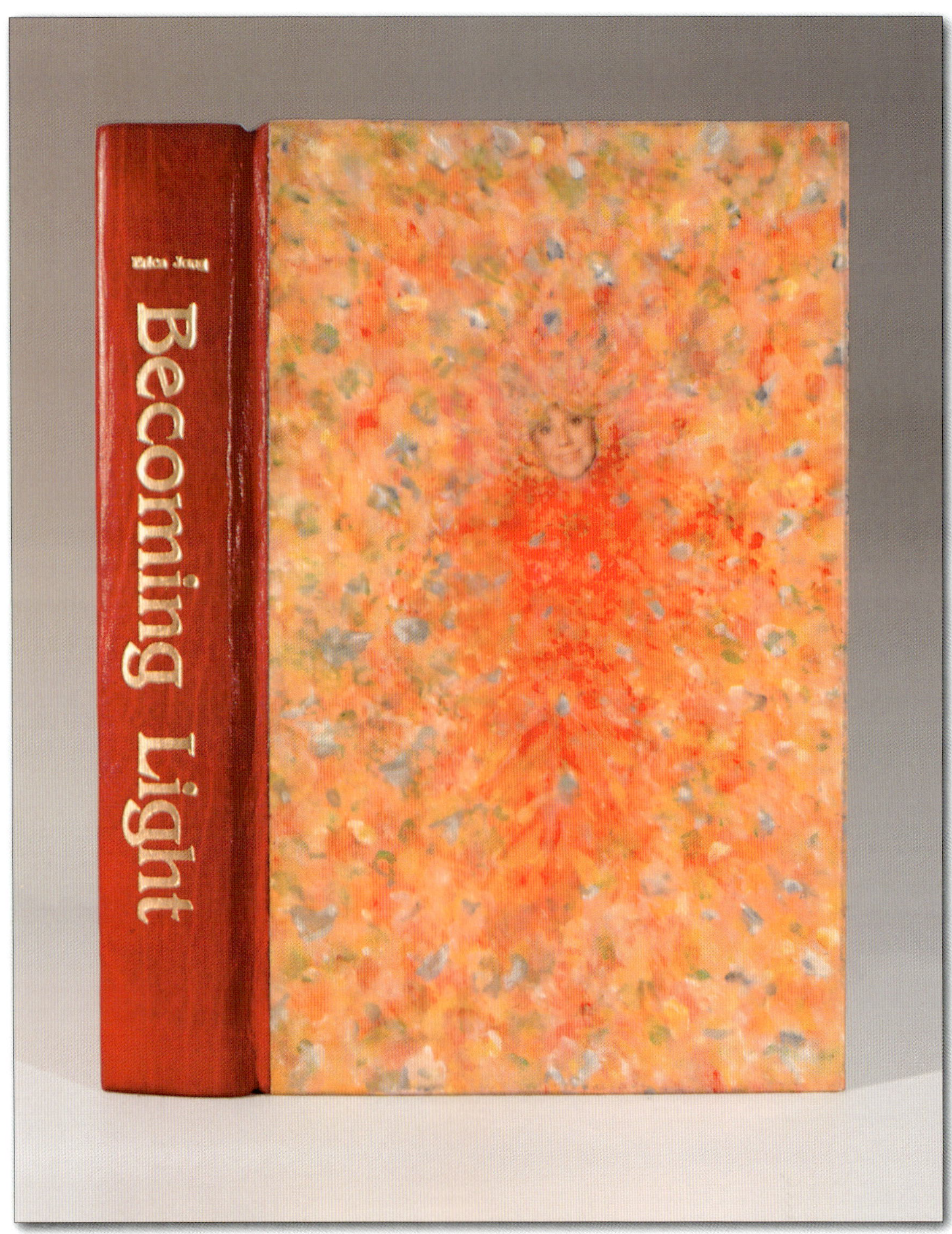

Becoming Light
by Erica Jong. HarperCollinsPublishers, 1991
Binding by Minsky, 1992. 9.5 x 6.5
Back cover and spine of Nigerian goatskin with 23k gold stamped title. Front cover is a lacquered panel of acrylic over a photo of the author.
Collection of Erica Jong and Ken Burrows, New York

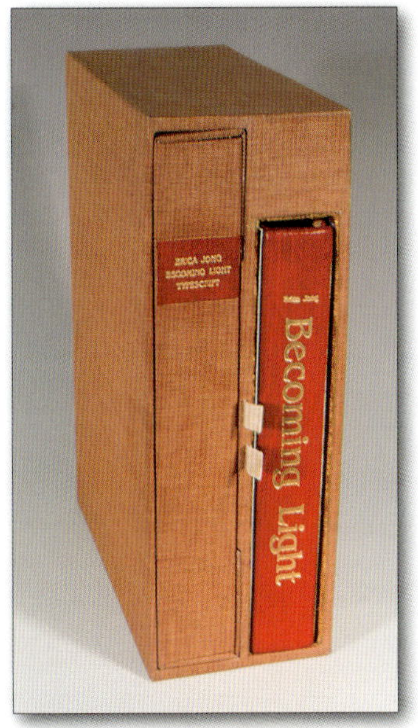

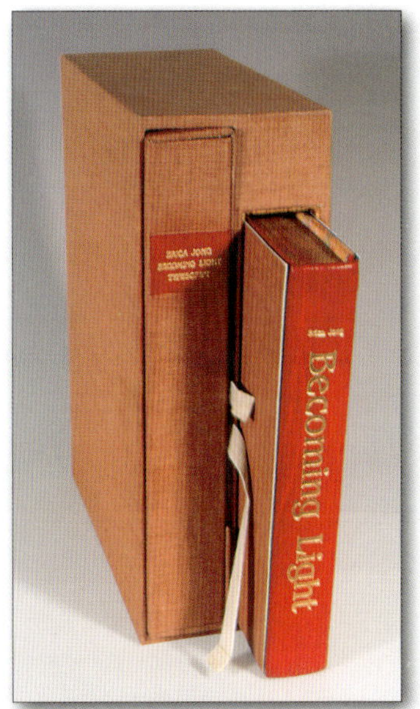

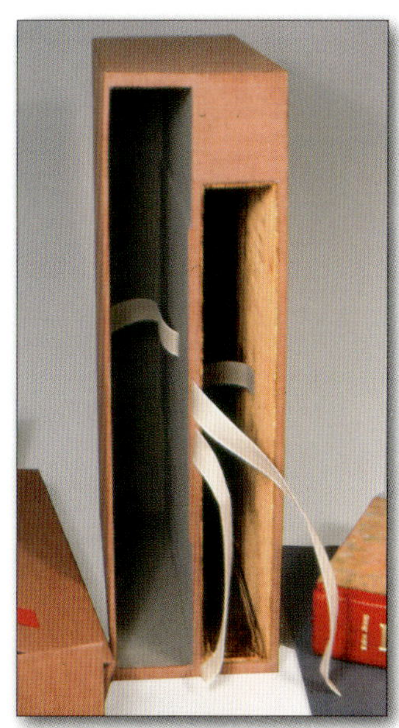

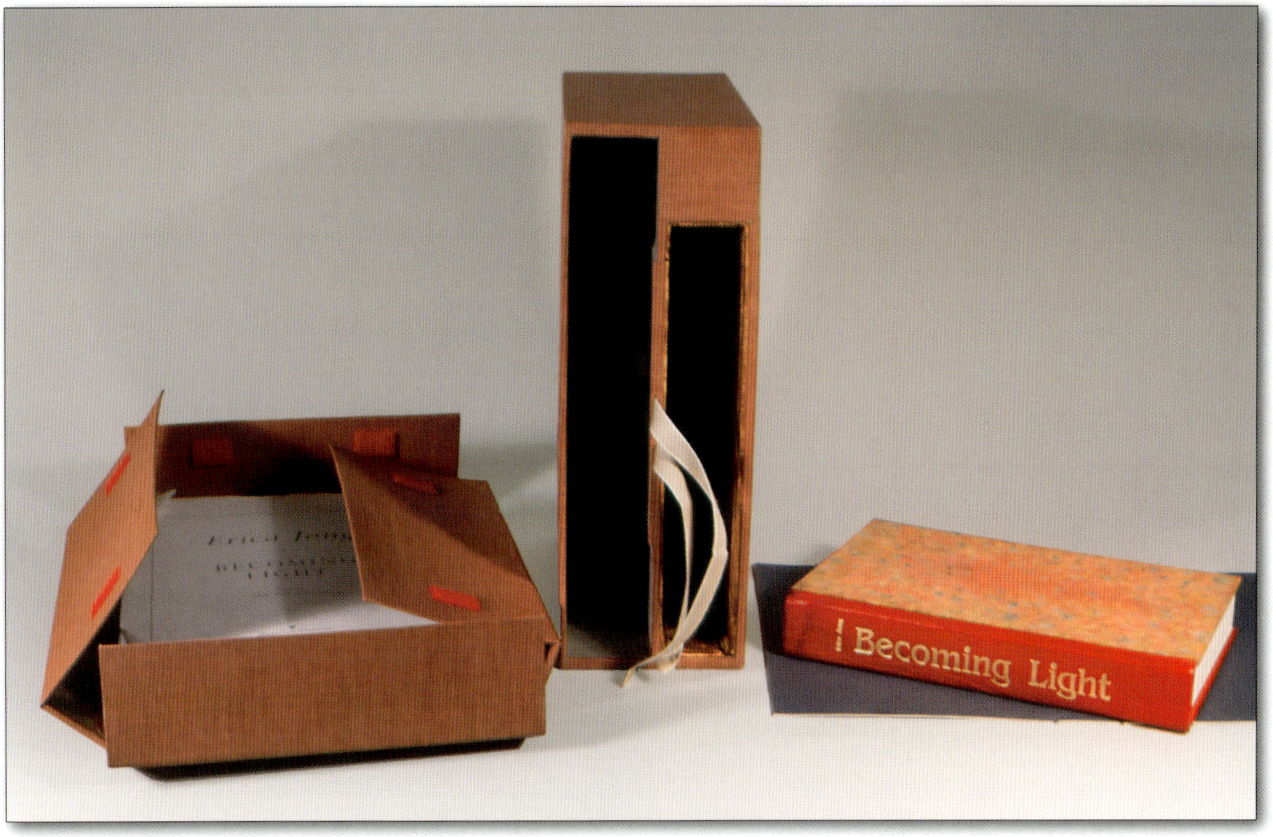

Becoming Light

Slipcase for book and typescript, 12 x 9 x 4

The binding has a paper chemise that slides into a velvet lined double slipcase. The original typescript is in the other side of the slipcase, in a folder with Velcro closures. The inside of that part of the slipcase is paper lined, and has recesses for the flaps of the folder. Linen tapes come through the edge of the slipcase between the two openings. Pulling a tape advances the book or typescript from the case. Either may be removed without taking the case from the shelf. Unlike ordinary slipcase tapes, these move through channels inside the boards, so when the book is removed the tape does not fall down, but remains in position ready to receive the book. Replacing the book in the slipcase pulls the tape back into the edge of the board.

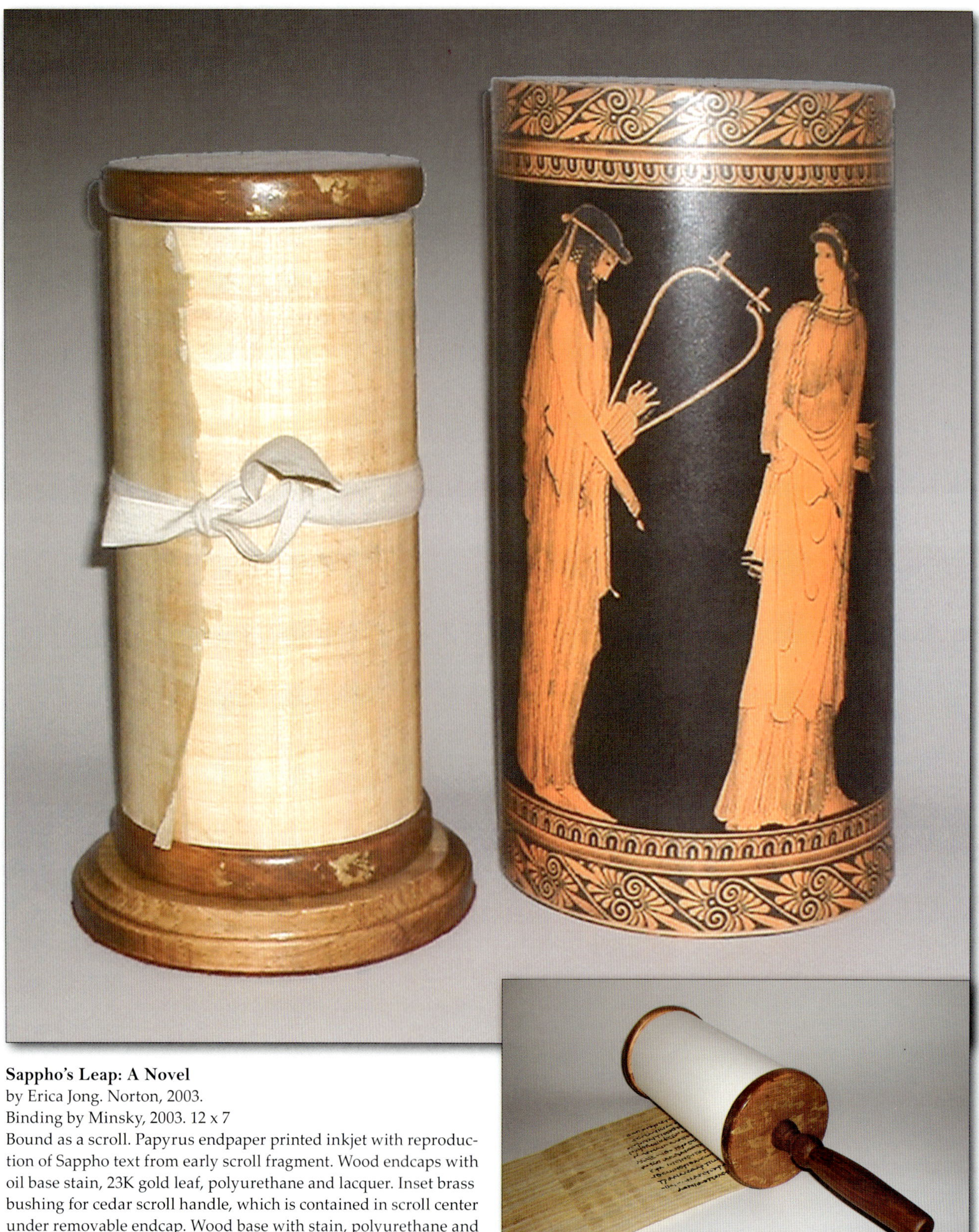

Sappho's Leap: A Novel
by Erica Jong. Norton, 2003.
Binding by Minsky, 2003. 12 x 7
Bound as a scroll. Papyrus endpaper printed inkjet with reproduction of Sappho text from early scroll fragment. Wood endcaps with oil base stain, 23K gold leaf, polyurethane and lacquer. Inset brass bushing for cedar scroll handle, which is contained in scroll center under removable endcap. Wood base with stain, polyurethane and lacquer. Scroll cover is lacquered inkjet adapted from Greek Krater image of Alcaeus and Sappho.
Collection of Erica Jong and Ken Burrows, New York

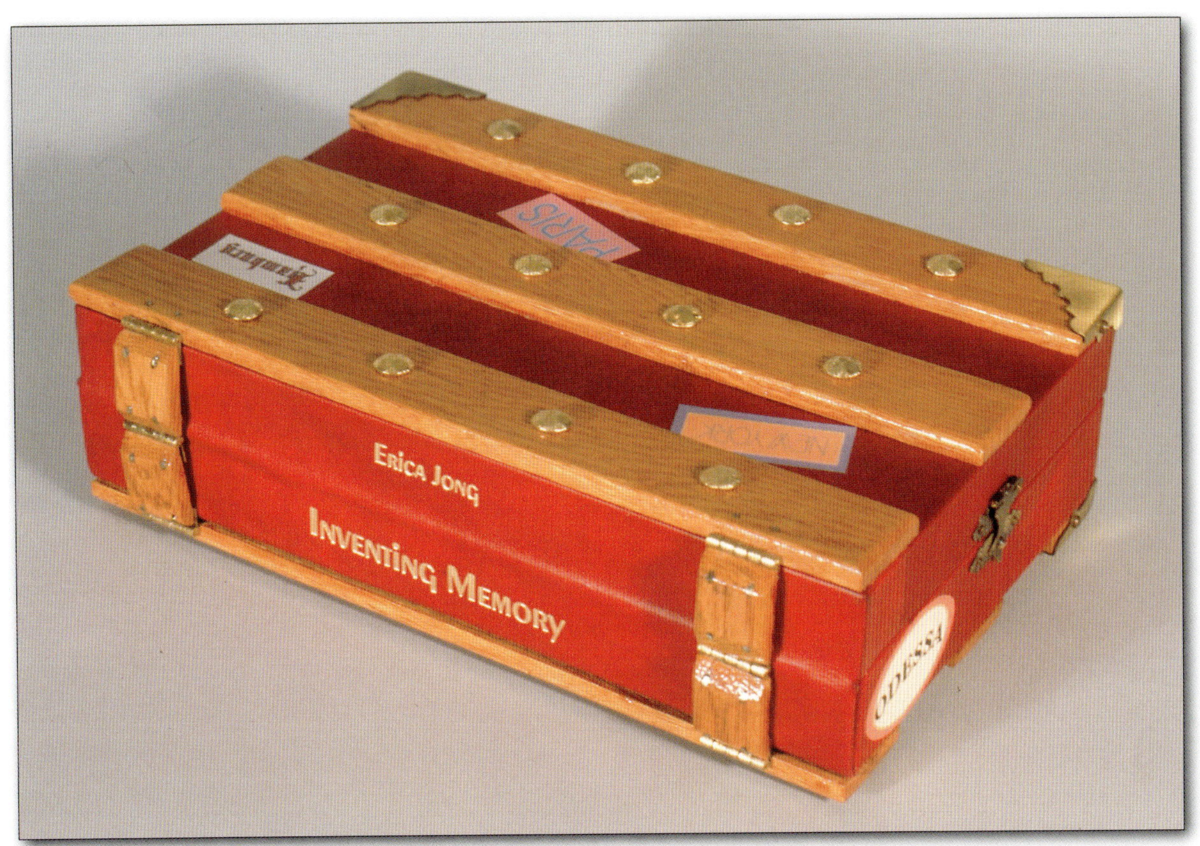

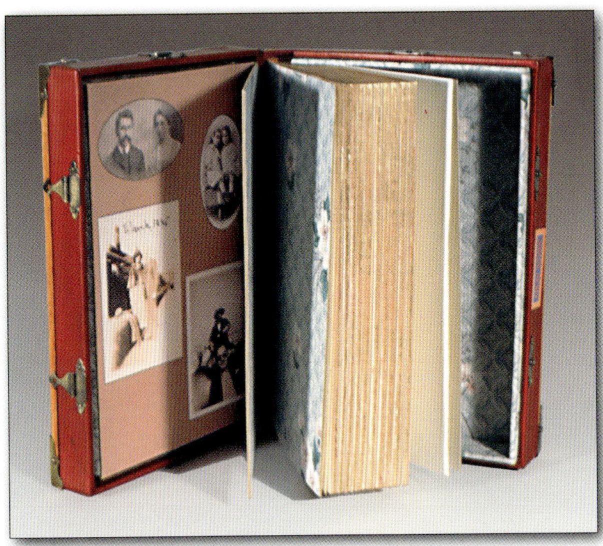

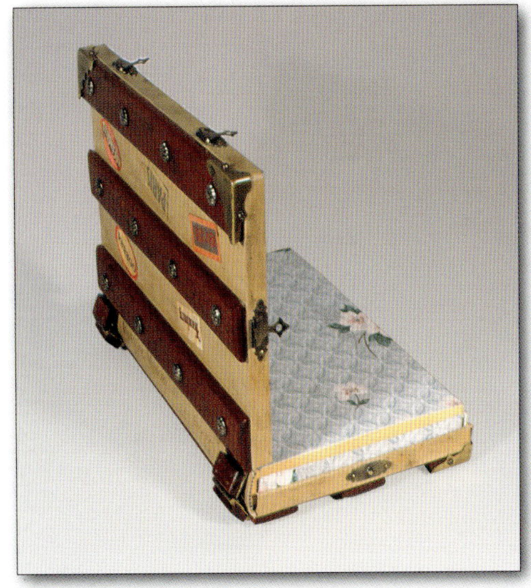

Inventing Memory: A Novel of Mothers and Daughters
by Erica Jong. HarperCollinsPublishers, 1997.
Binding by Minsky, 1998. 9½ x 6½ x 1½
Calf dyed by Minsky, gold stamping, oak, brass hardware, wallpaper endsheets, inkjet photomontage and labels. Edges of Armenian Bole and gold leaf. Hinged oak straps across the spine. This binding is created to give the feeling of a steamer trunk, with destination labels relating to the travels of the four generations of women in the novel. On the right is the prototype in bookcloth and mahogany. The text is integral to the structure [for another box-binding, see p. 106].
Collection of Erica Jong and Ken Burrows, New York

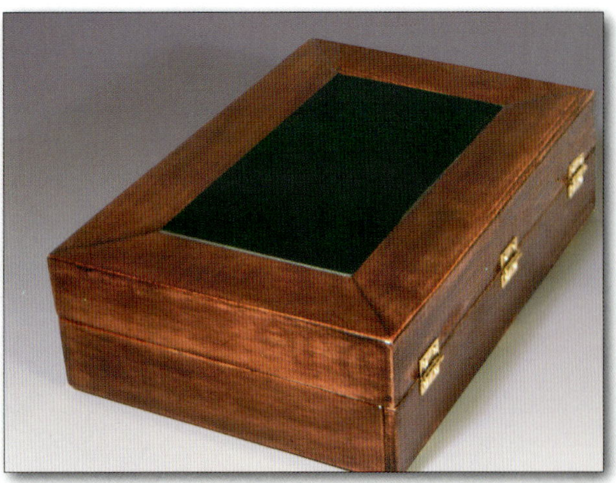

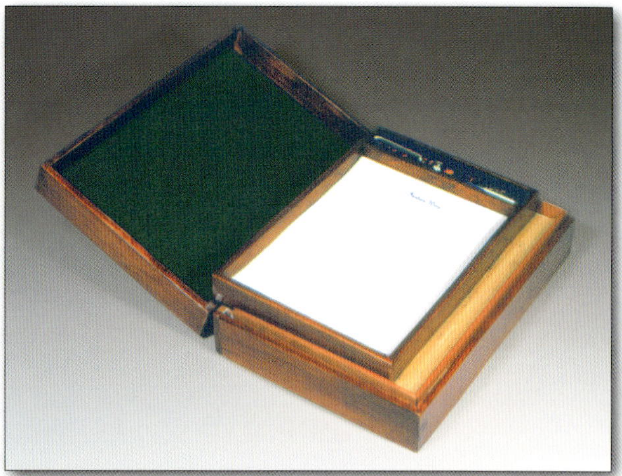

This binding treats the book as a woman's private diary, hidden from the world, disguised as an anonymous writing box. Opening the box reveals a tray containing writing paper and a fountain pen. Four different women's names on the stationery: Isadora Wing, Leila Zandberg, Erica Jong and Mechtild Maes. Isadora is a fictitious author created by Erica Jong. Leila is a character of Isadora's, who maintains a dialogue with her creator throughout the novel. Mechtild commissioned this work.

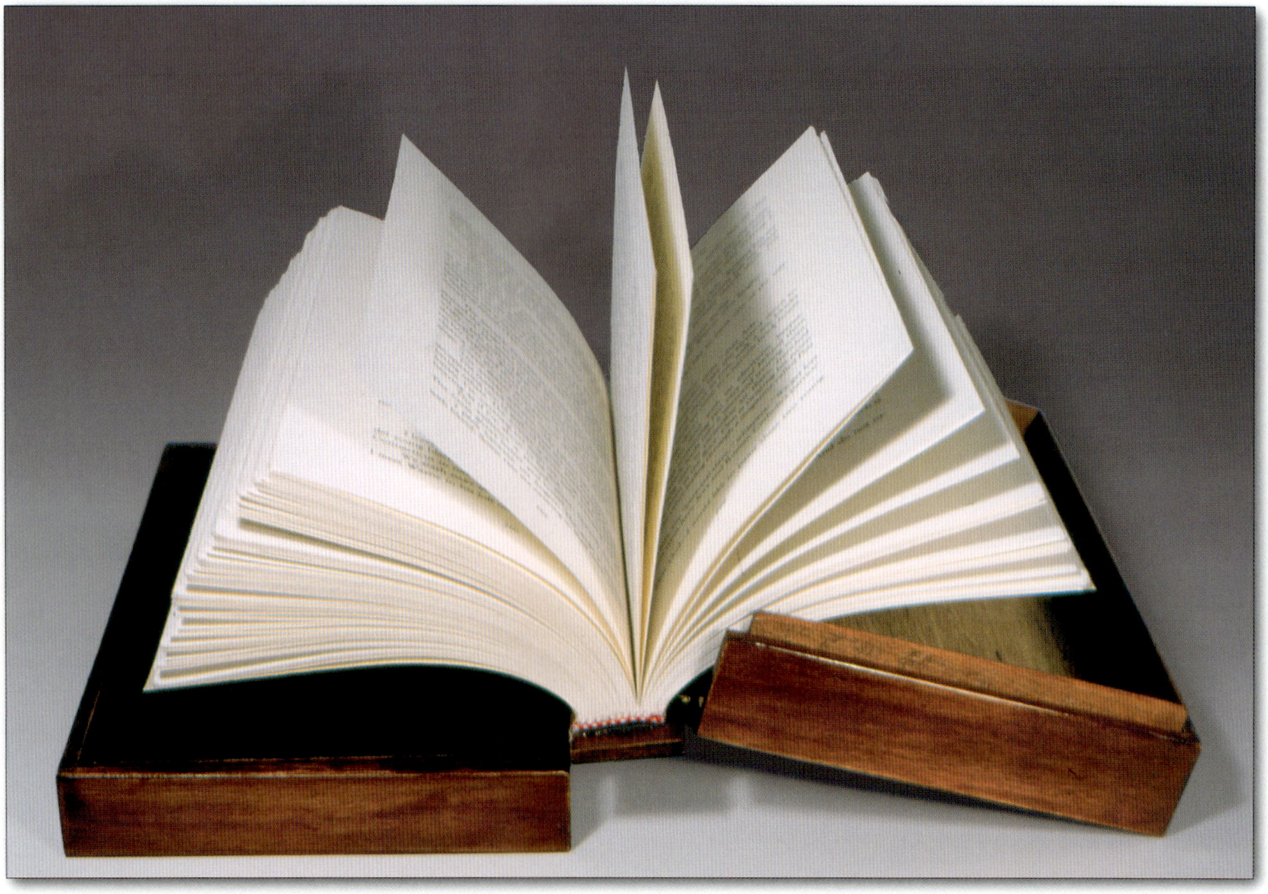

Any Woman's Blues: A Novel of Obsession
by Erica Jong. Harper and Row, 1990.
Binding by Minsky, 2000. 10 x 7 x 3
Stained wood and wood veneers, inset leather panel.
Collection of Mechtild Maes, Amsterdam

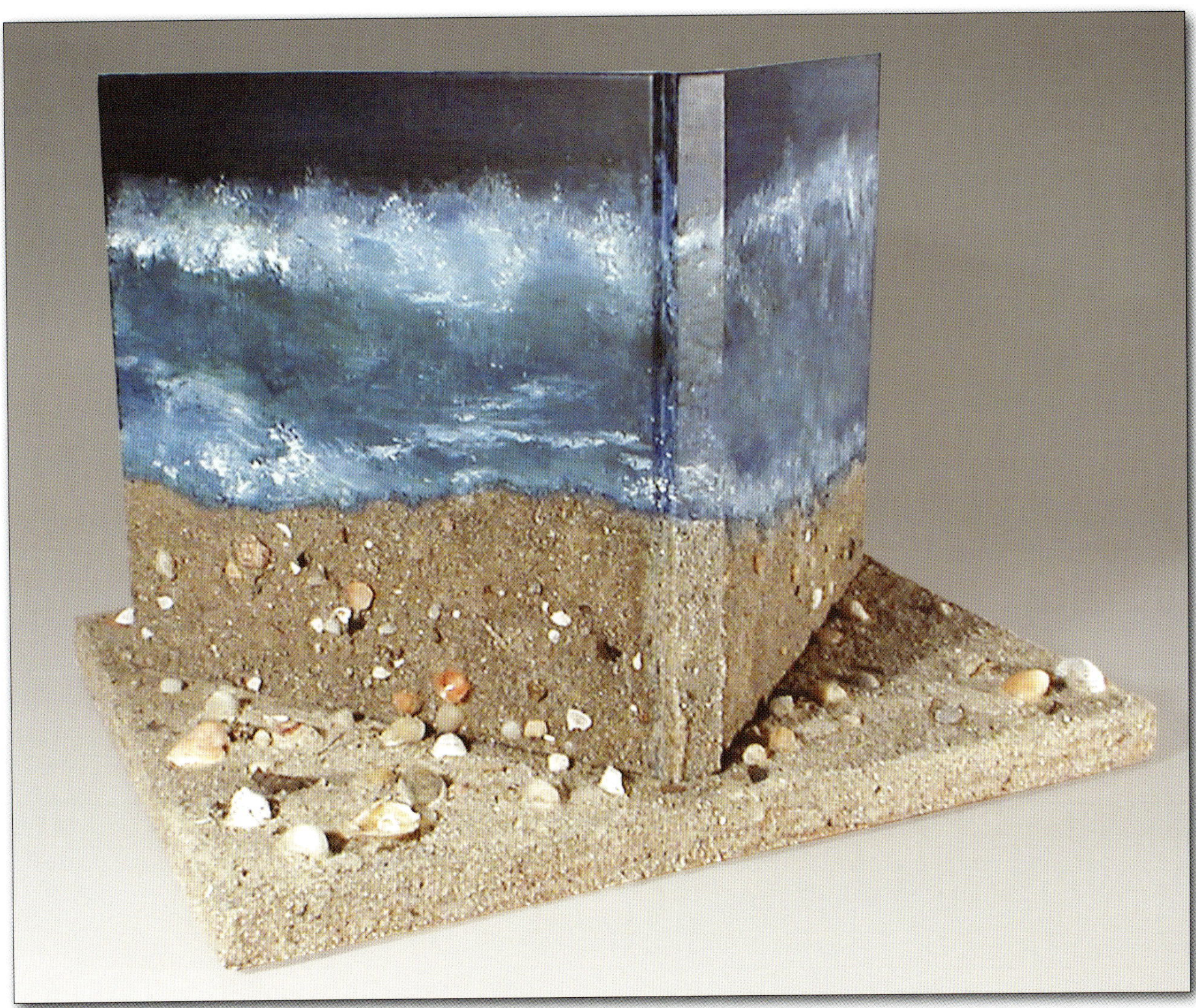

The Hamptons
by Susan P. Meisel and Ellen Harris.
Harry N. Abrams, Inc., 2000.
Binding by Minsky, 2000. 10½ x 10
Acrylic, sand and shells from the Hamptons.
Collection of Susan P. Meisel

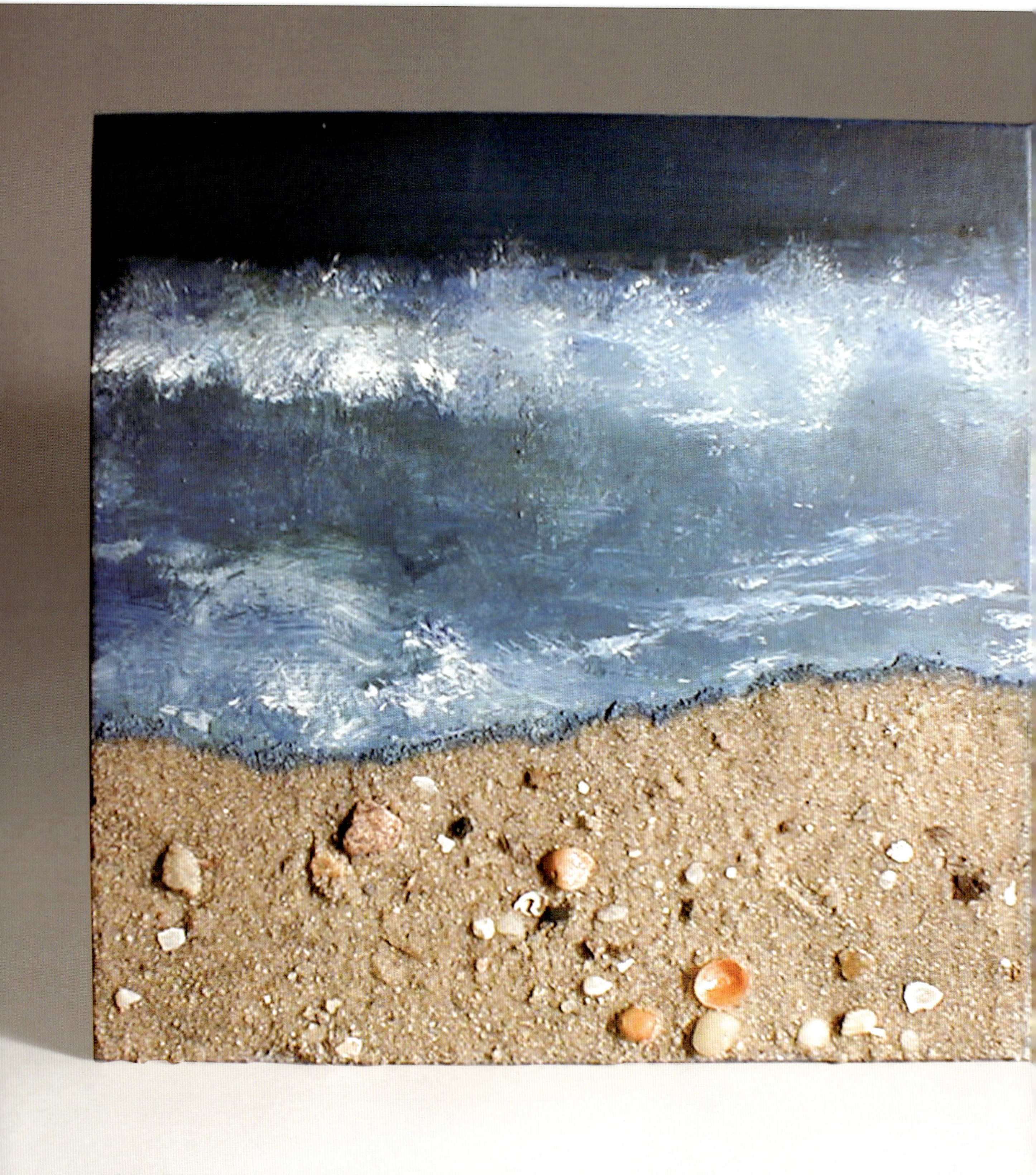

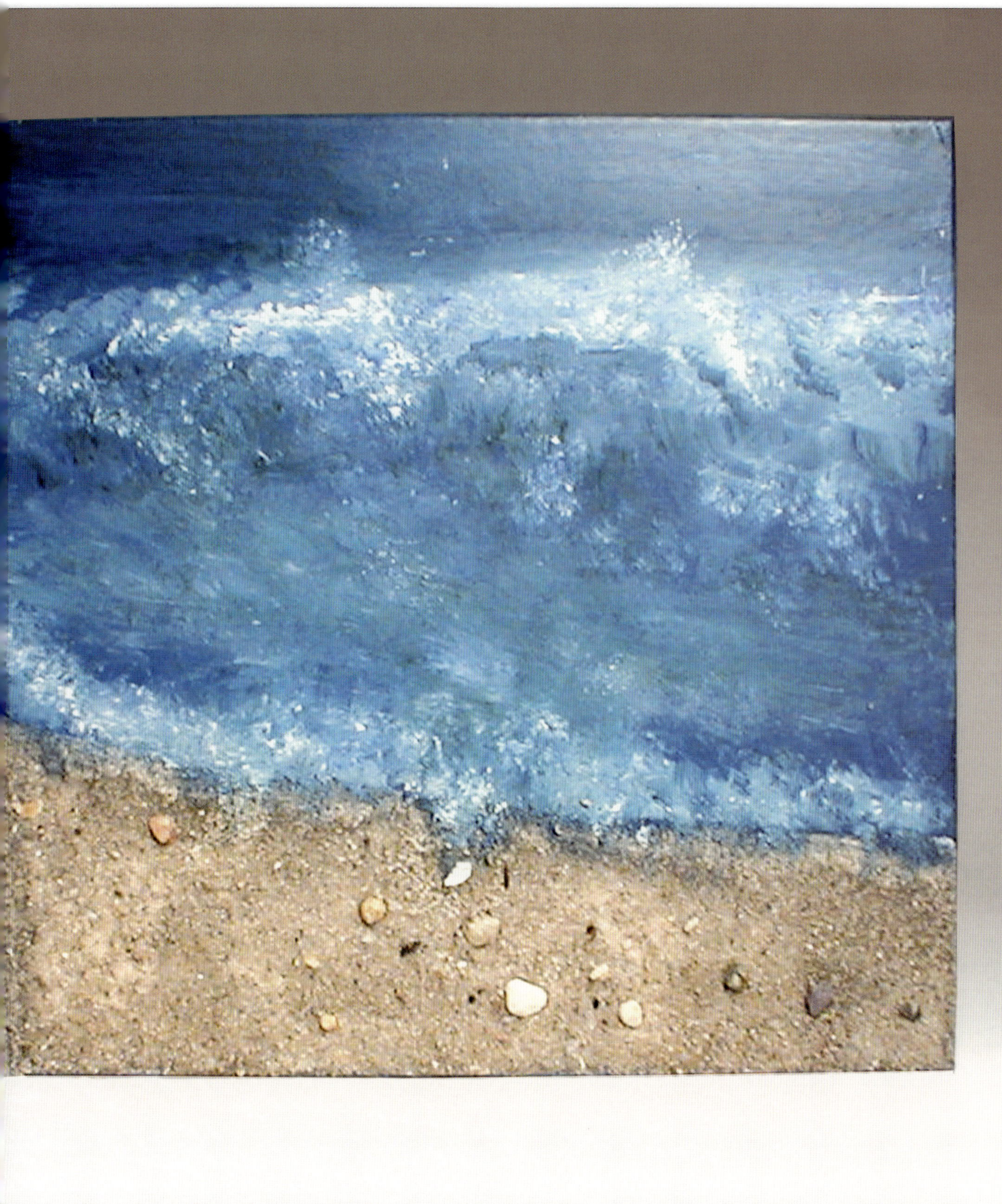

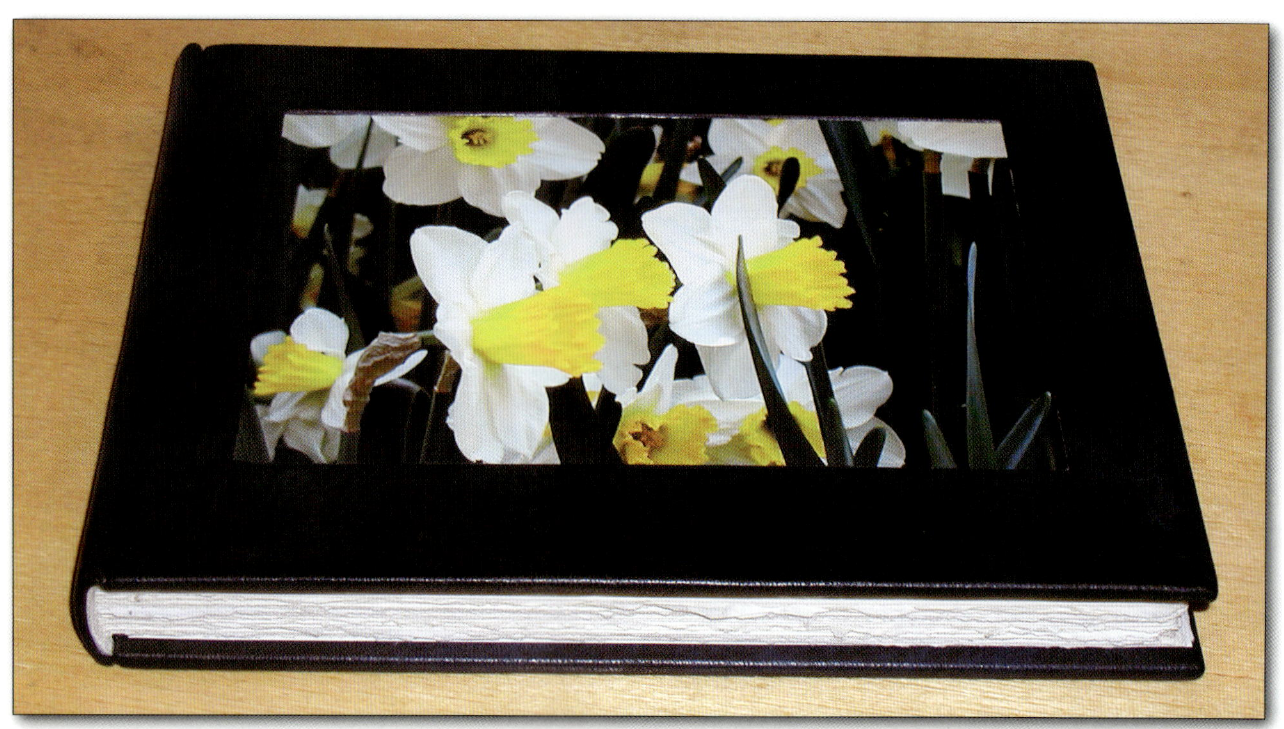

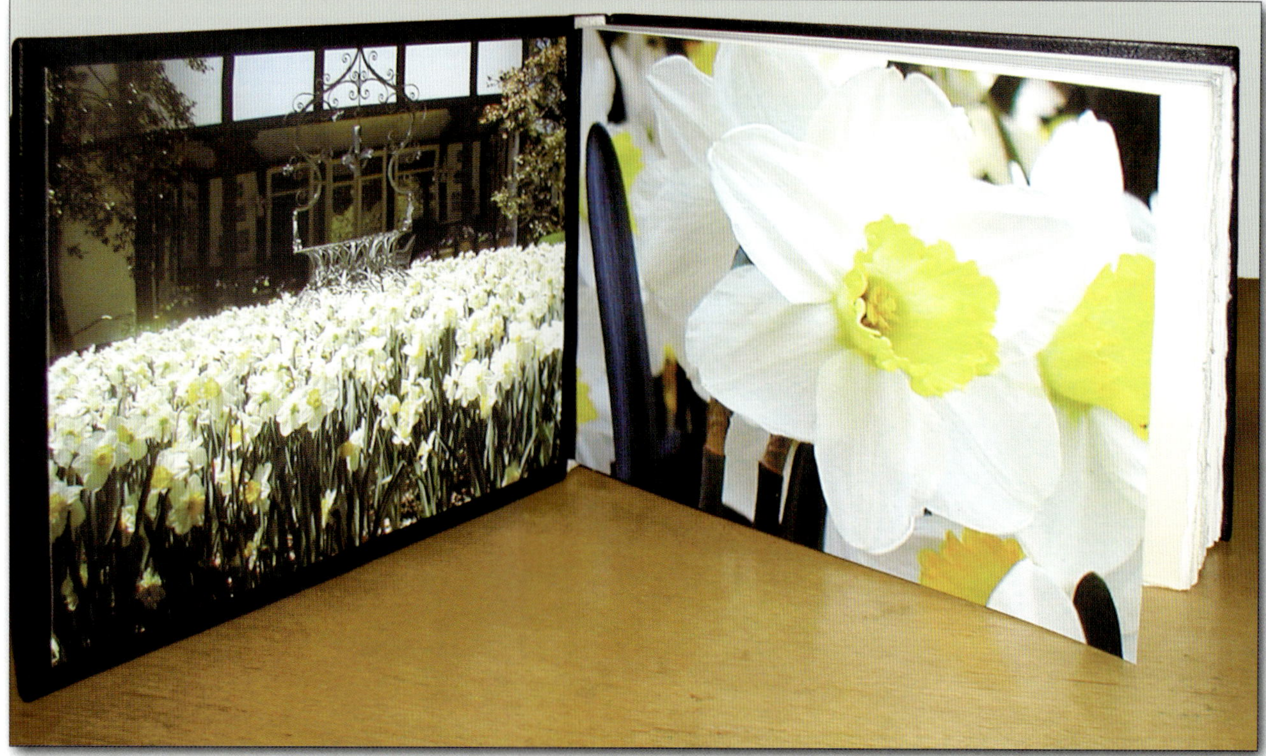

Guest Book
2003. 9⅛ x 12
Goatskin with inlaid lacquered inkjet on paper of Jonquil photograph by Minsky, endpapers are lacquered inkjet prints. Linen headbands over a core of goat vellum laminated to alum tawed pigskin.
Private collection, Long Island

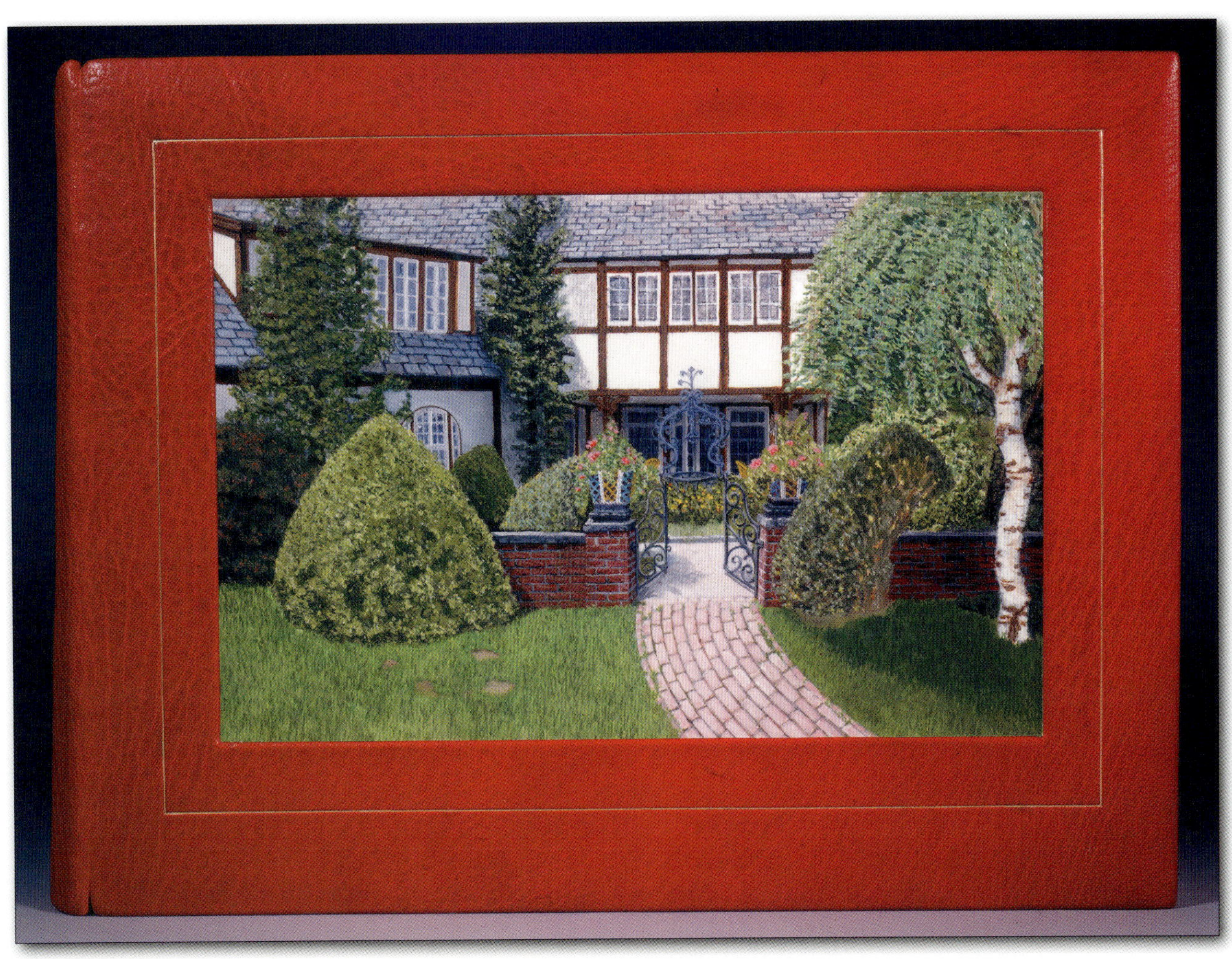

Guest Book
1986. 9⅛ x 12
Nigerian goatskin, recessed 6 x 9 panel is lacquered acrylic paint on Rives BFK.
Private collection, Long Island

Zabriskie Gallery, 1988

FOR THIS EXHIBITION, seven books on social and political themes, mostly bought at the $1 table outside the Pageant Book Shop on 9th Street, were iconified in "material meets metaphor" bindings. *Laying Waste* was displayed in a black plywood box, with a radioactive trefoil in yellow and purple and a viewing port. A switch on the side enabled the viewer to control the light and see the phosphorescent death's head. The inclusions extend the meaning of the work to ways we poison ourselves

Also shown were *The Geography of Hunger* [p. 36], *Tragedy and Hope* [p. 44]. *Holy Terror* [p.114], and *Hunger Fighters* [p. 115].

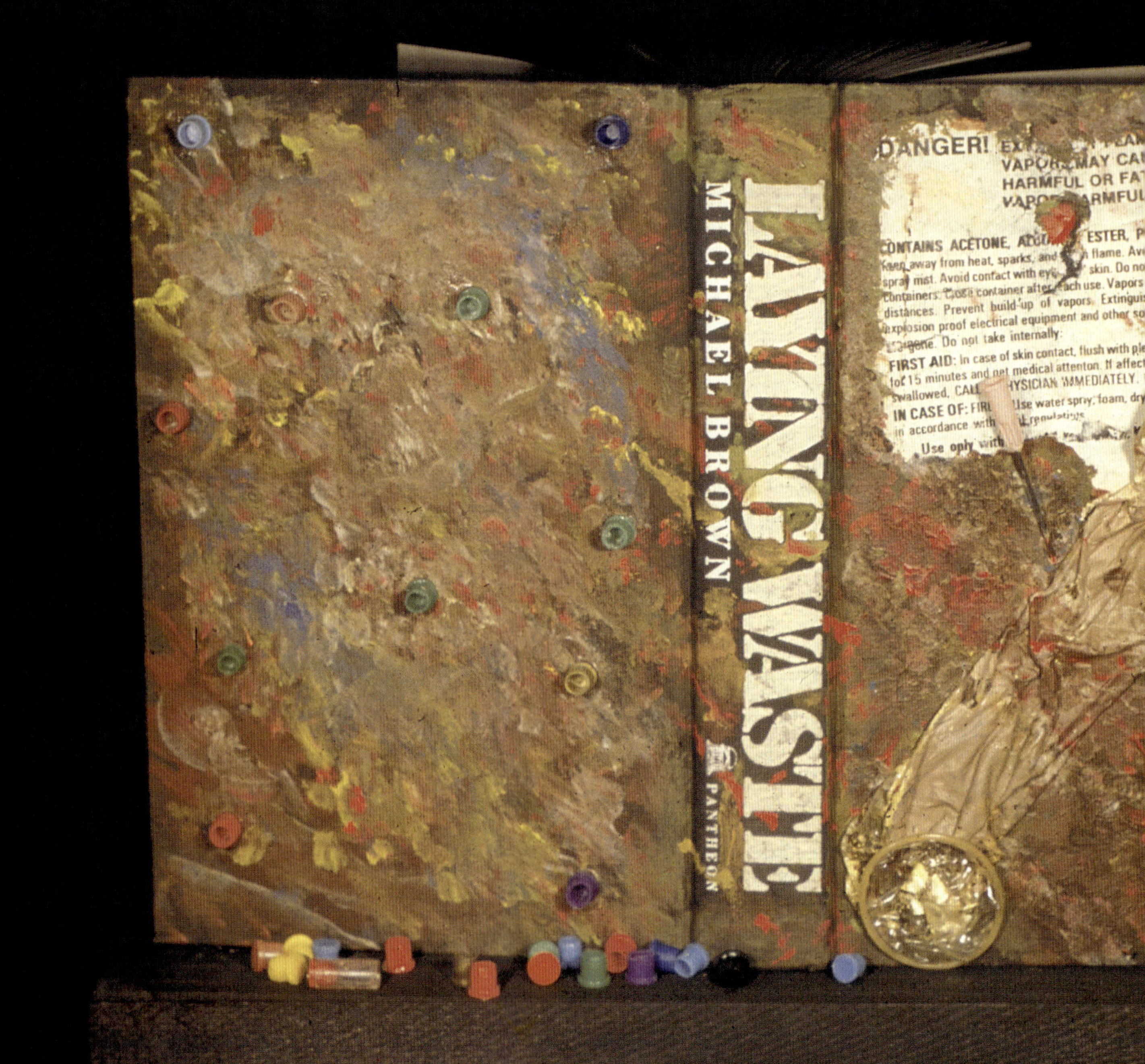

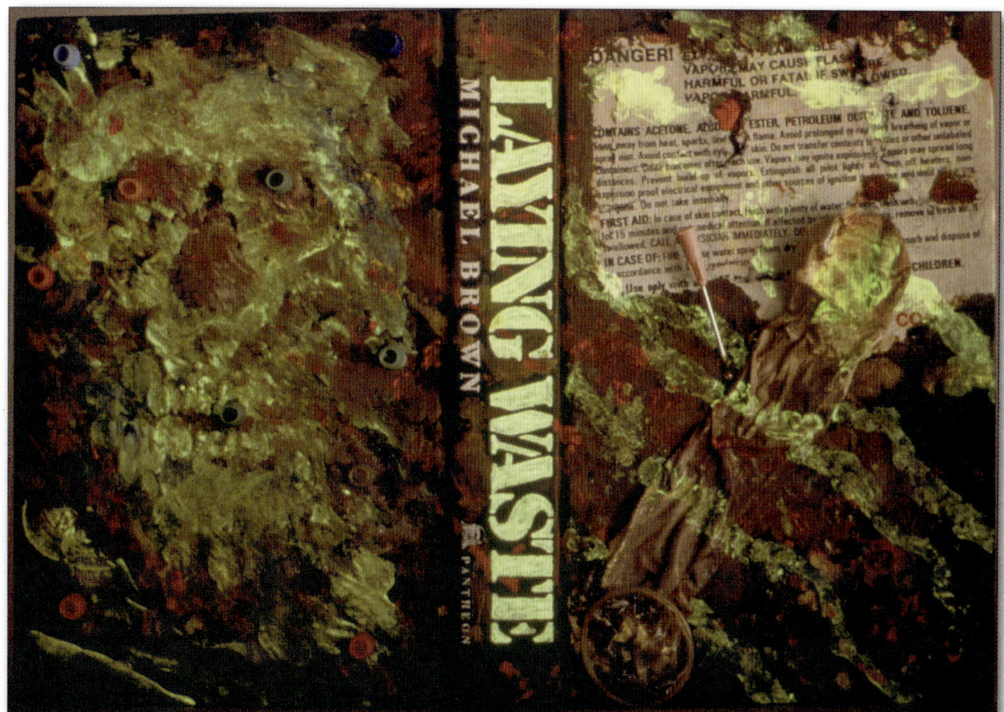

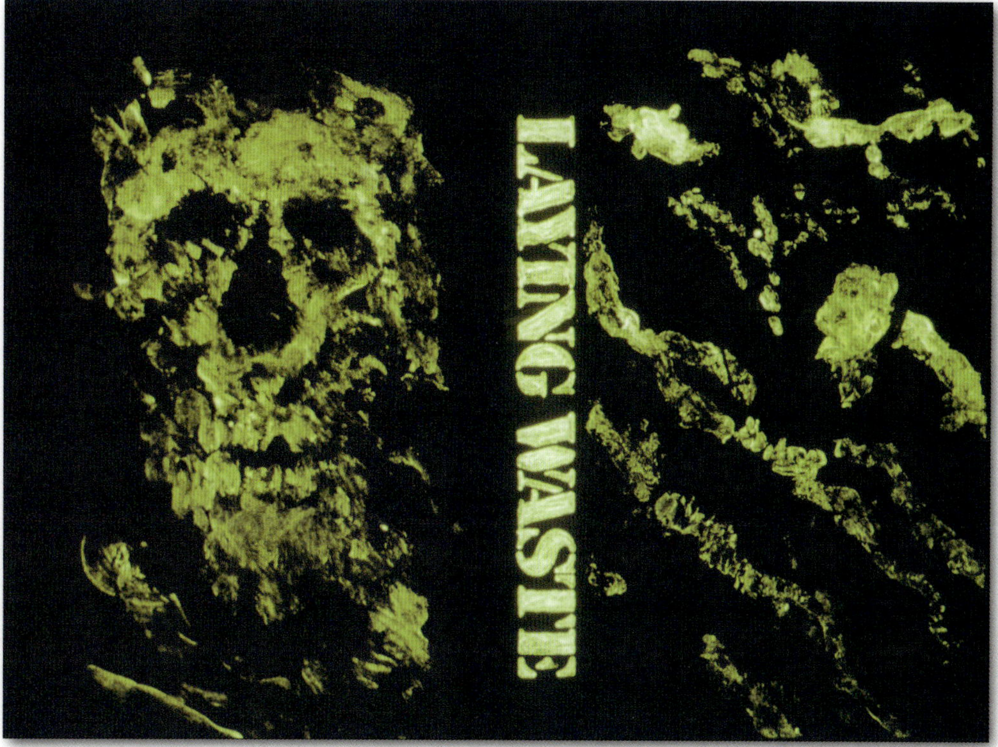

Laying Waste: The Poisoning of America by Toxic Chemicals
by Michael H. Brown. Pantheon, New York, 1980
Binding by Minsky, 1988. 8 x 5¾
Trade binding, with added hypodermic needle, crack caps, condom, collage (the artist's toxic lacquer thinner label), acrylic and phosphorescent paint. Photos above show the book in dim light and no light.

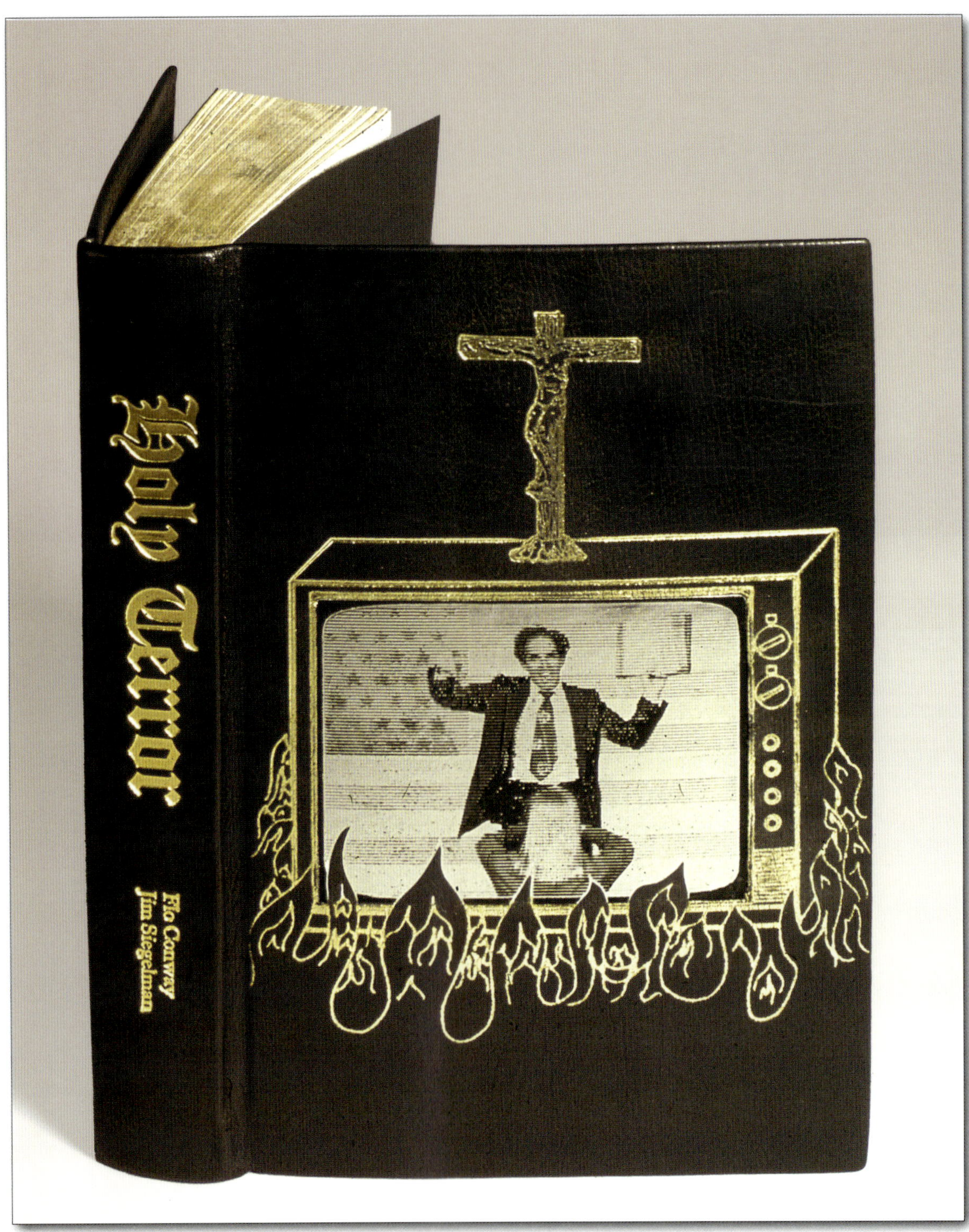

Holy Terror
The Fundamentalist War on America's Freedoms in Politics, Religion and Our Private Lives
by Flo Conway and Jim Siegelman. Doubleday, New York, 1982.
Binding by Minsky, 1988. 9 x 6
Nigerian goat and Hewit calf, gold and white metal foil hot stamping.
Collection of Clare Stone, New York

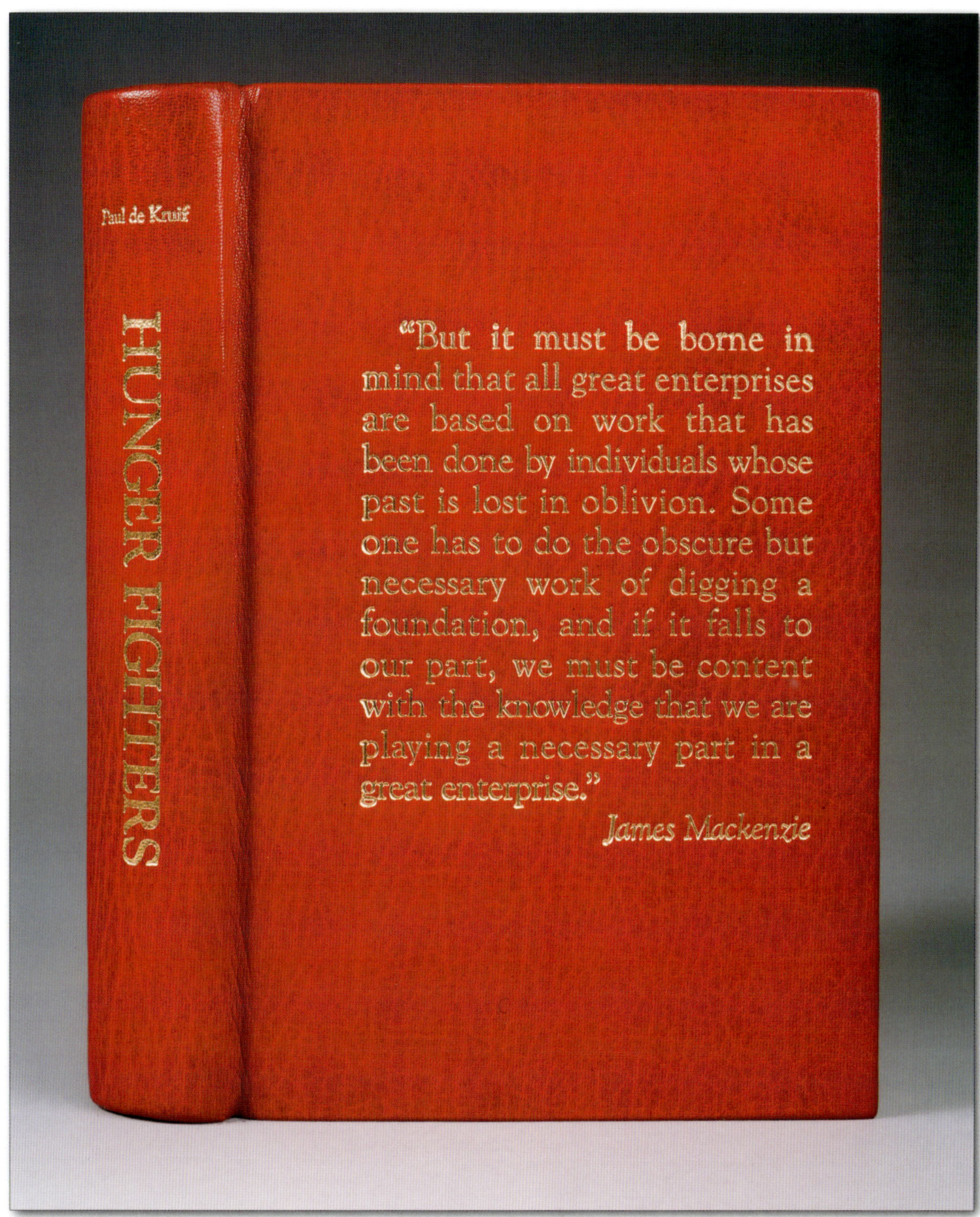

Hunger Fighters
by Paul de Kruif. Harcourt, Brace and Company, New York, 1928
Binding by Minsky, 1988. 9 x 6
Goatskin stamped in 23K gold.
Private Collection, New York

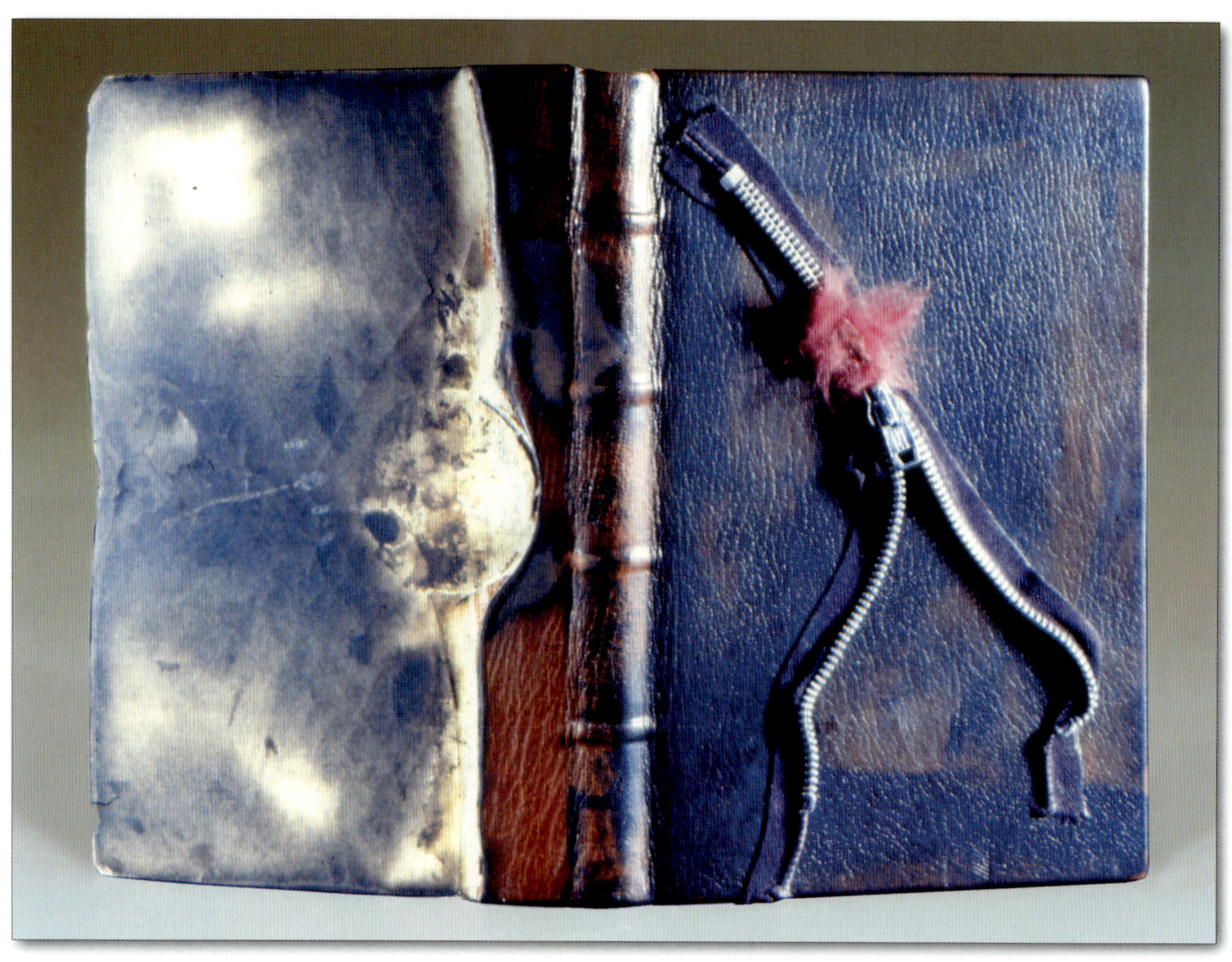

Achieving Ecstasy During the Apocalypse
Blank book, 1980. 9¼ x 6¾
Goatskin partially covering paper-lined binder's board,
zipper, pink fluff, leather dye, burned.

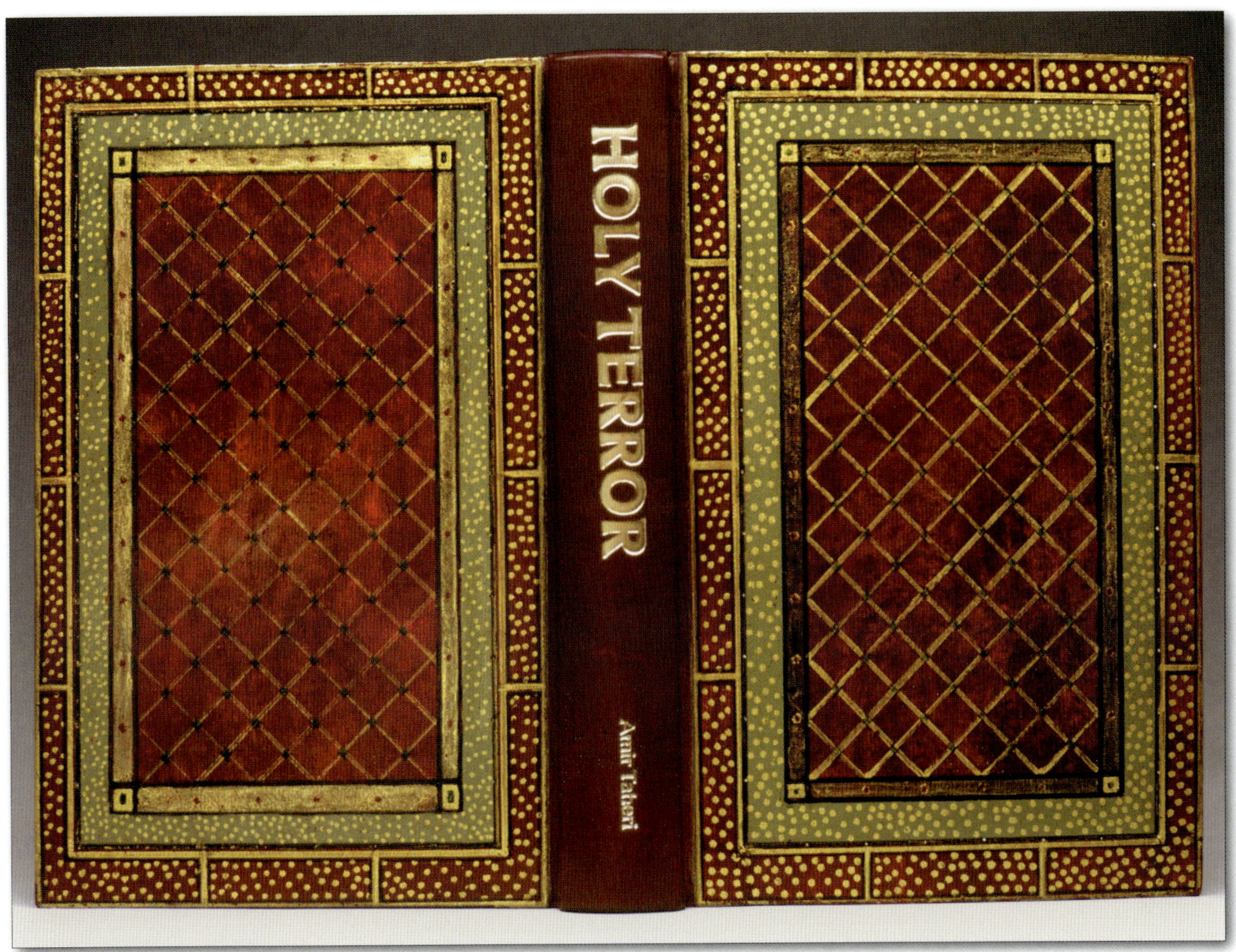

Holy Terror
Inside the World of Islamic Terrorism
by Amir Taheri. Adler & Adler, Bethesda, MD, 1987.
Binding by Minsky, 1990. 9 x 6
Quarter leather, gold stamped spine, lacquered acrylic on boards, flyleaf of gold stamped vellum.
Collection of Clare Stone, New York

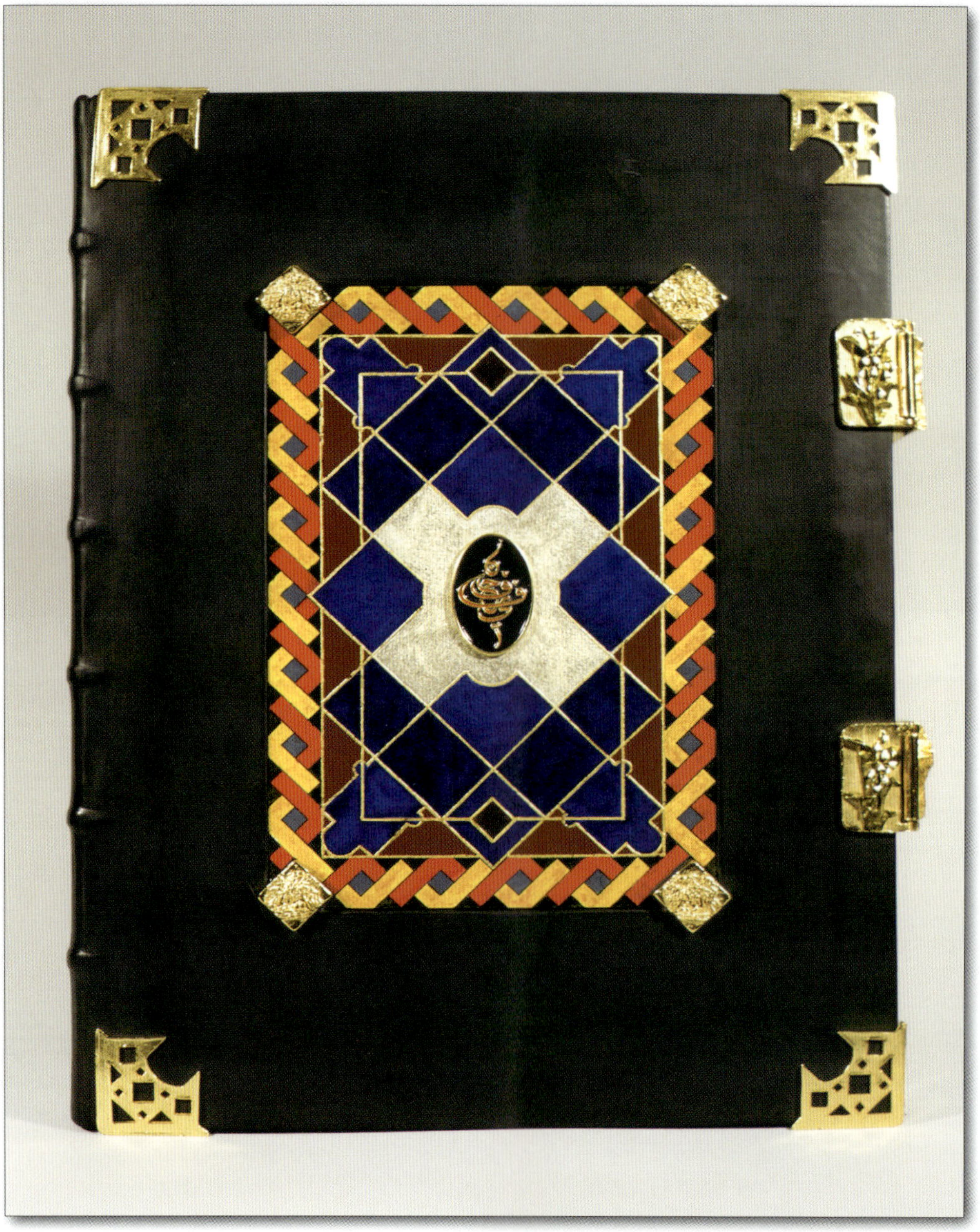

Chateau Guest Book
1994. 20 x 16
Blank book of various vintage handmade papers and sheepskin parchment. Green Hewit calf with inlaid panels of lacquered acrylic, gold leaf, and white gold leaf on Rives BFK. Lost wax cast 24K gold plated hardware includes central medallion filled with couleurs vitrail, bosses and clasps with heraldic emblems, and strapwork corners.
Private Collection, Normandy, France

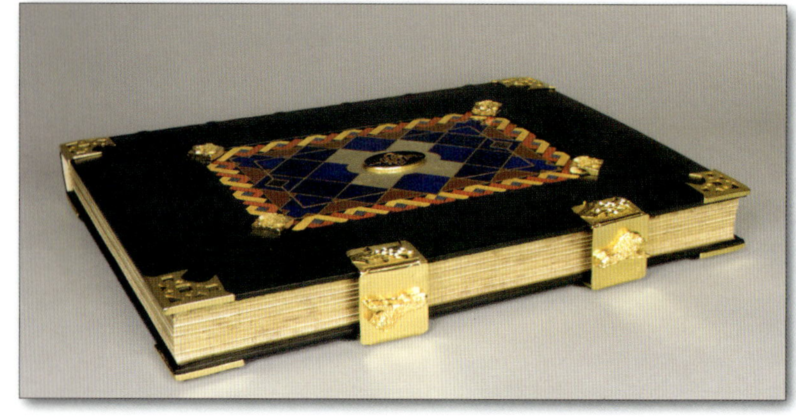

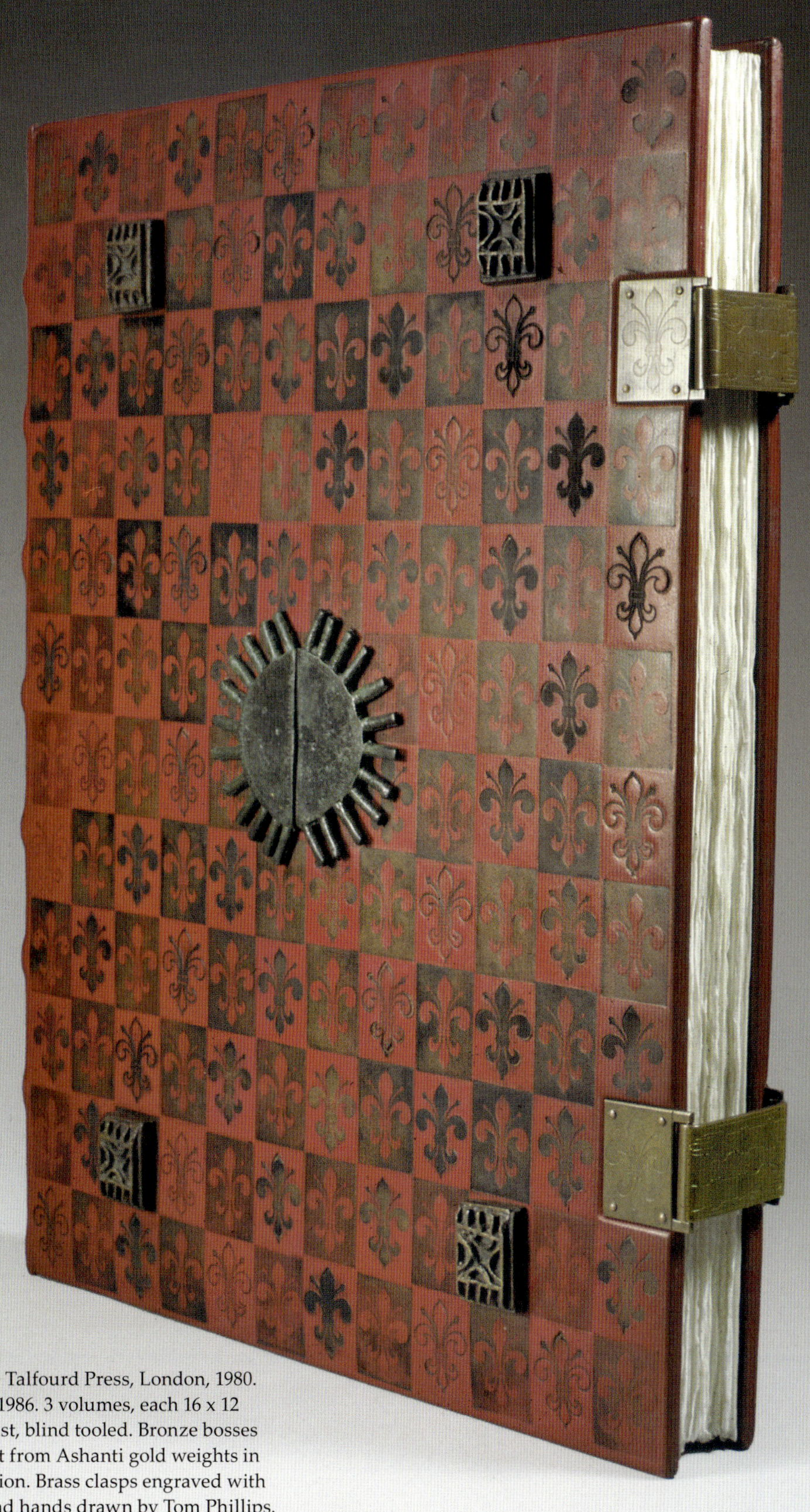

Dante's Inferno
by Tom Phillips. The Talfourd Press, London, 1980. Binding by Minsky, 1986. 3 volumes, each 16 x 12 Calf dyed by the artist, blind tooled. Bronze bosses and centerpieces cast from Ashanti gold weights in Tom Phillips' collection. Brass clasps engraved with the Florentine lily and hands drawn by Tom Phillips. Private Collection, New York

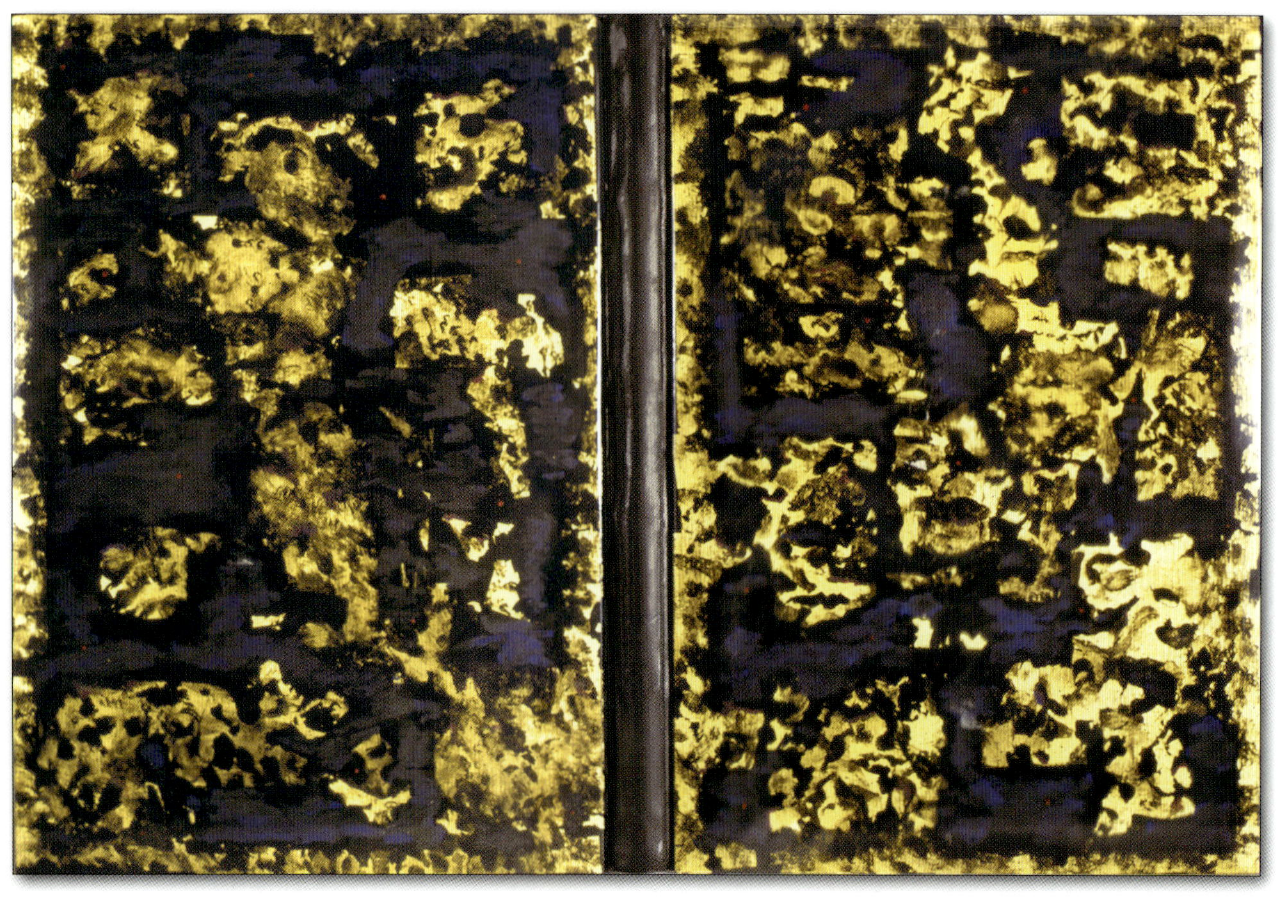

Blank Book
1986. 15 x 11
Black calf spine, lacquered gold leaf and enamel over gessoed boards. T.H. Saunders Paper
Collection of Clare Stone, New York

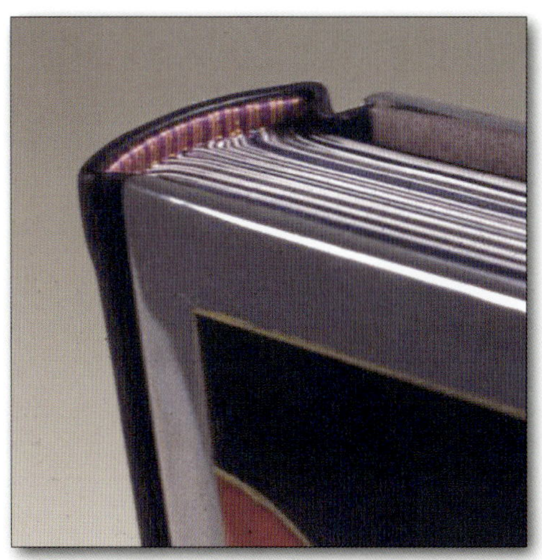

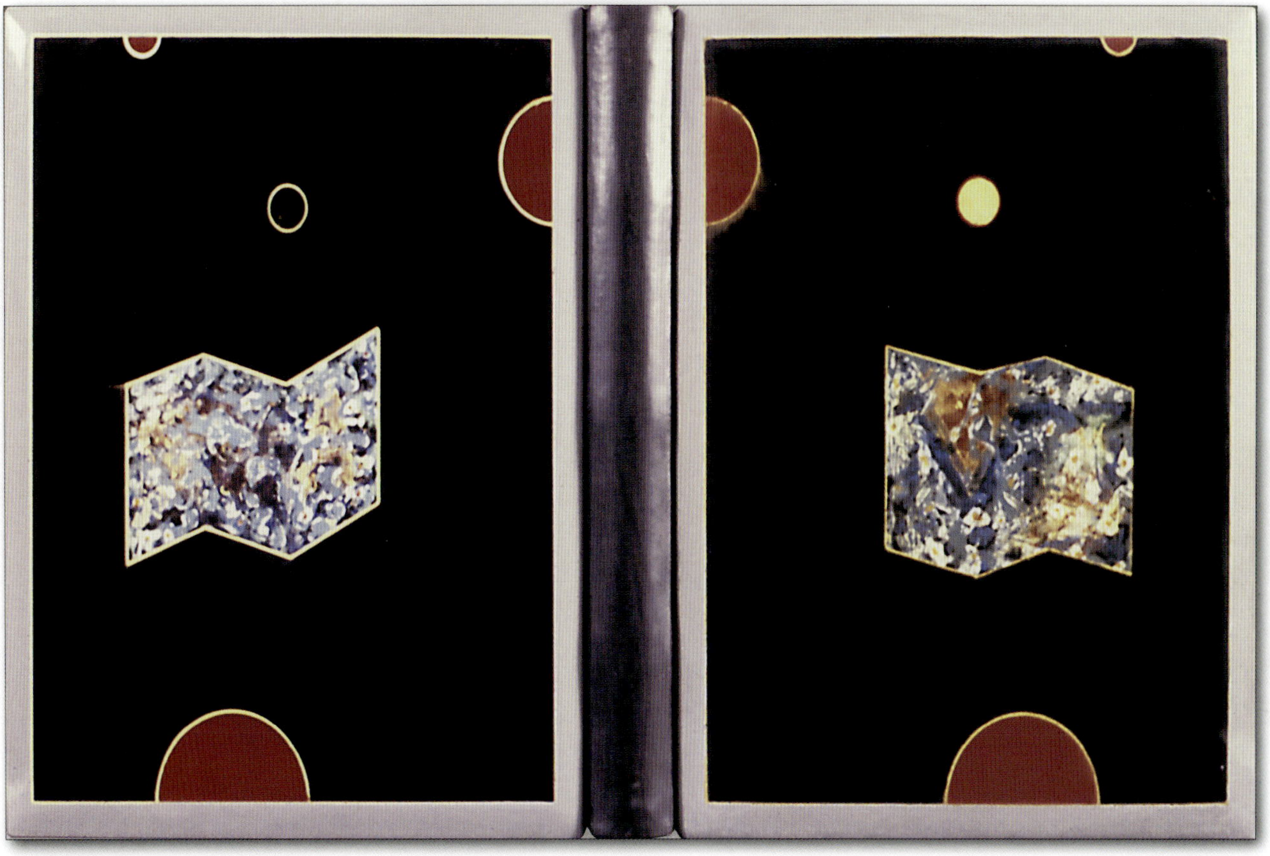

Blank Book
1985. 11 x 10
Grey goatskin spine, varnished enamel and gold leaf boards, acrylic and gold leaf endsheets, hand-sewn silk endbands [detail above].
Private Collection, New York

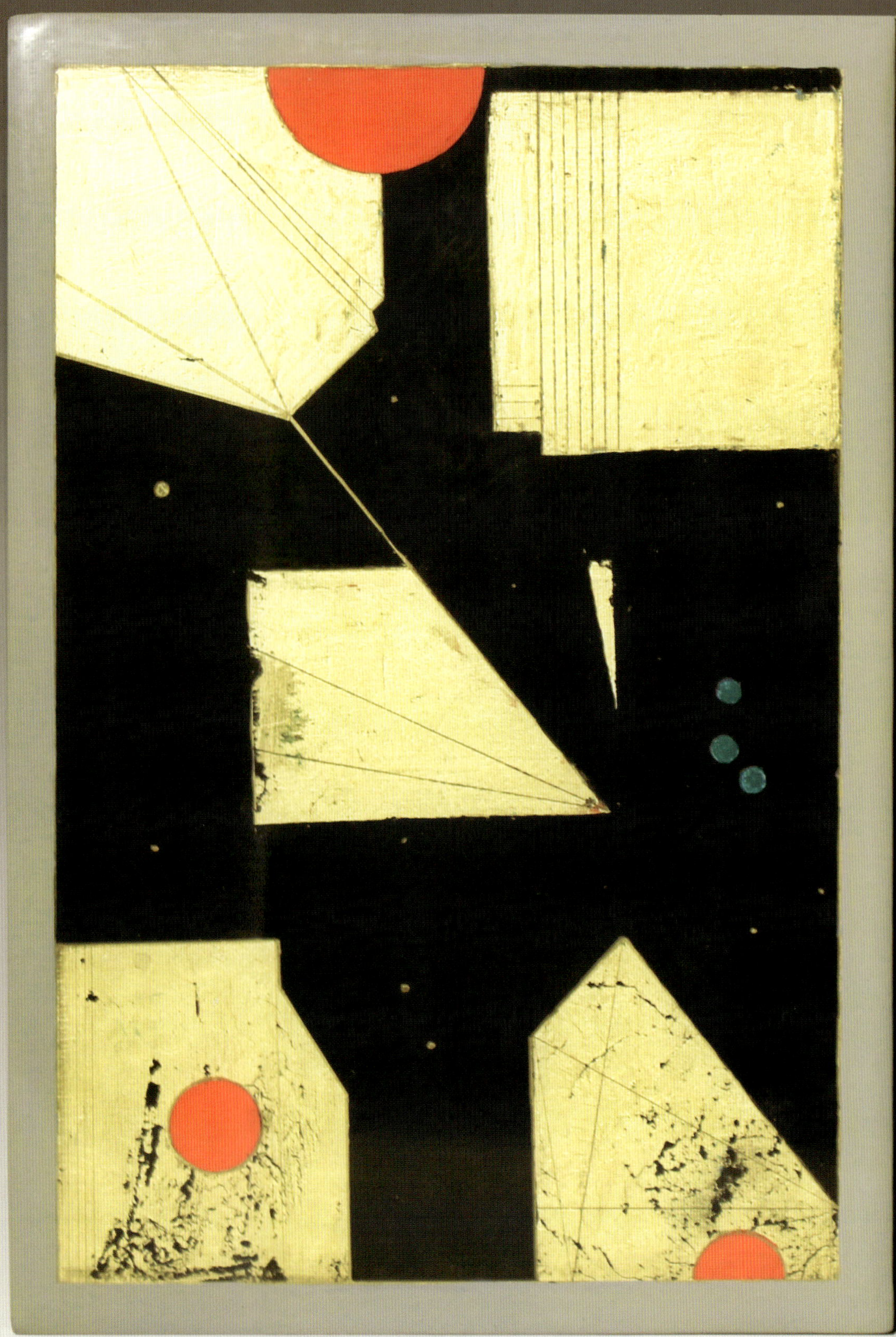

Blank Book
1985. 11 x 9
Goatskin spine, varnished enamel and gold leaf boards.
Private Collection, New York

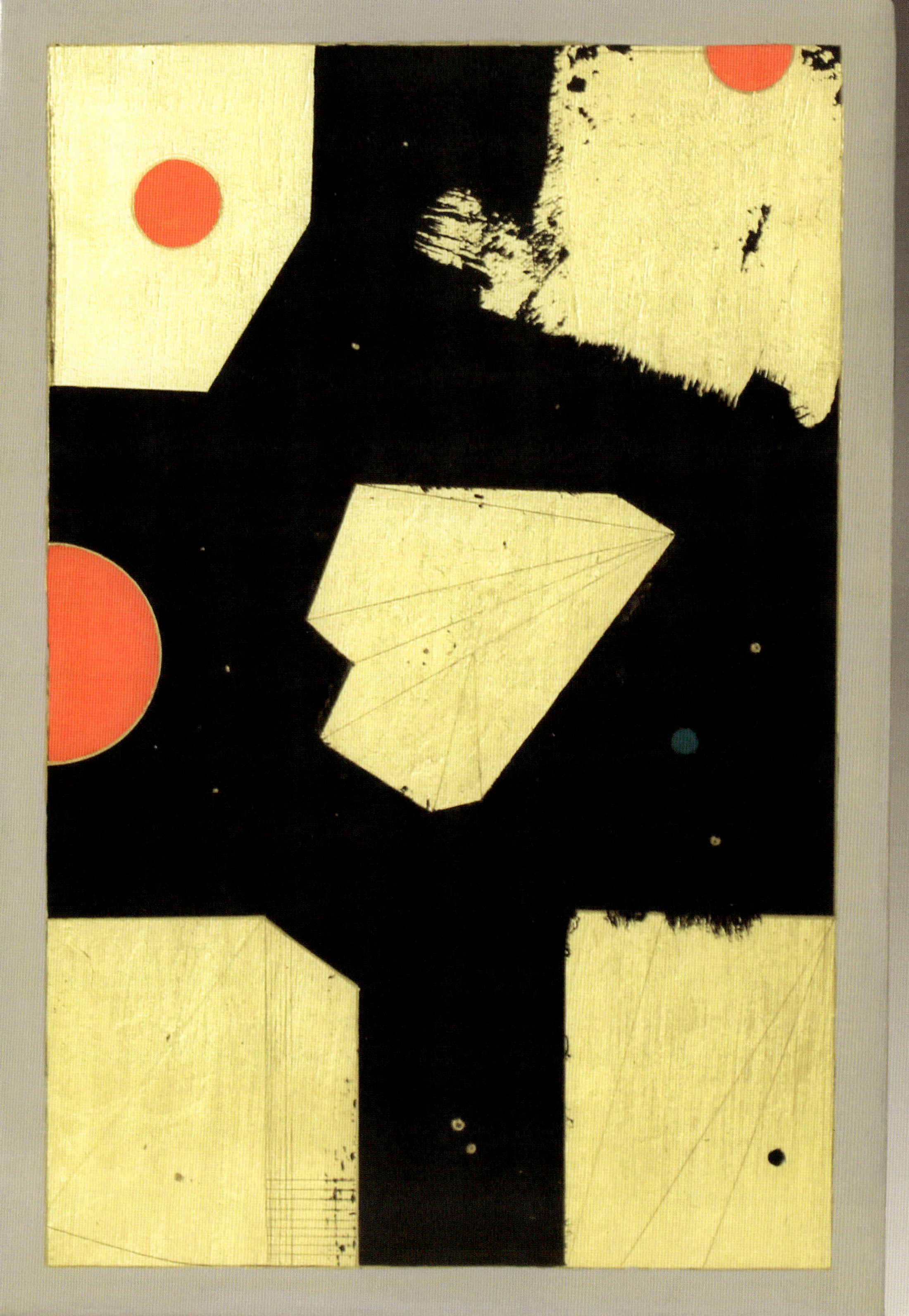

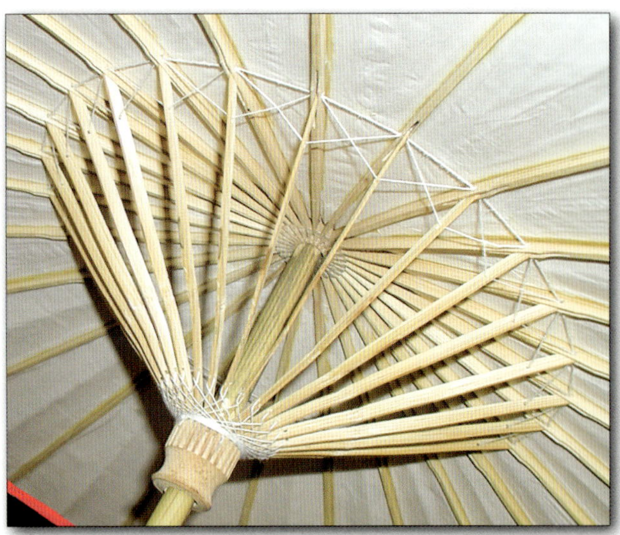

The Philosophy of Umbrellas

by Robert Louis Stevenson

THIS EDITION was created in 1968 while I was the von Hess Visiting Artist at the Borowsky Center for Publication Arts at the University of the Arts in Philadelphia, with master printer Lori Spencer running a Heidelberg KORS offset press.

It seemed like the perfect opportunity to make an edition in honor of Judith Hoffberg, Editor and Publisher of *Umbrella*, which celebrated its 30th anniversary that year as the main resource for information about contemporary artists' books, mail art and Fluxus.

The obvious form for this work would be an umbrella with a text, but what text? I asked Judith for a suggestion and she sent this essay by R. L. Stevenson (1850-1894).

The type is set in stanzas that form a spiral. When the umbrella is spun, the effect is hypnotic for the viewer. The pink color made by the text when spun stimulates the production of endorphins in the viewer, making them happy. Thus the umbrella itself is not the work of art. It is a tool for the performance of a happiness event.

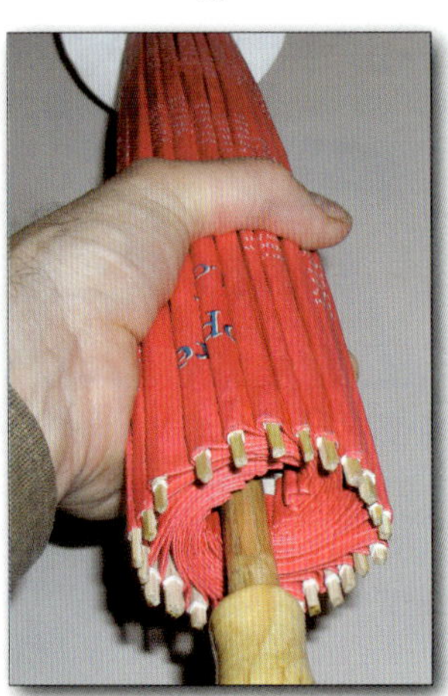

Judith was co-founder of the Art Libraries Society of North America (ARLIS/NA) in 1972. She died in 2009 and was honored at that year's annual conference. Her huge Umbrelliana collection is at the University of California San Diego, and her collection of artists' books is divided between UCLA and UCSB.

Edition of 100 copies printed on DuPont™ Tyvek® includes a cylindrical slipcase printed with the Preface.

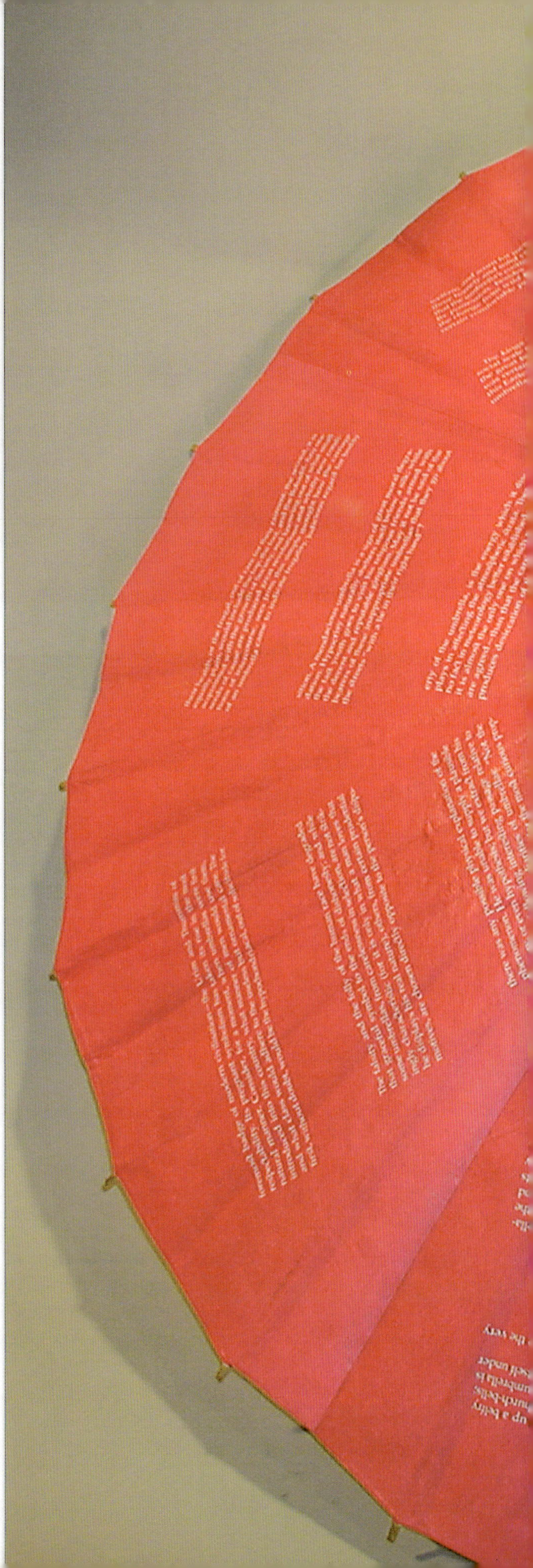

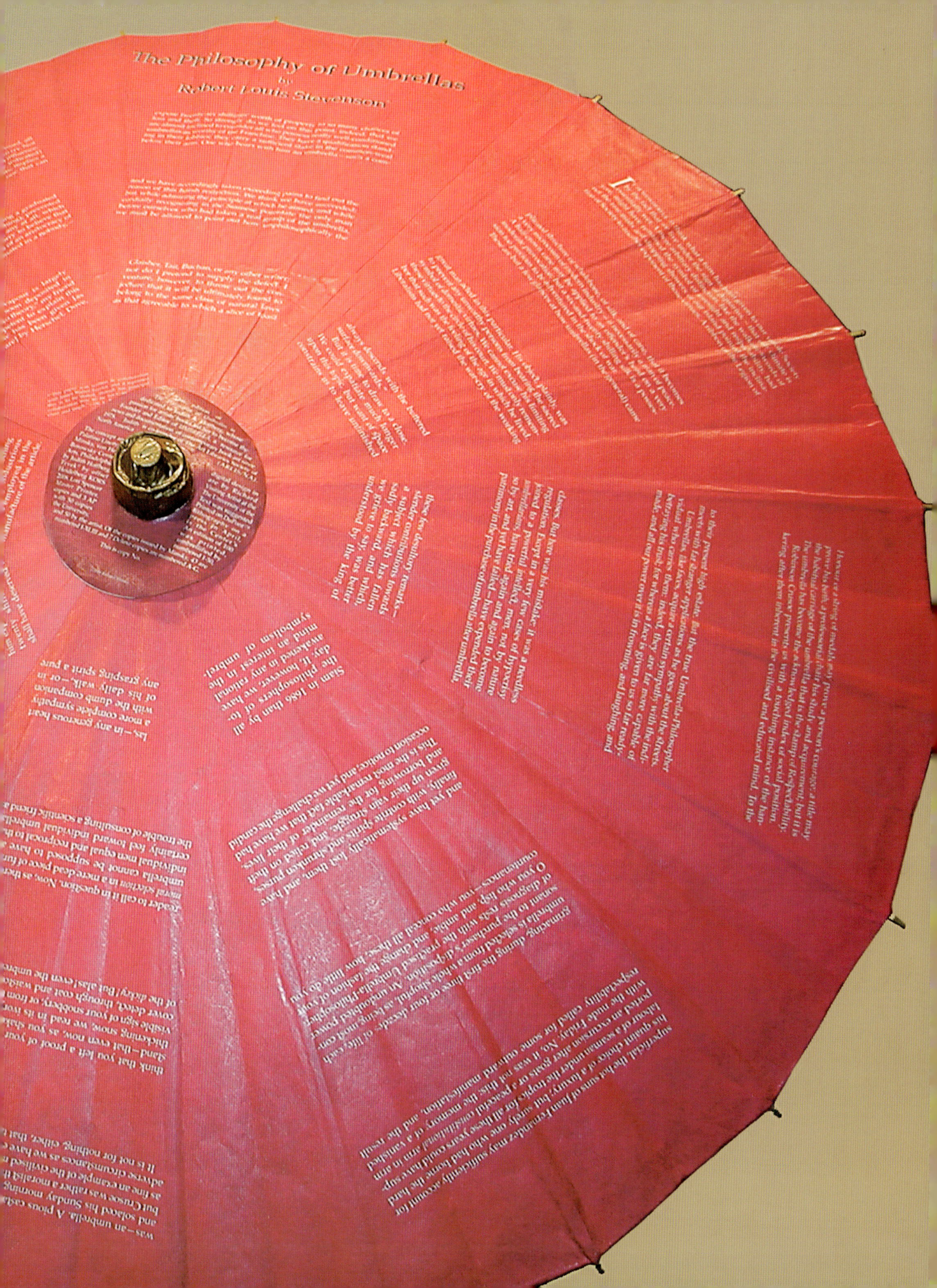
The Philosophy of Umbrellas
by
Robert Louis Stevenson

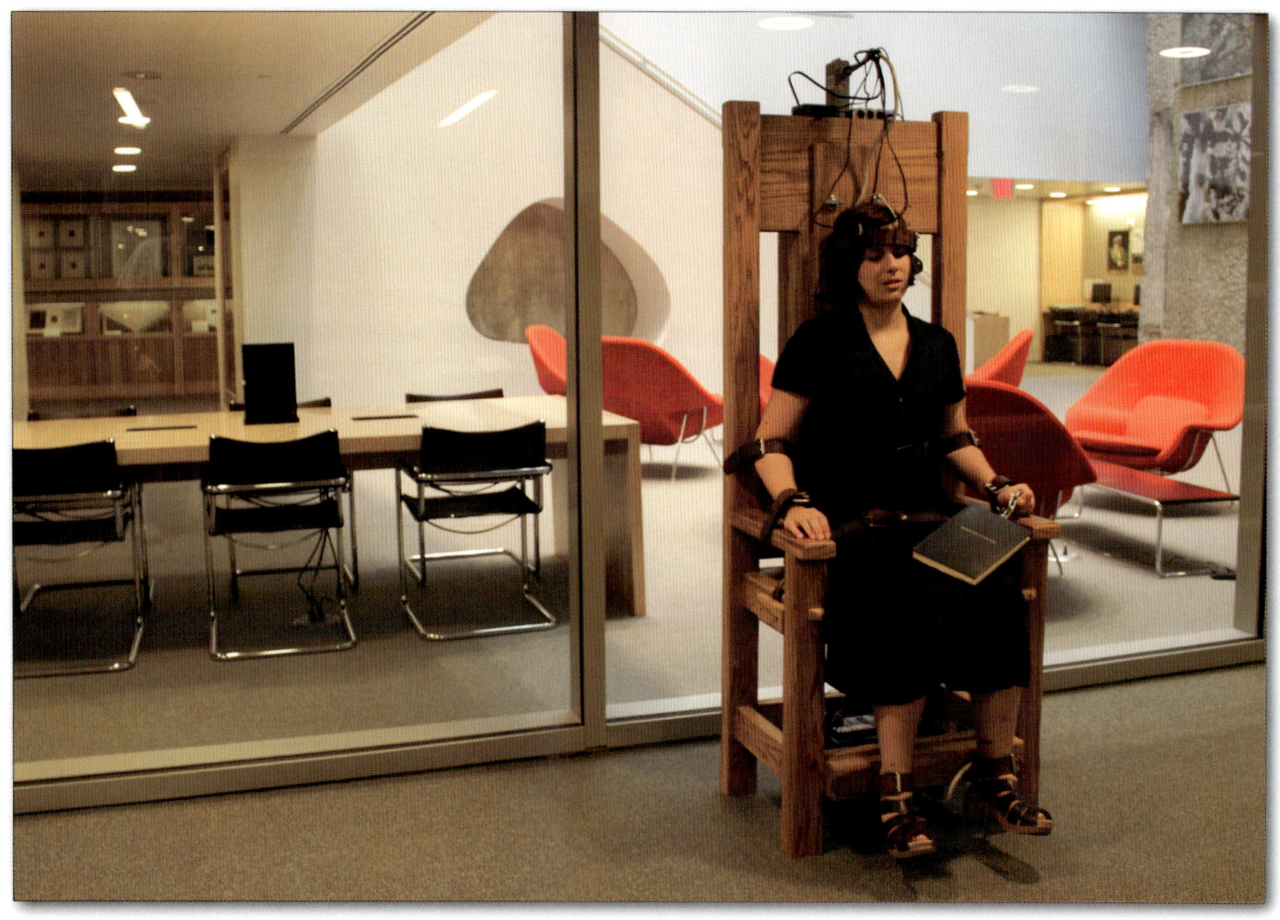

Installation at the Robert B. Haas Family Arts Library, Yale University, 2010. Strapped in the chair is Jae Rossman, Assistant Director for Special Collections and Curator of the exhibition *Material Meets Metaphor: A Half Century of Book Art by Richard Minsky.*

Freedom of Choice

Choose your death

"This work by Minsky pushes his 'material meets metaphor' philosophy to the extreme. *Freedom of Choice* permits the reader to engage his/her full body in the reading experience.

He created it for the exhibition *Somewhere Far From Habit: The Poet and the Artist's Book* sponsored by Longwood University.

For the full experience, the reader can strap on the head restraint with three electrodes, applying one electrode to the leg. An MP3 player on the head restraint plays Minsky's reading of the three poems, two of which concern shotgun suicides and one, an electrocution."

Jae Rossman
in the catalog of the 2010 Yale exhibition [see photo above]

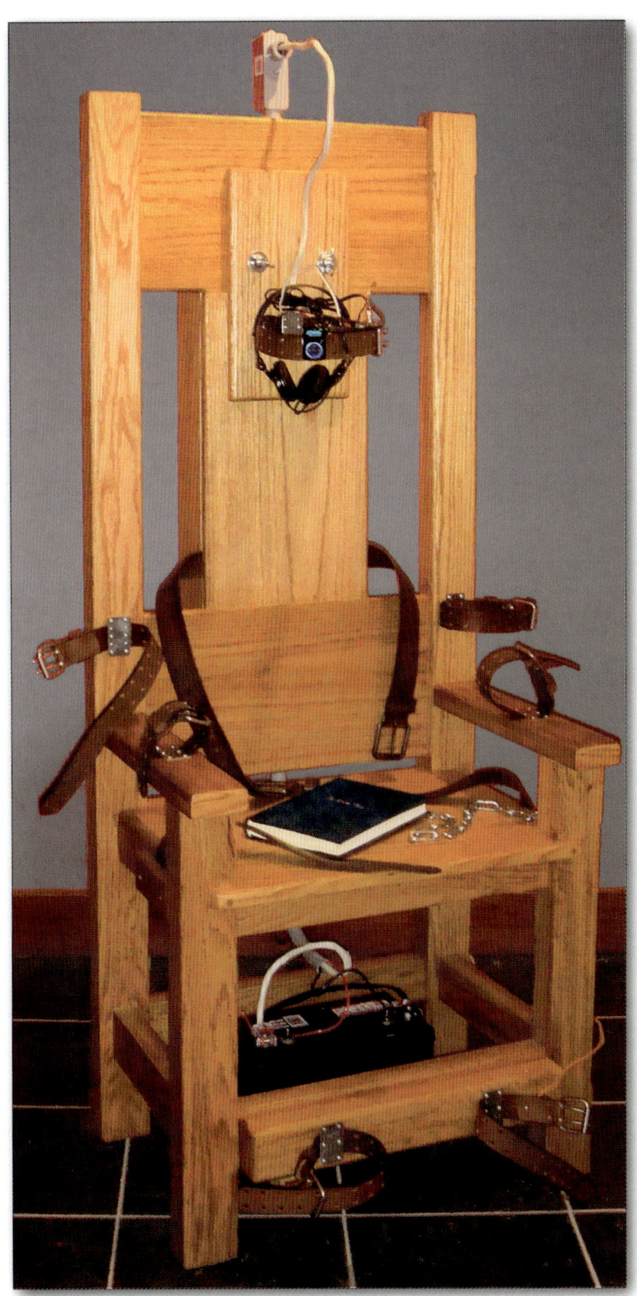
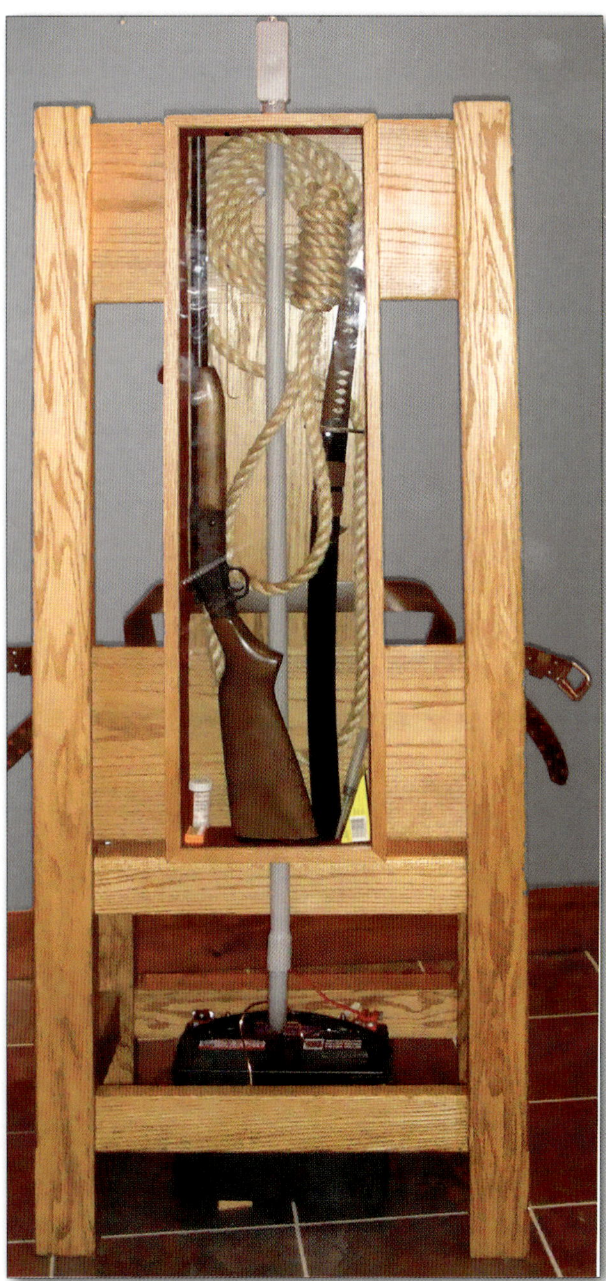

Freedom of Choice
Three Poems of Love and Death by Lucie Brock-Broido
Richard Minsky, Stockport, NY, 2009.
Edition of 5, printed inkjet on J. Barcham Green 1976 handmade paper. Copy No. 1 [above] is bound in dark teal goatskin with 23K gold title, chained to an oak electric chair built by Minsky. 73 x 26 x 24
On the back of the chair is a cabinet containing a 20 gauge shotgun, a Manila hangman's noose, a wakizashi sword, razor blades, poison and a hypodermic syringe.
Copies numbered 2 to 5 are bound in limp leather with gold title, no chair.

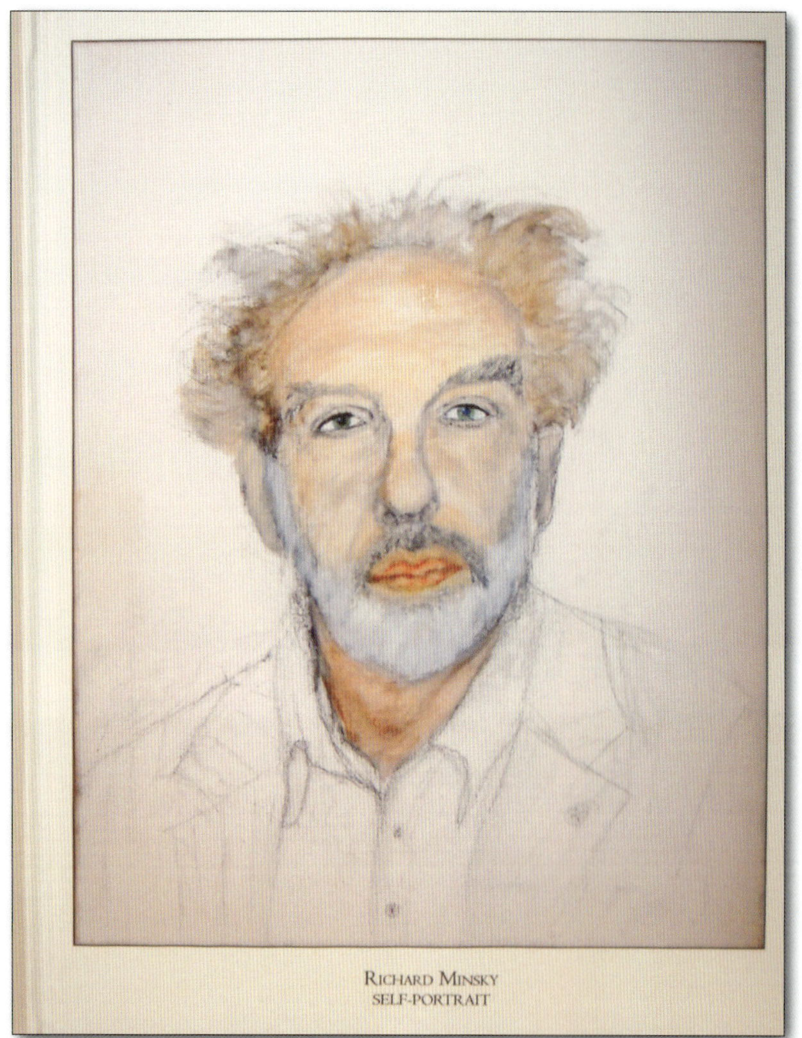

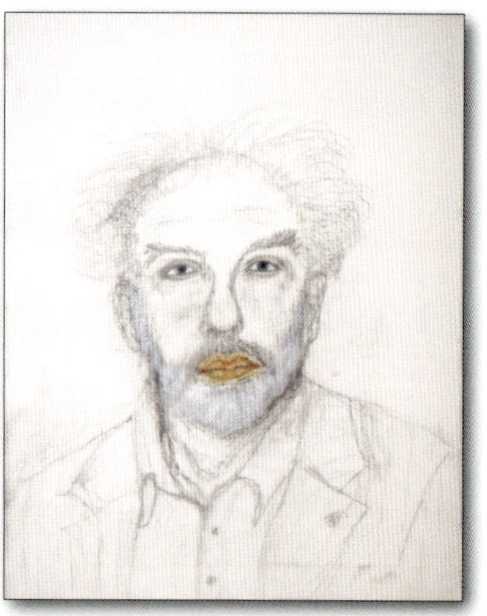

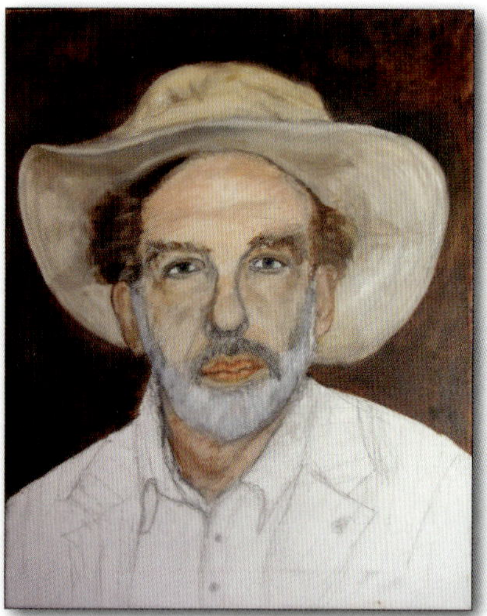

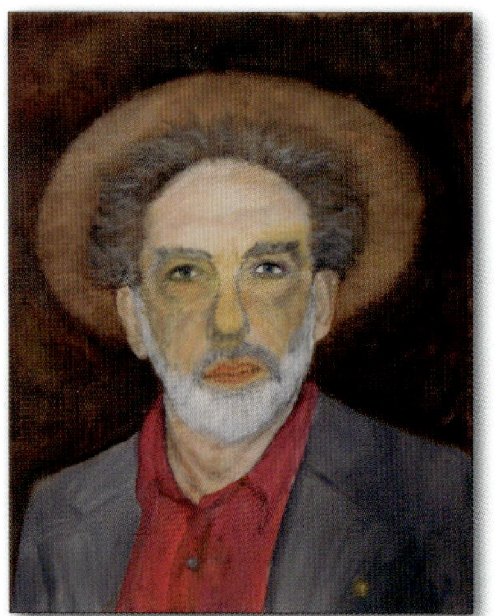

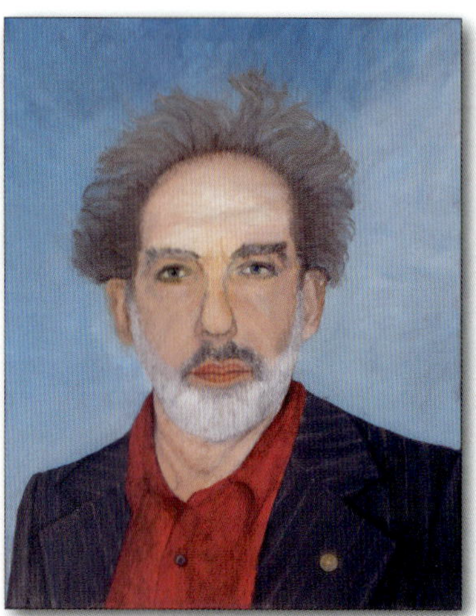

Self-Portrait
Richard Minsky, Stockport, NY, 2010.
Editions of 25 copies 9 x 6
and five copies 12 x 9.
Inkjet on paper, cover of inkjet on canvas.
Snapshots of the evolution of a 16x20 oil painting on canvas from the first pencil sketch. This book, and not the painting, was exhibited in "Local Self-Portraits" at the Hudson Opera House, Hudson, NY, June 12–August 14, 2010.

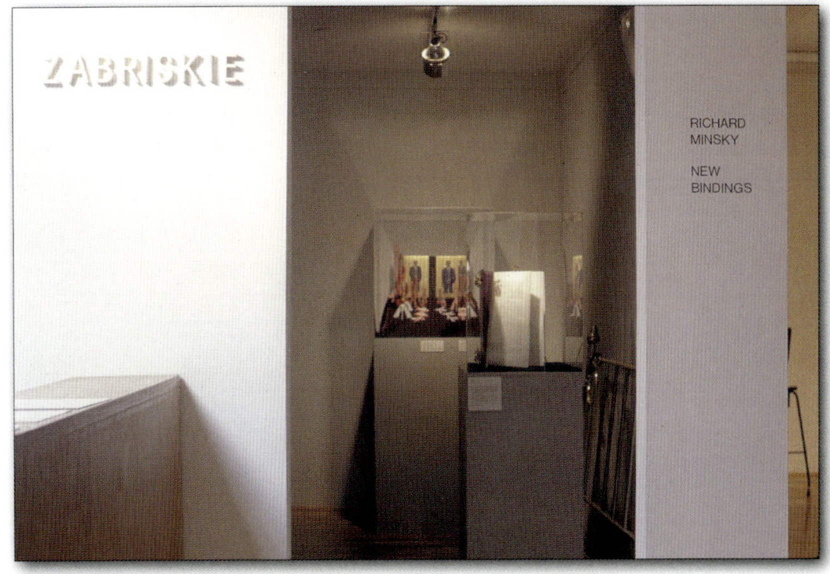

Exhibition at the Zabriskie Gallery, New York, 1988 [see p. 112]

Exhibitions

2010	Yale University, Robert B. Haas Family Arts Library
2005	Syracuse University Library, Syracuse, NY
2003	Minnesota Center for Book Arts, Minneapolis, MN
2002	Oberlin College Library, Ohio
	Louis K. Meisel Gallery, New York
1992	HarperCollins Gallery, New York (25 year retrospective)
1990	Twining Gallery, New York
1988	Zabriskie Gallery, New York
1981	Allan Stone Gallery, New York
1978	San Francisco Museum of Modern Art, CA
1976	92nd Street YM-YWHA, New York
1974	Zabriskie Gallery, New York
1972	AIGA Gallery, New York [Guild of Book Workers]

Group Shows

2010	*Local Self-Portraits.* Hudson Opera House, Hudson, NY
	Somewhere Far From Habit. Longwood Center for Visual Arts, Farmville, VA
2009	*Somewhere Far From Habit.* Pierre Menard Gallery, Cambridge, MA
2004	*What's in a Book?* Katonah Museum of Art, Katonah, NY
	The Book at the Back of the Mind. Rutgers University, Newark, NJ
2003	*Beyond Reading: Contemporary Book Art.* The Ellipse Art Center, Arlington, VA
	Love and/or Terror. University of Arizona Museum of Art, Tucson
	Visual Poetics: Art and the Word. Miami Art Museum, Miami, FL
2001	*Not for Publication: In the Spirit of the Book.* Hillwood Museum, Long Island University, NY
1999	*Legible Forms.* Contemporary Art Center of Virginia, Virginia Beach, VA
1998	*Legible Forms.* Chicago Public Library, Chicago, IL and Sheldon Memorial Art Galllery, Lincoln, NE
1997	*Inside Editions: A Literature of Punishment.* The Grolier Club, NYC, NY
	Legible Forms. Hand Workshop Art Center, Richmond, VA

1996 *Love.* Arlene Bujese Gallery, East Hampton, NY
The Alternative Page. The Gallery at Hastings on Hudson, NY
1995 *Redefining The Book.* Braunstein/Quay Gallery, San Francisco, CA
This Day in History. Center for Book Arts, New York
1994 *Waking The Book.* Rutgers University, New Brunswick, NJ
1993 *Not By The Book.* Pelham Art Center, Pelham, NY
Artists' Books & Art About Books. Pratt Manhattan Gallery, NY
Paper-The Essential Material. HarperCollins Gallery, NY
1992 *Completing the Circle: Artists' Books On the Environment.*
Minnesota Center for Book Arts, Minneapolis, MN and four other venues
1991 *Books as Art.* Boca Raton Museum of Art, FL
Objects of My Affection. Elaine Benson Gallery, Bridgehampton, NY
The Regilded Age. The Newark Museum, NJ
Creatures. Elaine Benson Gallery, Bridgehampton, NY
Dieu Donné Papermill: 15 Years. Center for Book Arts, NY
New Surrealism. New Jersey Center for Visual Arts, Summit, NJ
1990 *Prints of the Eighties.* Pratt Manhattan Gallery, NYC and Guild Hall Museum, East Hampton, NY
1989 *2e Forum International de la Reliure d'Art.* Basel, CH
In the Craft Tradition. Guild Hall Museum, East Hampton, NY
Handmade Paperworks. Aaron Gallery, Washington, DC
The Eloquent Object. Virginia Museum of Fine Arts and The Orlando Museum of Art, FL
Obsessions. Elaine Benson Gallery, Bridgehampton, NY
1988 *The Arts of the Book.* Rosenwald-Wolf Gallery, Philadelphia, PA
The Eloquent Object. The Oakland Museum, CA, Museum of Fine Arts, Boston,
and Chicago Public Library Cultural Center
Book Making: Practical and Provocative. Painted Bride, Phila., PA
Invitational Exhibition. Benton Gallery, Southampton, NY
Contemporary Book Arts. U. North Dakota, Grand Forks, ND
Off the Shelf: A New Look at Book Art. Fort Wayne Museum of Art and Sweet Briar College, VA
1987 *The Eloquent Object.* Philbrook Museum, Tulsa, OK
The Masters II. Long Island University, Southampton, NY
A Survey of Book Arts. The Queens Museum, Flushing, NY
1986 *Bookworks by Photographers.* Watson Library, Metropolitan Museum of Art, NY
1985 *Books as Sculpture.* Rutgers University, Newark, NJ
1984 *The First Decade: Center for Book Arts.* New York Public Library, NYC, NY
Ordinary And Extraordinary Uses: Objects By Artists. Guild Hall Museum, East Hampton, NY
1981 *The Birthday Party.* Oregon School of Arts and Crafts, Portland, OR
1980 *The Naked Book.* BACA Downtown Cultural Center, Brooklyn, NY
1979 *The Open and Closed Book.* Victoria and Albert Museum, London
1978 *The Book as Art.* Dayton Arts Institute, Dayton, Ohio
1977 *Crafts in The White House.* Los Angeles Museum of Craft and Folk Art
The Object as Poet. Renwick Gallery, Washington, DC and Museum of Contemporary Crafts, NY
1976 *The Center for Book Arts.* New City Free Library, New City, NY
and Larchmont Public Library, Larchmont, NY
1975 *The Book as Art.* Fendrick Gallery, Washington, DC
The Center for Book Arts. Creative Arts Workshop, New Haven, CT
Guild of Bookworkers. New York Botanical Gardens Museum and Yale University, New Haven, CT
1968 *Students of Daniel Gibson Knowlton.* Rogers Free Library, Bristol, RI

Exhibitions Curated

2003 *Open for Action: Political Book Art* [with Sharon Gilbert] Center for Book Arts, NYC

1994 *Out of Bounds* Creative Arts Workshop, New Haven, CT

1990 *Book Arts in the USA* Center for Book Arts, NYC, five venues in Africa, four in South America

1987 *The Effects of Time* [with Leonard Hansen] Center for Book Arts, NYC

The Bookworks of Tom Phillips Center for Book Arts, NYC

1985 *Book Artchitecture* T J Watson Library, Metropolitan Museum of Art

Publications

The Art of American Book Covers 1975-1930 by Richard Minsky. George Braziller, Inc. 2010.

Artist's books and limited editions published by Minsky

Material Meets Metaphor: A Half Century of Book Art by Richard Minsky [Yale exhibition catalog], 2010

Self-Portrait 2010 by Richard Minsky, 2010

American Decorated Publishers' Bindings 1872–1929 by Richard Minsky, 2006; vol. 2, 2009; vol. 3, 2010

The Philosophy of Umbrellas by Robert Louis Stevenson [with The University of the Arts, Philadelphia], 2008

Essential Liberty by Richard Minsky, 2005

The Bill of Rights [limited edition set] by Richard Minsky, 2002

Branches by Mitch Cullin, illustrated by Ryuzo Kikushima [with The Permanent Press, Sag Harbor], 2000

Minsky in Bed by Richard Minsky, 1996

Minsky's Animal Magnetism by Richard Minsky, 1993

Anathema Maranatha by Jonathan Williams, pictures by Bill Anthony, 1992

32 Studies by Richard Minsky, 1991

The First Time I Thought About Suicide But Didn't [broadside] by John Paul Lee, illustration by Robert Garey, 1991

Dreaming The Caves by Rose Slivka, laser prints from watercolors by Elaine de Kooning, 1991

Where Are They Now? (The Class of Forty-Seven) by Tom Phillips and Heather McHugh, 1990

Immortal Dreamers by Kathy Fire, 1982

Minsky in London by Richard Minsky, edited by Pamela Moore, 1980

Adventures In Ku-ta-ba Wa-do by Gerald Jackson, music by Richard Minsky, 1973

Bibliography

"Beauty and the Book" by Rebecca Rego Barry, Review in *Fine Books & Collections* April 2010

"The Breathtaking Book Art of Richard Minsky" by Stephen J. Gertz, *Booktryst* [blog] August 2, 2010

"It's About Art" by Scott Brown, *Fine Books & Collections* March/April 2007

No Longer Innocent: Book Art in America 1960-1980 by Betty Bright, Granary Books, 2005

"Making Books Speak: Book Art and Politics" by Richard Minsky, *International Gallerie*, Issue 18, 2006

"Richard Minsky" by Scott Brown, *Fine Books & Collections* March/April 2005

"Profile: Richard Minsky" *Bound and Lettered* vol 4,#2, April 2005

"Bookbinding as Art" *Stars* Magazine [*The Post-Standard*, Syracuse, NY] Sunday Feb. 20, 2005

"'The Bill of Rights' Exhibition Comes to Bird Library" *Syracuse Record*, Feb. 14, 2005

"Arts Library acquires the archive of pioneering book artist Richard Minsky" *Yale Bulletin & Calendar*, Dec. 17, 2004

"'Bill of Rights' bookworks bound to be provocative" by Thomas O'Sullivan, *St. Paul Pioneer Press*, April 5, 2003

"Artist Depicts the Bill of Rights in a World Out of Joint" by Ralph Blumenthal, *The New York Times*, May 20, 2002

"An Interview With Mr. Richard Minsky: Professional and Academic Perspectives of Book Art" *ArtSchools.com*, August 6, 2001.

"Nouvelles du front: les derniers travaux de Richard Minsky" par Joëlle Naîm, *Art & Métiers du Livre*, Jan-Feb 1998

"Richard Minsky" by Caroline Seebohm. *At Home With Books*, Clarkson Potter, 1995.

"A Time for Judging a Book by Its Cover" by Betty Freudenheim. *The New York Times*, July 3, 1994

"What Is a Book? Perusing Some Unusual Ideas" by Bess Liebenson, *The New York Times*, June 5,1994

"Don't write off fascinating show at Arts Workshop" by Judy Birke. *New Haven Register*, June 5, 1994
"Finishing Books" by Janice Friedman. *Bostonia*, Winter 1992-93
"Madonna's 'Sex' Binding" *A Current Affair*, FOX-TV, Oct. 21, 1992
"Naked Came the Bookbinder" by Lisa Interollo. *Avenue* Magazine, Summer 1992
"August Blues" by Ellen Keiser. *Dan's Papers*, August 21, 1992
"Richard Minsky/HarperCollins Publishers Gallery" photo in *American Craft*, June/July 1992
"Richard Minsky" by Jeanne Moos. CNN-TV, May 8, 1992
"Art Pick: Judging by Their Covers" by Catherine Drillis. *Manhattan Spirit*, April 21, 1992
"Traditions in a Bind"by Jerry Tallmer. *New York Post*, April 24, 1992
"From the Studio" by Rose C.S. Slivka. *The East Hampton Star*, April 9, 1992
"New Medium for an Urgent Message" by Mary Ann Grossman. *Saint Paul Pioneer Press*, March 1, 1992
"Books Cast as Artworks in Exhibit" by Gary Schwan. *The Palm Beach Post*, August 25, 1991
"Minsky in Bed" *East Hampton Star*, August 2, 1990
"Wordless Art of Bookmaking" by Jerry Tallmer. *New York Post*, April 27, 1990
"Bookbinder on a Cabin Cruiser" by Eric Wald. *Dan's Papers*, Aug. 18, 1989
"Richard Minsky" *Art & Metiers du Livre*, Oct/Nov, 1988
"Richard Minsky" *Arts* Magazine, May 1988
"Books as Art" by Darrel Koehler. *Grand Forks Herald*. March 25, 1988
"Faculty Show: Ranqe of Ideas" by Phyllis Braff. *NY Times*, Sept. 6, 1987
"On Art" by Amei Wallach. *Newsday*, August 21, 1987
"Alternate Autos" *Craft International*, April-June 1987
"Bound to Please" *Smart Living*, Feb 1985
"The Book Transformed" *ID Magazine/International Design*, Jan/Feb 1985
"Reading Matter With a Difference" *New York Times*, Sept. 7, 1984
"Art in Bondage" *Art & Antiques*, June 1984
"Ars Gratia Artist" *Money*, June 1984
"Art for Debt's Sake" *Newsday*, March 29, 1984
"New Company Issues a Debenture That's Secured by a Picture Frame" *The Wall Street Journal*, March 26, 1984
"Richard Minsky" photo in *The Athens Observer* (GA), Feb 11, 1982
"Richard Minsky" Review in *Craft International*, Summer 1981
"From Neo-Conceptual to Bodies" Review in *Artspeak* III,19, May 21, 1981
"Minsky in London" Review in *Artforum*, January 1981
"American Book Artist at Large" *Crafts* (London) February 1979
"Book of the Century" *Craft Horizons*, October 1977
"The Decade: Change and Continuity" *Craft Horizons*, June 1976
"Richard Minsky" Review in *Arts* magazine, October 1974
"Richard Minsky" *People Who Make Things* by Carolyn Meyer. Athenaeum, 1975
"You Can Always Tell a Bookbinder by His Cover" *Acquire*, December 1973
"Vanishing Breed" by Rita A. Black. *Book Production Industry*, April 1973
"Richard Minsky" by Rolland Smith. WCBS-TV *6 O'clock News*, May 17, 1972
"Another Chapter In Ancient Art of Binding" by Philip H. Dougherty. *The New York Times*, May 28, 1972
"Art Scene Comes to Queens" by Milton Adams. *New York Post*, May 16, 1972

COLLECTIONS WITH UNIQUE MINSKY WORKS OR LIMITED EDITIONS

The Sackner Archive of Concrete and Visual Poetry, Miami, FL
Allan Stone Gallery, New York
The Brooklyn Museum, Brooklyn, NY
Metropolitan Museum of Art, New York
National Gallery of Art, Washington, DC
Library and Museum of the Performing Arts, New York
The New York Public Library Rare Book Room
Joseph H. Hirshhorn Museum, Washington, DC
The White House
Gracie Mansion, New York
Center for Book Arts, New York
Los Angeles Museum Of Craft and Folk Art
University of Alabama, Tuscaloosa, AL
Yale University, New Haven, CT
University of Rochester, Rochester, NY
Indiana University, Bloomington, IN
Oberlin College, Oberlin, OH
Washington University, St. Louis, MO
Fales Library, New York University, New York City, NY
Amherst College, Amherst, MA
Minneapolis Institute of Arts, MN
Nelson-Atkins Museum of Art, Kansas City, MO
Honnold/Mudd Library, Claremont, CA
University of California, Davis, CA
Princeton University, Princeton, NJ
University of Idaho, Moscow, ID
Arizona State University, Tempe, AZ
Reed College, Portland, OR
The Morgan Library & Museum, New York City, NY
University of Michigan, Ann Arbor, MI
University of Wisconsin, Madison WI
Pennsylvania State University, University Park, PA
McGill University, Montreal, Quebec Canada
North Carolina State University, Raleigh, NC
Michigan State University, East Lansing, MI
The Grolier Club, New York City
The University of Chicago, Chicago, IL
Nelson-Atkins Museum of Art, Kansas City, MO
FSU/Ringlng Museum of Art, Sarasota,FL
Winterthur Museum, Winterthur, DE
California State Library, Sacramento, CA
University of Alberta, Edmonton, Alberta, Canada
Columbia College Chicago, Chicago, IL
University of California, Los Angeles, CA
University of Minnesota, Minneapolis, MN
University of Central Florida, Orlando, FL
Victoria & Albert Museum, S. Kensington, London UK
New Mexico State University, Las Cruces, NM
New Hampshire Institute of Art, Manchester, NH
Boston Athenaeum, Boston, MA
Amon Carter Museum, Fort Worth, TX
Getty Research Institute, Los Angeles, CA
Cornell University, Ithaca, NY
University of Iowa, Iowa City, IA
Bienes Museum of the Modern Book, Ft. Lauderdale, FL
Grand Valley State University, Allendale, MI
Brown University, Providence, RI
Ohio State University, Columbus, OH
Phoenix Art Museum, Phoenix, AZ
University of Washington, Seattle, WA
Johns Hopkins University, Baltimore, MD
The British Library, London, UK
University of Illinois, Urbana, IL
Buffalo & Erie County Public Library, NY
University of Virginia, Charlottesville, VA
Smith College, Northampton, MA

INSTITUTIONAL COLLECTIONS WITH SIGNED AND NUMBERED CD-ROM EDITIONS

Clark Art Institute, Williamstown, MA
Rhode Island School of Design, Providence, RI
University of Virginia, Charlottesville, VA
Georgetown University, Washington, DC
Art Gallery of Ontario, Toronto, Ontario Canada
Philadelphia Museum of Art, Philadelphia, PA
The Athenaeum of Philadelphia, Philadelphia, PA
Duke University, Durham, NC
Harvard College, Cambridge, MA
California State University, Fullerton, CA
Humanities Research Center, U. of Texas at Austin
Ohio University Library, Athens, OH
Virginia Museum of Fine Arts, Richmond, VA
Newark Public Library, Newark, NJ
Temple University, Philadelphia, PA
University of North Carolina, Greensboro, NC
University of San Diego, CA
University of Maine, Orono, ME

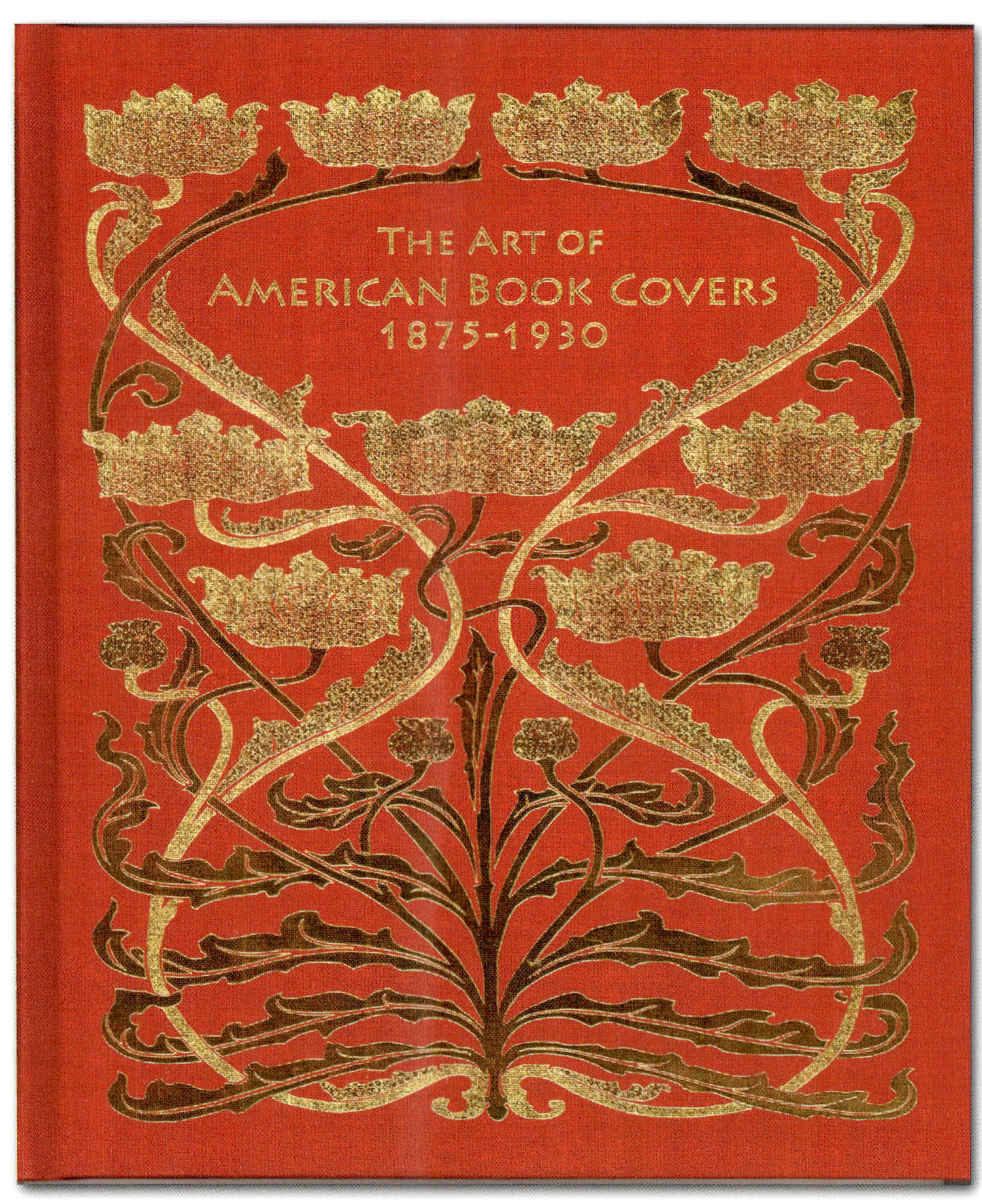

The Art of American Book Covers: 1875–1930
by Richard Minsky. George Braziller, Inc., New York, 2010. 9½ x 8¼
Cover design adapted by Minsky from an 1890s book cover.